Into the Arms of the Goddess

A Kundalini Awakening

Peter Nelson

NeoPoiesisPress.com

NeoPoiesis Press

Inquiries:
P.O. Box 38037
Houston, TX 77238-8037

Primary Address:
2775 Harbor Ave SW, Suite D
Seattle, WA 98126-2138

www.neopoiesispress.com

Copyright © 2012 by Peter Nelson

All rights reserved. No part of this book may be used or reproduced in any manner whatsoever without express written permission from the publisher except in the case of brief quotations embodied in critical articles and reviews.

Into the Arms of the Goddess by Peter Nelson
ISBN 978-0-9855577-2-0 (paperback : alk. paper)
        1. Spirituality. 2. Philosophy. 3. Memoir I. Nelson, Peter

Printed in the United States of America.

First Edition

Cover art designed and produced by Milo Duffin and Stephen Roxborough
"Mandala 4 Golden Spiral" illustration by ErinSparler.com
"Carina Nebula" and "Milky Way" Hubble telescope imagery courtesy of NASA

We were born before the wind
Also younger than the sun
'Ere the bonnie boat was won
As we sailed into the mystic

Van Morrison – Into The Mystic

I just know that something
Good is going to happen
I don't know when
But just saying it could even
Make it happen

Kate Bush – Cloudbusting

To the Beings we call Animals
Teachers to the Masters

But ask the animals, and they will teach you
Or the birds of the air, and they will tell you

Or speak to the earth, and it will teach you
Or let the fish of the sea inform you

Job 12:7-9

Until one has loved an animal
A part of one's soul remains unawakened

Anatole France

contents

overture: the lightning — ix

moon one: thirteen days — 1
new moon: e-stands for evolution — 113
first quarter: earth is talking — 123

moon two: i'm not seth — 131
last quarter: namaste — 149
new moon: the calling — 153
first quarter: the ghost and the rainbow — 157

moon three: granddad — 161
last quarter: vera and white feather — 167
new moon: grandma and jane roberts — 175
first quarter: we rise now — 189

moon four: bodhisattva — 197
last quarter: the blue jay — 205
new moon: parvati — 213
first quarter: jesus and siddhartha — 223

moon five: moon angels — 237
last quarter: in for a penny — 247
new moon: big-wigs and mr. green — 257
first quarter: time flies — 263

moon six: sea of feathers	267
last quarter: diwali and rex	271
new moon: alarm bells	275
first quarter: something in the air	279
moon seven: a glimpse of heaven	283
last quarter: through and through	287
new moon: the orbs begin	291
first quarter: the church	295
moon eight: christmas pigeon	301
last quarter: 2012	305
new moon: ascension	319
first quarter: believe	347
moon nine: merkaba	351
last quarter: look back with affection	355
new moon: steady as she goes	359
first quarter: you will be all right	363
moon ten: learn to discern	367
last quarter: no time to hurry	373
new moon: orbs and the red crystal	377
first quarter:	
the crow and the crystal serpent	381
moon eleven: what a song and dance	385
last quarter: be like the wind	389
new moon: passport to eternity	393
first quarter: sandra and the golden sparkles	397
epilogue: the holding	403

overture
The Lightning

Keep this to yourself for a while – okay?

That's what I thought after this phenomenal event had occurred. Many incredible things had happened to me over the years, and I'd so far shared all of them, starting with the dreams.

First it had been the precognitive dreams, especially when I'd been asking for an answer to a specific problem. My dream journal contained many dreams resulting from suggestions given before going to sleep, and if the dreams then manifested in the physical world, I would suddenly find myself living the dream I'd had a couple of weeks ago.

Then came the lucid dreams, and I mean full blown high-level lucid dreams, not just being aware of dreaming enough to wake up if something unpleasant was going on, but full reasoning consciousness within the dream, eventually leading to a great deal of control if that was the desire. Sometimes it was as much, if not more fun, to just sit back with that clear awareness and watch the dream unfold around me.

And the synchronicities in my waking life became closer and more astounding.

Next came the Out-of-Bodies or Astral Projection. Sometimes I would call them BLTs (bodiless trips) for fun, but on one journey while flying along, a fellow traveller had waved and called out to me, "Hey Windrider!" – so I latched onto the term, Windriding. There are some interesting tales to tell in this area – the entire bed vibrating before I was about to leave – trips just out and in the bedroom looking at my body – trips out and straight into other dimensions – trips to an in-between place, a neutral undifferentiated area.

As various abilities became stronger and more precise, the synchronicities worked their way into the past.

For instance, the first record I ever owned was "Rock Around the Clock" by Bill Haley and the Comets, a 45 rpm 7 inch vinyl disc given to me by my Auntie Vera, my mother's sister.

As I became older, I realised Rock Around the Clock was a perfect metaphor for this latest incarnation in physical reality where linear time is one of the ground rules – a place where time actually "exists" in the first place.

As I became yet older still, and with research being easier than it's ever been in history, what with the wonderful internet, I found out the song had been recorded on April 12, 1954.

My birthday is April 12, 1954.

So there had been a lot of things happening to me over the years, and most of my friends were also on a spiritual journey, so we always swopped stories back and forth, but this episode was truly something else again, and for some reason I wanted to hold this one close to my heart for now. I might need to think about this for a year or two.

This was just so... personal somehow. I really needed to put some perspective on this thing and see where it fit in. So here we are.

It was 2005, early afternoon and I was sitting on the bed with my legs straight out and my back leaning on the headboard. I was thinking.

There was no music or any other distraction going on, however the digital clock on the VCR was right in front of me at the end of the bed. In retrospect – how perfect this was, because I can easily tell you this incident took exactly forty minutes from start to finish. Forty minutes I will never ever forget, regardless of the wonders that have occurred since then.

Out of the corner of my eye I noticed... something. Knowing sometimes you can only see certain psychic visions this way – peripherally – I refrained from moving my head or my eyes for a minute so as not to maybe spoil what was going on. I needn't have bothered.

I slowly moved my eyes and I saw... a bolt of lightning.

That is the best description I can come up with, because that is exactly what it looked like, a jagged shape of white energy, a few inches long, and it was hovering horizontally about five feet off the floor over by the window. The curtains were closed so there was no direct light coming in from outside, but it wouldn't have mattered much anyway, this was *in* the room. And it was *growing*.

I looked back towards the clock, and the chronicler part of me took note of the time. I noticed I was excited *and* composed, which was an interesting combination, and I began to check a few things.

This object did not care whether I moved my eyes or my head, and being a bit afraid it might be gone when I opened my eyes again, I closed them for a few seconds... Still there!

This was not in my head like a vision you can still see, eyes open or not.

This was physically in the room, but for some reason I decided not to go that one step further and go over to touch it. Something told me to stay where I was.

I couldn't help but think of The Seth Material, and Robert Butts' circle of light that appeared in the kitchen during the early days of his and Jane Roberts' amazing experiences. I wasn't at all afraid, I had a context, and I knew I was seeing a bleed-through of some sort. This was transdimensional, or my vision had suddenly expanded to be able to see these frequencies that normally one doesn't see. I lit a cigarette.

By five minutes on the clock, it was around five feet long and half a foot high. The actually thickness of the energy I couldn't really see from the angle I was at, but I "felt" it was two or three inches thick. Somehow physical dimensions just didn't seem to really apply but old habits are hard to break, and it's only natural to apply the usual standards and measurements.

Ten minutes in, it was as big as it was going to get – a full twelve feet or so long, and about a foot high. This was fairly easy to determine as the bedroom was large – twenty by fifteen feet. I just sat there, watching it quiver and tremble – it seemed to flutter – it seemed to be alive. Lightning with no discharge.

I thought about trying to explain this to people. I thought about demonstrating it with thick ribbons of white silk or something. I thought about what this signified, and I thought about being at another stage in my own psychic/spiritual development. Mostly though, I sat and gazed in wonder and awe at this gift of magic from somewhere, and I kept my eye on the clock.

For a full twenty minutes exactly it remained, vibrating with power and shifting with its own life, and then just as it had grown, it started to retract back into itself.

Five minutes – half the size again, and then the last five I watched as it dwindled away, smaller and smaller until just a pin-prick, a point of light, until it said goodbye and winked out. Holy cow!

I must have sat there for another half an hour or so and just gaped at nothing.

Did this really happen? Oh yes, it sure did.

If it had have been for only a moment or two, I might have been able to explain it away somehow, a trick of the light or a trick of my eyes, but this was no trick. A full forty minutes from start to finish? That amount of time left no room for doubt – for second guessing. Something had happened – something larger than this reality had happened. It had happened to me, and I decided I wouldn't be saying anything about this to anyone right now. How odd!

I'd been given something precious and it would take a while to figure it out.

Maybe I would never untangle the whys and wherefores of this, and then I saw it really didn't matter, the experience itself was all I really needed to know.

The medium is the message – I thought, and laughed as I remembered that phrase from Marshall McLuhan.

This was a message all right, and it was about as subtle as a lead pipe.

I had to laugh again as I went a step further, and thought about everything mystical that had happened to me in this life, culminating so far with this latest event.

Maybe the message is – I'm becoming a medium.

Moon One
Thirteen Days
Day One

What is going on? I knew I was dying. I was as thin as a rail. I knew this was real. This was the moment we have all been waiting for and the wait was over. This is crystal clear. Do or die. I can't live this way anymore and I'm dying. Holy cow!

It was time to take stock of the situation.

1. I had just spoken to my dead mother, and my guide, through my friend Gordon, in the coffee shop.
2. My mum told me I had less than two years to live, but more like six months, if I didn't extricate myself from the suffering. And eat.
3. If I didn't make it I could live with her, but I still had time to make a "success" of this life.
4. My guide told me I had concentrated on my feminine side for so long, I was 70% feminine, and 30% masculine. Out of balance. "It's time to round-out your education," he said. (He? That's a shock.) And eat.
5. I have an overcompensating warrior life during the War of the Roses, where the man (barely) was described as a monster. Oh Joy.
6. Eat, eat, eat and a thousand times eat.
7. My dog is with my mother, and my second girlfriend's dog is with her also, waiting for his people to join him. This is good.
8. My dad is not with my mother. This might not be good.
9. I can't believe what I'm saying.
10. I am never alone. She said that.
11. The place she's in sounds absolutely incredible. Worth dying for. That's funny.

12. I don't doubt any of this for one second.
13. I can't walk a straight line. I'm actually staggering.

That's about it for the salient points, I guess. Oh, and with the understanding that all responsibility for suffering and joy, in any life or reality, lies with me and me alone, I can't blame anyone for the state I'm in. That would just be-lame. Well, at least I still have my sense of humour.

You Create Your Own Reality – is something I learned a long time ago.

Okay that's good, that's good, let's go back a bit further.

It was Saturday June 2, 2007, there was a full moon and it was a very hot summer day.

The day before at work, someone commented on the coming weekend – it's going to be a hot one! I said, well, we'll just have to roll with it.

I liked that, sometimes I would choose a mantra for a few hours or a day, or as long as I could remember to think about it, so I thought I would choose this for the weekend. Let's roll with it, no matter what happens, no matter how hot it gets. I didn't know this weekend would become the beginning of something, and the continuation of something, and the end of something, all three in one glorious implosion.

Today would become the epicentre for this reincarnational cycle.

Was it only four hours ago, I was standing on the busy corner waiting for my old friend Gordon Phinn? How old remains to be seen, as I know our friendship involves many different times and places, but anyway in this particular life, at this particular time, I'd met him thirty-five years ago in 1972, give or take a year. I would have been about eighteen at the time. He had a book on the market, "Eternal Life and how to enjoy it," and he had been kind enough to send me the manuscript for his next one, "More Adventures in Eternity."

I was early, and I was looking and watching and waiting and wanted to see his approach. There were only two ways to arrive, and somehow I missed them both and he was just – there. It felt to me as though he had *appeared.* And now I had my hand on his shoulder, touching his hair with a great degree of familiarity, and I was noticing this as if from the outside. What am I doing?

"You're shrinking." These were his first words.

"I'm leaving the planet, one pound at a time." These were mine.

All right, so I do like these ground rules, we're going to tell it like it is are we? Good. I knew I was dying and there's not much time is there? We went inside, and a word popped into my mind.

Toltec

That was funny. I hadn't read Castaneda in years, why was I thinking of him now? This old friend reminded me of Don Juan Matus from the books. This might be something more than just a simple how-are-you at the coffee shop – I thought, because I really didn't feel very well right then. I felt otherworldly and – finished.

Along a counter were the many coffee pots. There was a coffee pot involved with Carlos meeting Don Juan. This was very interesting indeed. We collected our cups and sat down – Gordon got himself a muffin.

"Aren't you eating?"
"No."
"Don't you care about your body?"
"I love my body!"
"Then why aren't you eating?"
"Eating's for happy people."

My head's down and I'm crying and I pull myself slightly together because I've actually scared Gordon, he thought I was having an asthma attack.

Look at me! I'm ready to bolt for the door. One foot is already two feet away from my chair, and I think I'm actually going to *run!* Don't hyperventilate right now okay, because you are! What the hell is going on? I felt like I was about to fall off a cliff.

The time-lines divide here.

Gordon gave me man-to-man advice, all good, all logical, and all but impossible, especially in the condition I was in, then he began a casual reading and things changed.

Quietly, after half-an-hour or so of enlightening impressions about me and my various incarnations, all of which struck me as being bang-on, and with people coming and going in this busy place on a Saturday morning, he offered three words.

"Your mother's here."

"My mum? Oh my." My voice was a shaky whisper. I need a handkerchief.

I heard these words issue from me, but now the coffee shop was fading away and there was only the two of us in a void. The "real" world was now gone and gone far away. I would never see it quite the same again, in this or any other lifetime.

"She's been here about ten minutes now." Gordon is speaking from somewhere.

My god, am I just sitting here? Where? Time is nonsense. I'm lost.

"You have to ask."

There he is again. Ask what? He's annoying. Then I got it.

"Can I say hi to my mum?" Should've said may I – I thought.

It was like flipping a switch. He put one foot up on the bench, closed his eyes and ran his fingers backwards through his hair. He checked his breathing, swallowed and wet his lips – his mouth opened.
I had never been so transfixed in my life and I've seen Leonard Cohen. What would *your* opening remark be if you'd been waiting twenty-three years for this?

"I know everything that's going on."

I bet you do mum.

What followed was a debriefing of my life so far with the points mentioned, especially the "you're almost dead" part, and then my guide following with the news of the necessary balancing act, just in case I *do* survive.

Who is this guy, and he's definitely male, is he? His name wasn't coming through.

I complained about not wanting to lose my gentleness, my character as it were, (what a whiner!) and for this he sent Gordon an image.

"Okay, I'm seeing an ocean, and there's a lightning bolt striking the water. Do you understand this?"

Not only did I understand, but I realised something odd was going on, as I could see this image myself now, and not just because of Gordon's more than apt description – I could see it *as* he was describing it.

The ocean is gentleness, the feminine underpinning, and the lightning bolt is obviously the male and aggressive, this was clear, and then the lightning struck the water and when it was over, the water was – unchanged. Many things became apparent here. I will not *lose* anything but we need more action, and crying control at crucial times would be nice. Calmness yes, but I mustn't actively suppress the masculine anymore. Indeed.

Many, many things were told to me until I sensed it was time, and if I didn't break the spell it would go on forever. Gordon seemed on autopilot. I asked my mum lastly if we would be able to talk again, and was assured we would – this would be very funny, very soon – then I reached out and touched his sleeve. He'd been in an altered state for a couple of hours at least, and I was drained totally.

The sun was bright and we were on the street now, climbing into his school bus. Almost four hours had gone by. We travelled a busy Saturday block or two.

I gave him a gift, my book – *Walk Softly in the Snow* – I'd picked it up at the last minute, on a whim. I took it back to scribble something on the fly-leaf. A moment later, he dropped me off and I realised it wasn't a gift at all.

an offering

I had a feeling it was actually an offering.

He pulled out and drove away. Bye. The school bus was appropriate – the teacher drives away and takes the school with him. There I was, head down, crying, and trying to be extra especially careful not to get run over at the lights, I began winding my way home.

Thinking I was mostly upset at what I was just told by my mother – that I was close to being dead – I focused on walking a straight line.

"It's okay."

I was hearing things.

He must've moved my assemblage point or something – isn't that the way it worked? There was that Toltec thing again. I realised I looked like a person who was talking to himself and weaving, because I was. I always did talk to myself, but now I was busy and this was in earnest. I must have looked insane and I didn't care.

What am I going to do? How can I change my life? I have no money. I have no assets. I do have a mediocre job, but other than that, I have nothing. How can I do it? How can I move forward? How can I stop the suffering I've learned to live with?

You're not going to "live" with it much longer – I thought.

My parents are dead, oh that's funny. There was no one to call – not funny. I did have an absolute when-all-else-fails-and-you're-on-the-street offer from friends, but they were 1300 miles away. My seven cats... Henry – I couldn't think about them.

"Peter."

I was hearing things.

I made it home. The house was empty. I was not alone.

What is happening to me? I sat on the back deck, a beautiful day, powerful sun, and I closed my eyes and reached up, pulling the sun towards me, and I made grandfather mine.

There's more to the sun than meets the eye. My friend had said something about sending a healing or a cleansing to the house, so I thought I would help and I put all I could into it. I imagined large swathes of fire and light washing down into me, deflecting out and around me and through the house, cleansing everything, washing everything with heat and light that comes with its own sound, making everything new. Electricity. Liquid fire.

I remember being amazed at how large my visualisations could actually be. It seemed easy to think on a planetary scale, it seemed easy to feel the Universe.

Hey, maybe I was actually good at this stuff? Maybe something was happening to me at last. I felt like Eleanor from "The Haunting." They called her Nel as well.

"But it's happening to *you*, Eleanor.
Yes. Something at last is really, really, really happening to me."

I really did my best, using all the psychic energy I could muster, then, I said "out," as though I had a clue as to what I was doing, and went inside.

I went to my room and got a large sheet of Bristol board and drew a rough sketch of lightning striking water. I wished I could draw better, but that didn't matter now.

My guide had used this image of lightning, and I thought about the bolt of lightning that appeared in the bedroom in 2005, the one I told you about. I thought about what it all meant...

a herald

A herald, I suddenly thought to myself.

Water. Wash away the tears nice cold water on your wrists your mum taught you that cool down cool down hang on calm down it's going to be okay water life giving water I am water this is incredible.

"Peter, stay calm."

What? Who's that? Mum is that you? Are you here, did you follow me home? I know you did. I think you did. My guide's here too isn't he? The meeting didn't end. My god what happened? Did I crack? I did, didn't I? I'm open.

open unto yourself

Was that you mum?

That just seemed to come from everywhere.

I sat and cried for five hours. Crying turned out to be a common factor for the next six months or so, a sure sign of energy in motion. E-motion. I also tried to establish what exactly was going on and if this was really my mother. I felt she hadn't planned on this. She and my guide had waited all right, waited all these years for me to finally go and see someone. It must've driven them crazy. Of all people in the world, I never once tried to contact them through a psychic. I'd waited for Gordon. What a laugh.

It was an ambush for sure – they pounced on me. Twenty-three years is quite a wait, but they hadn't planned on quite *this*. Something had happened. They were here.

Tell me something funny, you were always so funny, let me know it's you. Say something from Lancashire.

"Eee, I don't know love."

Okay, that's good – I can hear the accent – more like that, it's you, it's you!

"I owl you."

"I nose you."

Oh my holy god! That was my mother all right, I remembered those terms very well from when I was a little guy, and we were nose to nose. Oh I love you!

"If you would eat, I'd be in heaven!"

That's so funny – that's got to be you! I know you're right about the eating thing.

"I'm dead right."

I could hear and feel her laughing! How can this be?

In a flash I saw I'd mapped out the future in a way, a long time ago. I'd always thought maybe one day I would be in the presence of a really powerful psychic – maybe a Buddhist monk, or an Indian Guru – and suddenly whatever I had going for me would be jump-started, like getting a boost just to get things going. (This is called Shaktipat in the Vedic tradition.) For some people it was falling down the stairs or a physical trauma like that, and I'd done *that* recently – it'd been serious, another potential death – but I now saw I'd thought about *this* scenario seriously for ages. That coupled with almost being dead had done the trick.

"I think you're right on that score."

You always used to say that!

"I still do."

This is too much!

"This is just right."

Oh my lord, what is happening to me mum?

"Your mind is unfolding."

Will I make it through this?

"Your confidence convinced me of the afterlife – now I'm returning the favour."

Let me sit down before I fall down. I noticed you couldn't answer that.

"The difference between thinking and listening."

What's that? What do you mean? You don't waste time getting down to brass tacks do you? Is this happening?

"Lesson number one: The difference between thinking and hearing your own thoughts – and just hearing thoughts. The difference between thinking and listening."

That made sense. I must learn to feel the difference.

I was wide open, should I be worried? Could I worry anymore? I understood what was going on enough to be okay for now, and I also understood something else. In the spirit world right then there were a lot of holy cows going on, a lot of searching for the right page. A probability had clicked into place – this was a new timeline. This was a good one. In this one I didn't die in the coffee shop.

At that moment I realised one of me *had.* When Gordon thought I was having an asthma attack, (my head down and choking/crying), that would've been the moment when I died and probabilities changed. I managed to become the me who didn't die, and had an awakening. Is that what this is?

Lucky, lucky, lucky. Then again, there is no luck. There actually is a very beautiful scheme. Your scheme – and you create it all.

My alone time was running out. What was I going to do? The next immediate question was whether or not to say anything at this particular moment. I could hardly believe it myself anyway. Everything I'd read, I realised, had laid a foundation for what was happening now. I had a context. Everything we read, all of this stuff, it's all just so we have some kind of reference when it finally happens. Thank god for that. Seth rules. This was really happening to me, this wasn't somebody else's story, this was my very own and I had to say, this was the best one I'd come across for a long, long time. Then again, how could it not be? I was living it. This was only day one and I somehow knew this would play-out forever.

Now I understood why I'd been listening to "Into The Mystic" by Van Morrison incessantly for the last two months, along with Kate Bush and "Cloudbusting." I'd be walking down the street and find myself looking at the sky, singing – 'cause every time it rains – you're here in my head....

I decided I wasn't going to say anything to anyone. This decision was the fastest and the safest and I felt I could truly be going insane anyhow. I kind of enjoyed the idea of this just being mine at the moment, and I also understood very clearly somehow, that voila, insanity was born and I had to be very, very careful. In fact the more I thought about it, hearing voices I'm sure was the first thing ever. The first symptom of the first mental patient! When you think about it, a lot of those people over the centuries were probably just poor enlightened folk in the wrong place and time. When the spirit world isn't accepted – of course you're insane. I guess people learned to keep their mouths shut – tightly.

All right then, I was on my own. All will be wondrous well – I thought. Then my partner came home.

That first experience speaking to someone in the flesh so to speak, while another voice out of the flesh was waiting to talk to me, was disconcerting to say the least. It was a combination of panic and exhilaration – astonishment and awe. This was the most exciting adventure I'd ever been on in my life... and it's not even a day old!

Adventure. It was one of my favourite words from childhood to be sure. Fortunately I stumbled through, feeling transparent as glass and a thousand times more delicate. Lines from my favourite movies were now being used to comfort me. For instance, I was thinking – can this actually be real?

The line I heard, clear as day – "And you know it, and everybody knows it!" from "Some Kind of Wonderful."

What was just as amazing was what I was now told. Jane had not had an average day at her not average job. She was a correctional officer, a jail guard at the oldest historical jail in the largest city in Canada, and sometimes her experiences were spectacular and unique, this was both. I listened, hoping my face looked as normal as possible considering the tears of the last few hours, and the shock at what I was now hearing.

As I was weaving my way home, Jane was making her way to work, and would've arrived there at more or less the same time as I arrived home, so this may have occurred as I was invoking the sun, or shortly thereafter – close enough. In fact, in terms of the universe, and events such as these that were now unfolding, the timing was impeccable.

She had arrived at work and a situation had developed. The situation was an inmate dying in front of her and another officer. The body voided on her. This was death in her hands and on her clothes, and a new spirit at her side! She was in the presence of a new spirit – he was looking at her, probably saying what the hell is going on – and no doubt the part of her who was psychically mobile, would've been saying, hello, I'd say you're dead. And this was happening at this moment, at this time! What a synchronicity!

Maybe Jane and I have more unfinished business than I thought.

I couldn't believe my ears, I couldn't believe my life, I couldn't believe her life, I couldn't believe what was happening.

This was the most extraordinary day, in what had so far been a fairly ordinary life from the outside. What did I do to deserve this? I've read a lot of books, and I've done a lot of thinking, but have I done the work necessary to warrant this? People give up everything to attain something like this, so where did I do all the work?

I know spirituality, music and animals have followed me through the majority of my lives. Okay. I must have paid my dues somewhere. I also must be working my fingers to the bone in the sleep state. That must be it. Good for me, that's all I could think of, and I realised again my opinion of myself would never be the same.

This wasn't a flashing glimpse of something, I felt this was big. Really big. I mean, I've learned a lot I hope, but this doesn't happen every single day! I was pretty sure of that, but then I had more to learn on that score, and was I going to make it through this anyway?

Once alone, the thought of water was very enticing indeed. I was thinking a lot about water, a lot about being clean – clean clothes down by the river. I realised I should be bathing in the Ganges. Six months in a cave sounded really good right around then.

Some things are so old, so ancient, they are always here. Does that make sense?

The ancient rituals of washing under the waterfall and wearing the finest, cleanest linens were on my mind now. Ceremonial robes?

That made me think of my monk's robe, true to the time, it must weigh five pounds. I have a monk's robe, I have been a monk. In fact, I copied manuscripts, and that's why I just spent the longest time ever at a single job, a printing/copying company. How not surprising! This I'd already put together on my own, but I was used to a revelation per year or so, and even then it was more about belief and hope than *knowing*.

I had to get in some water.

Heading for the bathroom and thinking about the scented bubbles I was about to use, I took a breath and suddenly inhaled fragrances from *out of nowhere*. The air was filled with a spectacular bouquet and this is straight out of the Buddhist texts! Is that jasmine? Do I even know what jasmine smells like? I think it's jasmine.

I closed my eyes as the perfume continued for a moment, and then was gone in a manner that was not of the general way of things – bath time's getting interesting.

I'd always thought of the bath as therapeutic – I did yoga in there too – but now it was a sacred oasis, and my mind drifted through all the rites and rituals connected to the water and I have no idea how long I've been standing here.

"You must eat, that's the first thing. That's the only thing."

Holy cow mum, I really can hear you!

Could I actually now have a reason to eat, could I have a reason to live? I decided to get the bath ready whilst examining the intricacies of my new thinking. It seemed to come down to a few categories.

The first one: I knew I was clever enough to be creating this myself. No time to worry about the arrogance of that. I figured I had the wherewithal to completely fabricate this out of a desire to keep the meeting going, to keep the meeting going without the medium. I could pull this off. I wanted this, and instead of being actually completely insane, I was intelligent enough to create this seamlessly, with all the embellishments and intertwining to convince me I was communing with the spirit world. Until there was something I was not possibly just remembering and weaving in, I wouldn't be sure.

So I had to ask myself, why would I be doing that? For what possible reason?

Okay, because I've always wanted my psychic abilities to flower, and now I'm just going to pretend they are? I saw my friend Gordon, I have a good excuse, he triggered me and here we are. Now I'm going to go around pretending to be a psychic, there we go!

Well I guess I wouldn't get very far doing that, so what would be the point? There certainly would be no referrals for a phony psychic, so just to keep it to myself and...? That didn't make sense to me. I couldn't see why I would go through the extremely complex mental exercise to attempt to completely fool myself for no apparent reason. This led to…

The second one: my mum and guide had actually spoken to me through my psychic friend and given me the dire news and now, I'd cracked up. I hadn't cracked open – I'd just cracked up. I was now completely insane with the original madness. Might as well just try to enjoy whatever psychedelic head trips I can, with whatever time I have left, until *they* catch up with me and put me away.

The third one: I was dead. I really was the dead one, and just didn't know it yet. This made a lot of sense to me, in fact this one kept me company for quite a while, but at this stage it was a new thought, and it was one to savour.

Well well, I was so used to checking the current state of my reality for dream work, specifically lucid dreams, that there was something deliriously familiar now about checking this seemingly normal waking reality for clues to my actual demise.

So I went about the usual drill. My current favourite checking mechanism is attempting to push my finger or hand *into* something, sometimes my own body, including my head. If I was dead and this was the astral realm then it would behave as the dream state behaves, that is, when I touch my finger to the wall and push, it will yield, and then it will congeal again as I pull my finger back out. So I tried the wall, I tried the palm of my hand, I jumped up and down to check the gravity situation and I looked at the cover of a book, looked away, and then looked back to see the title had indeed remained the same.

Matter was *not* pseudo matter, I did not start to float around the room, and Tao Te Ching, didn't sneakily turn into The Tea Shop, right down to the type style. You really have to look.

All right, so everything seemed to point to me being alive and in the regular world, albeit a new probability for me. The funny thing was the feeling I had, my overall feeling. I felt dead. I was pretty sure this was what being dead probably felt like. My life-review had started in the coffee shop hadn't it? I could tell I was going to be facing some unique situations – some you normally face after you're dead. I was right about that one.

The fourth one: this was really happening. Now I knew why someone had said to me recently at work, "It's really, really real. She really did die! (Unfortunately, that was the situation.) It really happened, I can't believe it!" That line was now in my head. It's really, really, real. Yes, this was the fourth possibility.

There was that feeling again. Open. A feeling of being very, very, open and I wondered again if I should be concerned about this. I knew enough about protection, and opening and closing the Lotus flower, and I also knew I was lit up like a Christmas tree and I was doing nothing, at least nothing I was consciously aware of. Must come back to that thought. Also, I have friends on the other side, right?

I looked at the mask on the wall, the one my son Jonathon had made in school that looked like a demon to me – a devil. With that candle underneath it, two horn shadows actually appear on the wall. I said hello, I need to deal with you I guess. I thought of Seth, and "I wish you peace," to the negative entities, and I thought of the real problems people have had with the darkness, the negative, the evil, if you choose to use that word. "Live" backwards – indeed.

The funny thing was, I knew how open I was, and I knew how terribly off balance I was, not to mention also thin, weak and in some serious concern over my actual sanity, but overall, I felt safe. I decided at that moment to be safe. There would be some things to deal with, definitely, I didn't think I would never feel fear again, but things were very different. Falling and loud noises are all people are born fearing, right? I felt strong and correct. This was normal. This is what happens to people, this is what's been happening to people for millennium. Something else occurred to me with as much surety as anything I'd been thinking about – there was no going back. I was absolutely certain about that. So certain, I said – "You have full access to me mum – you and my guide." I said it out loud as well as in my mind. For some reason I thought it was important to do that – to say that.

"Go to your room."

My dead mother is telling me to go to my room – this is hilarious!

I had to meditate. It was something I just hadn't bothered much about for all these years. I seemed to just drift around all over the place anyway, so I never really seemed to feel the need to pick a place and sit down. This was different, now I felt I absolutely had to meditate, I had to go in my room, I was being told to go to my room, and I had to sit on the floor. I raised my arms to the universe and felt energy pouring down into me. I drew it in with a kind of fervour... I was in rough shape.

the firming

The firming? Okay, not my mum's voice. This sounded really cool and I understood where they were coming from. Things had to be firmed up now, they were in position but very shaky.

I kept getting the visual of water and how it fits into the shore, but the idea being the water designs the shore before it seamlessly moves in. The shore was being designed. This wasn't just water taking the shape of whatever container it was poured into, it was creating the container first.

This can't be happening. The firming. I was to hear this term many times over the next few days. Once again, I found myself simply saying the word "out," and standing up, sensing that enough was enough and I was losing focus. I was tired and elated beyond my wildest dreams.

"Have that bath."

I needed to be bossed around. I didn't have a problem with that at all, and it was my mother's voice again.

Okay, let's get in there. I need to be good to myself, careful with myself – that was first and foremost. The sense of being looked after was overwhelming. Could I do my part and care for myself as well as they wanted me to?

"Love yourself the way *I* love you" – my mum had said through Gordon.

I'm so tired. I *was* so tired. Let's not be tired anymore. I'm alive! This is my second chance. And as soon as I thought that, I heard my own song "Second Chance" in my mind. My mother was playing it for me, and somehow at the same time letting me know it's one of her favourites. This would certainly not be the last time my own words and music would be used to affect me in a sublime manner. Pretty smart.

> I'm going to find me a second chance
> Going to find myself a second chance

"You have Peter."

I lit many candles and made my bath beautiful, slowly climbing in. Something ordinary, something normal, bliss in a bucket of water. (The next six months of continuing to work would be another testimony to the power of habit or ritual for helping to cope with an experience such as this.)

Just me, the water and the entire universe – that's what it felt like. I was plugged in and I didn't know how to stop it. I didn't want to stop it, why would I want to stop what I've been waiting my entire life for? Why would I want to stop what all of my lives have been leading up to?

There was something else. I could feel a part of the plan. I knew the idea now was to bore me out so to speak, to blast the channel wide so it would never close, and I also sensed it could be a risky business.

As I started to wash, I was somehow informed it was time to sit at the board table and make some agreements, or not to. I say somehow informed, because some knowledge was just there, without any words. Seth again. The Inner Senses. It was a direct knowing, or you can call it anything you want.

It's all coming together – holy cow! Can you see how this is fitting together oh man oh man oh man what is going on? Am I dreaming? Am I dead? This is beyond incredible this is unbelievable but I believe it I've always believed things like this but I still can't believe it how funny I'm the perfect candidate and I can't believe it myself god this is incredible!

ten years in one week

It came from everywhere. Oh this is just like me it really is, where would be the adventure without the danger?

"Ten years in one week?"

Let's say it out loud. I'm a child in a bathtub playing with the spirits. Hey, I can talk out loud if I want to, just like the old days. Ha ha. Or I could start a sentence out loud, and finish it in my mind! We are redefining the word fun!

you must agree for this to occur

This came from everywhere again. Okay mum, you're the italics in quotation marks with the first word capitalised and the period.

this is the fast track, the crash course, you asked for this

I did ask for this, I knew that. You get what you concentrate upon, there is no other main rule. Seth again. Oh how perfect! Almost dead rag doll of a man with a second chance that could also kill him. This is so like me, at least the free, fantasy me. Could I actually be like that? Be like this? Could I have daring? Could I be heroic? Are we all heroic? Jane Roberts had something to say about that.

you don't have to

Well there it was. You don't have to. It's all up to you. Well, I knew what was behind me, and there really was no choice, no question, no option, no dilly-dallying. I was going to be dead in six months anyway right? Mum?

"You have a home with me whenever you die – I told you that."

She wasn't going to help me make this decision, and I didn't blame her for that. This was a big one, the biggest so far in this little life. I could overload, burnout, and that was basically it. My knowledge of electricity and electronics came to mind – I saw things smoking....

Well you don't know where you're headed
But you know where you're coming from
So at least you're halfway there

It was another song of mine playing now – "Centre of the Circle."

There has to be that one time, that one time when you know it's your turn and all those things about destiny and fate and your one shot, are right now. I wasn't going to put the brakes on this just as I'd started to feel the wind in my face. If I was crazy now anyway, it didn't really matter.
At this point I realised I had one condition.
How do you like that? Good for me! I was standing up for myself, there was something I needed to know, and without being very certain about it I wasn't going to make this deal.
Okay, here we go – I thought, here's what I have to know. I think you'll like it, you should expect it, and I guess with things being the way they

are, you already probably know what I'm going to say, but my one stipulation has to be that – this is for the GOOD OF ALL, or not at all.

I expressed the necessity of this with every fibre of my being.

I thought this awakening was a more personal thing, meaning personal between me and the universe, my own spiritual destiny/history merrily going along on its own way, independent of the earth. I didn't know about the Ascension then, but I thought if all this is just for me, without any real benefit to anyone or anything else, it would be unacceptable, or uncomfortable, or just not right on the money. This also made me feel I wasn't completely on my own and the rest of the world was with me. I felt the *universe* was with me, but suddenly, humanity meant something to me deeply.

How long had I been saying to people, whether at work or anywhere else – we're all in this together. At the same time as I felt *that*, I also felt more alone than I'd ever felt in my life. This was the biggest thing ever and I had to be alone. I understood that. I've always been that way, always figured you could just do anything alone in a room, and that was my style. In retrospect, I can't imagine anyone around me at that time. However, I've learned absolutely anything is possible, and I know if someone *was* there, they would have fit into the situation perfectly because that's the way the universe works, as I was beginning to see.

It was made clear to me, extremely clear, that this would be the case.

FOR THE GOOD OF ALL

I was made to understand that the channel or frequency was already clean enough and clear enough for there to be no distortion on this matter.

> *we know how serious this is*
> *be calm, be clear, be confident*
> *and you just passed the first test*

Was that my guide? We? Him and my mum? All right, well passing a test was good. Gordon said my guide was a man, and that was still very surprising to me, but he couldn't get his name, and neither could I. I need a bit more hot water in here.

Now my guide chose to show himself to me, and I was in for the shock of my life. It wasn't that he presented himself as a Hindu, and not a white man – my desktop background picture at work is an ascetic Indian guru in a meditational yoga pose – I love these guys!

No, no the shock was I couldn't accept this. I mean, I couldn't accept this at all! I mean whatever had happened so far today and whatever magnificence there may be in the future, I was ready to throw it all away! How can this be?

I couldn't believe my feelings. I hadn't had a bigoted notion in my mind for as long as I could remember. When you have believed in reincarnation for this long, and you realise you've been many different people of both sexes and different races, all of that falls away. I thought.

Tears were streaming down my face into the water – time became meaningless – it couldn't end like this before it had really even started, and then I thought of England, and why we left. I could hear it as clear as day, "We're moving to Canada for a better life for you and Sandra, and also because *the Pakies are taking over here*."

It was in my history, it was in my upbringing, it was a gift from my father – one he didn't know he'd left me – or worse yet it was from another life, or both.

A core belief! I had just found a core belief buried so deeply inside of me I had no idea whatsoever it was there. And it felt ugly. It had to come out.

I struggled with the feeling of not being able to accept this beautiful guide, and the shock and disgust of not knowing this disease was inside of me – it was invisible on the outside. Oh god!

I had a vision of the East Indian man just down the street from where we lived in England, and my mother showing an odd concern about me having gone into his house to see his tape recorder. I now knew it was just the usual mother's concern about any strange man, but I was being impressed that this was important. Come to think of it, I never did see this man again.

I was seven or eight and we had talked about music, the piano, tape recorders, (my life would be forever involved with these, and wouldn't it just make sense if this was a truly mystical event from my past, and I was only now finding out), he gave me some orange juice, and now I knew there was a connection between this man and my guide.

Maybe that's why I never saw him again?

Was that my guide visiting me when I was a child?

Have I completely lost it and my mother had simply told me to never go near him again?

There was something going on here, I could feel it. How interesting is this! But what am I going to do? This is like a life review – this is like going into the light! Holy cow! I'm purging – I'm being cleaned out! The bath seemed the perfect place for this purification and please take this poison out of me.

A timeless time went by as the irrepressible tears joined with the bath water and powerful, breathtaking surges of emotion threw my head back, until all of these things flew through my mind like startled birds and then found their bearings and flew away.

It was gone. The problem was gone. That old, tired belief from another time and place was laid to rest forever.

No one is superior.

A final wave washed over me and I realised I'd passed another kind of test, or cured an illness. Powerful medicine.

That was some entrance sir, I thought. I'm so sorry – and thank you.

I came to my knees and added some more hot water to the bath. The temperature gave me some indication of time actually going by as all this was happening. I washed my face with my hands and brushed the hair out of my eyes. My hands found each other in front of my chest and I took a deep cleansing breath.

That was just the preliminary.

Now I saw documents in the air. So *this* was how I was going to do it, signing my name with great sweeps of my arm, signing a deal with the universe. A promissory note to God.

I couldn't help but think of deals with the devil, I couldn't avoid that. Faustus. It's too pervasive and integrated into our society, and I had to be *that* sure, and *that* confident everything was right. So I thought, well, I am a soul, it's not something I have and can therefore lose, I don't sense a devil or the slightest negative *anything*, and it's my mother and my guide for goodness sake! How much more security do I need? Take a chance Nelson. The game of Risk, I never got that one as a kid.

"I do agree. I do agree to this."

I said this in my mind and also out loud to any who were there to hear.

Now there was another serious moment as it was made very clear to me that anything could happen because of free will, and there could be some "challenging" situations ahead. That's one way of putting it, however with my mother's involvement things actually were a lot more to the point – she had never minced words. So, what I actually got was more like – there might be times when you are scared out of your wits and wish you had never done this, if you say yes, you say yes to everything.
I get it – but for the good of all, right?
I've waited forever for this – where do I sign?

"I will agree to this."

I was also thinking – who the hell am I? My hand went up, I imagined a very fancy pen, and I signed my two names. Peter Nelson. There's nothing else to it, I don't have a middle name. I did this three or four times – just writing in the air with my invisible pen – over here, and then over there – then I got out of the bath.
My briefcase please.

After drying, I dressed in the freshest, loosest, most comfortable night-time clothes I could find. I had visions of prophets and their stylish spiritual wear. I needed clothes like that.
I barely had time to get dressed – the house was asleep – and now the tears just came in waves. Someone I had lost, someone I'd been separated from twenty-three years ago was now in my head, and that love was there amplified, magnified and merged into something else, something new – she was a different person also.
Information and feelings were flowing into me.
I felt like an indoor cat who finally gets taken out into the backyard and shrinks down at the sheer size of the sky.
I couldn't stop it and I didn't want to stop it and I knew what I'd agreed to.
Suddenly 11:11 that we'd all been seeing for years on our clocks meant balance to me. Balance was something I realised I would see reference

to in many places until I addressed the issue within myself. There's more though, it's not that simple – I thought. 11:11 means a lot of things.

Once again, I didn't realise how much everything related to what was happening to our earth herself at this time, but I soon started to learn. I thought it was funny the earth was ready to say enough, to the masculine, and to return to the sanity of the feminine, when I myself seemed to have too much feminine energy. This was pretty funny actually. Was there some particular use for my own personal imbalance in the other direction?

Alternating periods of laughing and crying within a few moments of each other were quite frequent now as I sat in my room and tried to calm down.

Frequent. Frequency. Hysteria anyone? I watched myself and tried to see the humour, thinking I must be okay if I was still somehow the cool, detached observer.

Things were moving so fast I could barely keep up or stand up.

Ten years in a week? How about a month or so in a couple of hours? Oh, I guess that's about the same actually.

I had to get this down, I had to record it somehow and share this with people! I had to attempt to remember it all. I was a writer wasn't I? I write songs and I write poems, and I write, well... words. Also, I just acquired a handheld digital recorder, and I mean just acquired it. How not surprising! I can just talk, maybe that will work.

All the time I was thinking this, I knew I shouldn't interrupt the flow, and then...

don't take notes

Oh my what's happening to me I wanted this to happen you know you wanted this to happen I always wanted this to happen I've been working towards this for years that's all I've been doing that's all I've ever done that's all I've ever thought about I bore people to death I bore people to tears and never stop talking about it death that's it that's all I've ever wanted to figure out and it's here it's here I've been given something I can't believe it I just can't believe it it's incredible my god Seth and everyone were right he was right the magic is real the real is magic and it's incredible am I going to make it through this I can't believe it breathe breathe I've got to breathe slow down slow down just slow down okay Neli slow down breathe in the room and take stock.

I managed to calm myself down and I was so tired, but I'd never felt so alive.

I was elated beyond words.

This had been a day more than anything I could ever have imagined, and as I was sitting on my heels with my palms on the floor, the voice from everywhere told me I would be trained – be taught.

Can all my dreams come true in one day?

it's all true Peter – The Magic is Real

That's what I heard, that's what I felt, and that's what I knew.

I could feel history. I could feel *my* history, and maybe it was the same? Maybe I was part of all of it? Didn't Gordon say, "You've been here since the beginning."

Was I going to be able to sleep?

You'll never be asleep the way you were Neli.

When it comes to abstinence, it's been tied to spirituality forever. I dare say any energy you save from one particular area may then be used for another. But this energy I could feel everywhere, it felt like bliss, I could feel the beginnings of an ecstasy, it felt like sex times a million. I would not be an adherent to the abstinent point of view, in fact if I didn't have an orgasm soon I was going to die, I was going to explode. I'm not sure how to put it any more delicately than that, and it made total sense to me, the feeling of creation.

I had a notion that the orgasms we experience, for all our complaining about their duration, are probably as much as we can handle at this particular stage or frequency.

Orgasms connect us to God, of this I am now sure. Relatively short but extremely potent reminders of what we have in store for us – connectors to our source – like dreams. There was more here, something about this connection being one of the few things we have left, something that could never be taken away no matter how much we forgot – again like dreams.

Let me report there was a definite reason for coining the term, "Cosmic Orgasm." Remember that one? I thought I might physically die.

This was to continue for quite a while.

Day Two

"Peter – it's okay – it's okay – it's okay."

Glad to hear it mum.

"Good morning."

All right, it wasn't all a dream, but I still might be dead.

Listen mum, (now the recording engineer came out), if this is really you, could you go in the left channel, I'll go in the right, but you go in the left, okay? More of your humour would be good too.
My mum is one of the funniest people I know. "Acting the fool," was something she thoroughly enjoyed, and thought more people should engage in, (me probably) and another one of her favourite sayings was/is, "the more the merrier." One other thing you should know about my mother, she didn't hold back, and would probably say what everyone else was thinking, but wouldn't say.

"How's that?"

Well that's you all right, and on the left side too! On second thought, never mind the left channel thing, I have to figure this out for myself. Amazing you can do that though.
It was Sunday, thank god for that, and this has been a very long reincarnational cycle, I thought.

the denouement of a long cycle is fireworks!

I'm starting to see that! Where did that come from? It came from everywhere.

I always thought I'd probably chosen a fairly conservative number of lives, with a lets-gets-it-over-with kind of attitude. Now I felt differently. I felt it had been a great many lives, hundreds I thought, and this was really starting to give me a completely different feeling about who I was. Maybe there was a lot more to *me* than meets the eye.

All these lives happen at the same time, I knew that, and I've been here since the beginning right? I had this new and exciting feeling that I spanned all of it with my various personalities. Or maybe it was this other new feeling that really, we as human beings, in more or less this form, and with more and less this consciousness, have not been here all that long. Or maybe I was sensing all times at once, or all my personal times at once, and so nothing seemed very distant. Yeah, not writing is probably a good idea right now.

History – there's that word again. It's absolutely astounding the amount contained in one word or one number. I thought of my monk's robe again, and I have sealing wax for letters. How can you not be interested in history, or the future for that matter, when the chances are there's a part of you there – right now?

Once again, I was blessed with a day to myself, and the universe knew it was necessary. Now, I was having spontaneous, visualisation/meditations, as I called them, and I could just go off at the slightest thing. Again, I was pulled to the sun, and I found myself outside drawing the liquid life into me.

I felt semiconscious, and that I could be tipped over by a feather breeze. Delirium. The last time I felt this way, was when I was vaccinated with smallpox before coming to Canada, and my mother, sister and I spent three days in the same bed not knowing who we were. My poor father, he was the only one on his feet thanks to his Royal Air Force inoculations, and it must've given him second thoughts seeing his entire family that ill.

Later, after doing some research, I knew that sometimes this phase of Kundalini rising was referred to as an illness, a sickness.

For now, I couldn't research or read anything at all. I don't think I could have anyway, but it was made clear not to do so. Hard not to go with the flow when you've been swept away so completely as to not know which way is up. I was learning a different way of thinking, of being, and I sensed I would have been too susceptible to any outside guideposts at this moment.

My foundation had started here when I read The Seth Material at eighteen, not long after I'd dropped out of the Protestant Church, but the real beginning was many lives ago. A-go. Another go in a different time that's happening now. (If you gently open words you can sometimes find a treasure.)

I had to "go" with what was inside me now, and I should be okay – I thought, there's quite a bit in there, at least I'm not too badly off when it comes to the *theory* of the situation. Then, there's what I don't know I know – the vast unremembered, maybe we should call it.

You write the screenplay, decide to direct the movie, be the star, and when you walk in front of the cameras both they and the crew disappear and you make one of the most amazing agreements in the universe. You agree to forget just about everything. You agree the movie is real and is happening *to* you, and that you don't know what death is or where you were before, basically.

Cue the birth of religion.

I'd never been more excited in my life! Maybe I could become well known, famous even. Maybe I'll win the lottery now! Maybe I could get my teeth fixed! I could see myself on TV, like on Most Hauntings, being the psychic consultant guest of honour who wanders majestically through the surroundings, gathering up all his impressions into a tidy little segment. It made me think of one particular TV psychic, someone from my part of town in Northwest England – that much was evident from his accent. He was constantly speaking to his spirit companion as though not quite catching what was said, and needing to ask out loud for clarification.

"What's that Tom?"
"What, can you say that again Tom?"
"Eh, what's that Tom, I'm trying…can you show me… what's that… a, a lady?"

No doubt this was for the benefit of anyone around, who just may have been doubtful he was actually speaking to a spirit at that particular moment. That wasn't for me, although I could easily see how it had probably developed from the simple need to get the point across, that yes, I am talking to spirits, right now.

It made me think of English Music Hall and Vaudeville. He really seemed to have his stuff together though. Would I ever be as gifted as he appears to be? He does it on TV as well, that must be difficult, or are there hours and hour's worth of edited-out drivel? Regardless, my mother and I decided without reservation, this was not the style for me. We gave it a trial run anyway.

"Sorry Edna, what's that…?"
"Wait a sec... I'm almost...."
"What's that Edna... could you just… hold on… I'm getting it!"

No. What fun this is though! And I could really use a new career. I thought of different kinds of psychics, mystics and the like, from the most famous to the most infamous. Would there be any way I would fit into this lot? Late-night talk show circuit? I didn't think so somehow – I never was that good in the spotlight.

Then again, nervousness just didn't seem to be the same thing it was a little while ago, even just the idea of nervousness felt different somehow. I knew the universe leaned in my direction, as it does for all of us, but I didn't realise how much the universe would begin throwing herself at me in a dramatic and relentless fashion. I could do no wrong it seemed, and if this was being crazy, it was the most elaborate and creative scenario I could imagine! What a way to go out! What was my mantra? Roll with it – that was it. How not surprising.

I didn't really want to go into trance – not yet anyway. I didn't really want to close my eyes thank you, I think I find staring down at the floor at just this angle to be perfectly suitable. For, things... you know... whatever I'm going to do.

Oh my, I'm turning into Jane Roberts! I could hear her saying – I'm not lying down, not like Cayce, and I'm not closing my eyes! Okay, well there you are, I *am* creating this.

"*You create everything Peter, all the time.*"

Well yes, I know that mum, and I'm not going to get caught up in that one. That's just using my own beliefs against me in a way, trying to convince me I'm not crackers. That's a good one though.

"*You're not going crazy.*"

I bet you say that to all the crazy people!

"*Have a shower.*"

Clean, clean clean clothes I'll get clean clothes I'll go in the closet

I'm crying again my head is against the wall and I'm crying again but not like before oh no not like before these aren't tears of despair these are tears of amazement and joy and the love I feel the crushing love it's almost unbearable it's almost too much my mum it's been twenty-three years oh god mum am I going to make it through this.

"Now."

Oh good, tell me what to do, actually right now that's the very best thing for me, that's the best thing you could do for me. Just tell me what to do, I'll do whatever you say, I'm in your hands and in the universe's hands and in everyone's hands okay, what's next, shower? Not a bath? Okay I'm on my way. Normally I would shave first, but I think I'd better get in there fast. All right, water coming out of my eyes, so let's put some water back in.

I opened the taps and got the water going, I knew this house very well and it was going to take a few minutes for the water to get hot. We all knew the low pressure intimately, and the call, "I'm in the shower!" resounded frequently through the house.

Finally it was hot, and I got in and began to wash. There was only one other person in the house, Jane's dad who lived in the basement apartment, and the water usage there, when it did on occasion cause a change, effected the pressure first, and then the temperature. So imagine my surprise, or not, when upon standing with the centre of my back to the hot water for about a minute, the water decided to turn full cold without any drop in pressure, whatsoever! In this house, that is simply impossible, and at this moment I had a vision of someone going through whatever this was I was going through, in a natural environment. They would be jumping off a rock into the icy cold waters of a sacred river. I needed the shock.

Ancient.

This is what I thought as the shock took hold.

This is so very ancient, and now it's happening right here in Toronto in 2007 on a residential street in a neighbourhood near you. Turn it off!

Well, that worked, I've got to hand you that one, my head space is completely changed – reset. Let me blow my nose. I can't believe this, but I know these events are as natural as the earth, and each time period presents unique tools that can be used by spirit, in this case, the shower. What time is it?

11:11

Of course.

roles change – loyalties don't

Okay – that makes a lot of sense to me reincarnationally – a lot of sense.

relax into yourself

That was a good idea.
Was that my guide or the universe talking? I can't tell yet.

I was having these feelings about crop circles, and another one was all about animals, and talking to animals. I knew I was going to talk to animals.

I remembered a lucid dream, with the crow's mouth moving as we casually spoke, just like in the movies. If you *want* them to that is. Otherwise it's mind to mind and facial expressions, equally amazing. When it comes to dying, I can hardly wait to talk to animals properly – however I had to feign being overwhelmed, and it wasn't too much of a stretch.

Talking to animals? Right now? Could you just hold off for a minute please?

I couldn't believe I was saying that, but I actually kind of meant it. I have seven cats and I had a vision of them walking into the room all talking to me at once. Animals, music, and books are my holy trinity and this is as good as it gets but I really need to breathe...

Give me a sec will you?

"Are you okay?"

Yes mum, I'm okay. I thought it and said it.
"Okay" didn't fit on any scale I could recognise anymore. Is this a *new* okay?

"1625 Constantinople."

You have a life in 1625, in Constantinople? I knew that's what she meant so I already knew the answer, but I wasn't used to this kind of knowing, so usually you ask someone to elaborate don't you?

"A lady of the night."

That's one of my mother's lines all right, and somehow it just seemed very appropriate, considering everything I knew about her, that a life like this would be part of her makeup.

My, my, we will have to give you a stern talking to about this kind of nonsense, but before that – give me all the details!

I was given an introduction to this life of hers and I was enthralled. She has a great fondness for this one, and I could feel it inside of myself as she was telling me about it. I could share the excitement, the wickedness, and the real danger she and her friends would sometimes find themselves involved in around here. It was a raw life with many lessons.

I suddenly realised tomorrow was Monday, and my own raw life was almost upon me. I had to go to work in the morning, and I realised it was probably the best thing for me, but I had no idea how this was going to work. I saw the pun – going to work.

I climbed into bed and pulled the pillow down tight to my shoulder. That idea had just popped into my head. I remembered my mum telling me years ago about other mothers saying, "Edna, he looks so comfortable," when I was an infant, and this was her secret.

Popped into my head? No, she'd put it there. My mother was tucking me in from another world.

Day Three

It was Monday morning in a new reality. I was excited.

comport yourself with dignity and humility

It was another one of those messages that seemed to come from everywhere. I supposed I would learn to sort the voices out, or maybe some messages were meant to come from everywhere on purpose. Knowledge was everywhere, wasn't it? All is one. An interesting way of accentuating something I thought, by having it come from absolutely everywhere. A cosmic highlighter. I will definitely do my best with the dignity and the humility.

I'd always been very interested in sacred hand gestures – mudras – so I was not surprised when there was an upsurge of thoughts and images about this. I'd been doing my Dr. Strange conjuring hands for years from the Marvel comic (Dr. Strange: the master of the mystic arts – Sorcerer Supreme – was my new desktop background picture on my computer at work) and of course, "Live Long and Prosper," with gesture, from Spock and Star Trek. It turned out Dr. Strange's favourite gesture was the Buddhist Karana mudra which incidentally, is the same as "I love you" in sign language.

I *was* surprised my hands now started to attain various positions all by themselves! I was really starting to see how everything connected, everything was tying in. Comic books from my childhood were involved, everything was involved – *everything*. I could feel this with certainty when I didn't think I was making the whole thing up, and if I survived all this I could have an amazing life! If I'm not crazy.

I had to go to work, and nobody alive on this planet knew what had happened to me. Some kind of fun! Nobody in the body knew, unless Gordon realised something was up before we parted on Saturday. I was bawling my eyes out as he pulled away in his school bus, but after four hours of crying solid in the coffee shop, I don't suppose I seemed particularly different.

Nobody knew, and I'd never had a more powerful secret in my life, but the strange thing was, everything knew, the entire universe knew, every molecule of air knew, every bird flying by. It was hysterical really. If anything was *not* a secret, this was it. It all depended on who you were and what you thought, and what frequency you vibrated at, basically. I felt like I was stirring up the world as I moved through it. I got my bike, probably the best, most meditational activity for me other than walking, other than sitting, other than watching creatures, other than daydreaming... oh never mind, I got my bike, and rode to work.

Open channel D. This was the joke now from the old "The Man from U.N.C.L.E." TV show – open channel D. Now it stood for open channel dead, and we both laughed at that. She told me everything was going to be okay, she was just as surprised as me really, and now my new life, my real life had begun. There was the song "Second Chance" in my mind again that she'd made reference to earlier, and she now connected it to The Second Cup where I'd met Gordon. The Second Cup was now the Second Chance.

There's also a school on the corner where The Second Cup is located, two actually, and this also attained special significance for me, especially when I thought of the school there before the newer one. It was a stately old building and much more noble. I really liked that building but learning swirled here regardless – teaching was on this corner... a Yoga school too.

The first lesson, the difference between thinking and listening, never stopped. Over and over again it was impressed upon me how this was the basic thing I had to concentrate on at the beginning, and from this ability would come all confidence with what was going on.

Confidence. Confide-ence. To be sure enough of yourself to possibly tell someone else? Words are crumbling to something simple and beautiful. What am I saying?

I still felt as open as was probably possible and this gave me some cause for concern. Lots of light and love, I guess? Shouldn't I sprinkle salt in a circle or something? What about this whole protection thing? There's something I need to figure out. It's weird because I still can't feel anything but grace – the universe is safe.

The Universe is Safe. Pick your side once again. Thank you free will and the universe is safe. I hope I don't fall off this bike.

On the way past the hydro transformers, I called for my groundhog, hoping I would see him as he lived there, but not this morning. He was probably still asleep. It didn't take more than fifteen minutes to get to work, and that was taking it easy. Once there, I locked up my bike, and took a moment to compose myself. What was this going to be like? Would anyone notice? How could they *not* notice? This was the most incredible adventure ever. I closed my eyes. I had the same vision I was to have over and over again in the first thirteen days – water creating the perfect shore, before easing into it. Even though water would fit any shape, double comfort for it first to design the shape of its boundaries. And I saw the water, I saw it coming along and creating a vessel for itself. And all was refining that shape, and all was becoming more comfortable. I opened my eyes and went inside.

Familiarity is a powerful thing. That's why everything seems so permanent isn't it? It makes us comfortable – it makes this training-ground very comfortable. So the familiarity was like an old coat, but one I might not need for next season. There's the machine, there's the job, and the phone is ringing. I plunged in, it was that kind of job and I was the only full-time employee. I ran a lot of the show at this point in the company's history. I started copying serious documents about serious situations mostly, but now, the numbers and the significances and the synchronicities were flying off the pages. I was in heaven. I was in some kind of heaven that was for sure. I'd waited a long time for this, not just this lifetime, a very long time.

People came into the room, there were only two other employees and the boss, and the two part time employees were both at work that day. Within moments of coming within my vicinity, there was a marked change in the demeanour and behaviour of these people. They became happy! They became very happy! They were not normally like this. I'd worked here for eleven years – I had worked with these two people for eleven years and I knew them very well. This was not just because I seemed to be in an okay mood and had a grin on my face. They were laughing, they were talking, they were in a good mood and they were fine with their Monday morning, all was well with the world ring that bell. Can this really be happening to me? Break time.

"I'm here love, are you okay?"

I'm okay mum. This is the most incredible thing I've ever experienced in my life. Is this really happening? I know I keep saying that but I just can't believe it. I'm so open, I just feel so open. This is funny having break with you.

Before going back inside, I noticed an ant on the wall of the building, and bent closer to have a look. Visions of Ant-Man, or The Atom, depending on which comic you preferred, rose in my mind. Ant-Man could communicate with the ants using a high-tech helmet, originally described using words like frequency and vibrations. Now I felt *I* could communicate, or at least merge for a moment with this ant.

Don't resist the urge to merge – I thought, and how perfect it's an ant at this moment!

I'd never forgotten Seth saying years ago, "You could learn a lot from the consciousness of an ant." I imagined my consciousness funnelling towards this beautiful insect. I thought the word insect must have come from, in sect-ions. How obvious that seemed! Everyone must know that.

My mind entered this creature and from a sensory point of view, I saw through the ant's eyes and the way was laid out as though it were a tunnel. There was no straying from this path, and the feeling culminated into the word, "dedication." After all these years, I finally got to know! I thanked the ant profusely.

Do I deserve the magnificence of what's going on?

Back on the job, work goes by in a dream. There's a very large wall calendar for each month, and I started scribbling on it now like a madman. Is it okay if I jot down just a few key words? I was reminded of all those books and movies of insane people constantly scribbling on every inch of every wall in their rooms, then the floors, the windows. Most of it spiritual in nature I was willing to bet. I imagined straying far off the calendar and covering the walls with sacred, cryptic, arcane symbols. This is fun, but I'd better be careful, and then, I'd better be careful.

I realised I would have to tell my longest friend Susan, as we'd just started getting to know each other closely again. Her sister Lindh, my ex-wife, had somehow mysteriously been taken out of the picture at just this moment, having suddenly lost her job with no warning, and subsequently the use of the work computer. She didn't have her own computer either. The timing didn't escape me.

I'd found "The Haunting," (Susan's favourite movie) on DVD, and sent it to her. Yes, that movie again, how appropriate is that? She was miles away, perfect for the way I was feeling somehow, and now I had my own computer at work she would want to know how the "meeting" with Gordon had gone.

I'd told her on Friday I knew I was in "trouble," so I knew she'd be concerned. I also told her Gordon had a brand new website one week old, and she should have a look at it. She had wished me luck.

I checked my mail, sure enough there was a note from Susan, she'd sent it at 8:36 am, but this had been my first chance to look – Happy good morning! How's your new keyboard? How was the meeting with your friend? Hope you had a really good time.

I had to laugh at the universe – yes, it was a really good time all right.

I managed to bang out some kind of a reply, it was all over the page, but I told her I wasn't the person I was on Friday, and explained that my mum and guide had been waiting, and told me I really *was* in trouble. Contact made! I said, but I don't seem to have much time....

Then the clanger – and they were *still here!*

In less than an hour I had a response – she said I absolutely *had* to listen to my mum and I could never go back. Oh my god this is so great a thing, she added, along with – I became all tingly as I read your mail.

She'd felt something in her heart and *believed me* without a second thought! There is no substitute for someone you've known for almost forty years.

I had an ally.

She also took care of Lindh by telling me she'd give her a call tomorrow and let her know what was going on – that was good.

One last thing, she said – when you said you were in trouble, you can fix that right?

Yes Susan, I'm going to fix it.

I thought I'd better start doing that right now so I went out at lunch time, even though I didn't have a lunch time, and I bought chips (french-fries) and a milkshake.

I could sense my mother's relief and approval even before she said anything, and we both remembered how I'd discovered strawberry milkshakes when we came to Canada, and I wanted them wherever we went. If I'd have known about milkshakes, it would've been a lot easier to drag me over the ocean. I so didn't want to leave England at ten years old.

All they had was chocolate at this place, but good enough. It was a start.

I made it through the day. I just applied myself and worked, was in awe, and worked. The next thing I knew the day was over, and if I had anything to show in my wake from the new me it was happy people. There was no way around it – their vibrations had been raised up just by being in the same room as me! I'm the luckiest person on earth!

It was just this feeling of being open to anything that would've made me nervous, if I'd been able to feel nervous.

I flew home on my bike – hey there Mr. Groundhog! And once home we tried to make me feel "as if" I wasn't so open.

First we had The Vacuum Exit, which was supposedly the sensation of *them* actually leaving. Kind of a swoosh off to my right.

This was followed by The Absence, which was an artificial sensation of emptiness. Ho hum, it sort of worked for an hour.

Then the idea was to get my attention as subtly as possible, and this we called, The Gentle Prod. This quickly fizzled out also.

So, the vacuum exit, the absence, and the gentle prod, ridiculous little notions that helped for a short while. Then we tried saying, "private time"– complete with a psychic bulletin board for leaving messages if necessary – but it didn't really work for long either. We tried it for a few days and the last time, I just started talking away half an hour later and completely forgot I'd imposed a private time. It was a joke, but I didn't know if I could ever be alone again, so it seemed important to try and figure a few things out.

Would this be the price I would pay for this particular "agreement?" Or was it just part of the preliminary business, and once things were secure, I would have, or would be given or develop, control and finesse possibly? Maybe I just needed to get *used* to things.

Then, I marvelled at my own mind, and it wouldn't be the first time I did this and hopefully it won't be the last. The human mind is really something to behold, and I must have really needed to feel that I had some kind of control over what was going on, and that I could actually stop the communication for a while, so my mind erected a barrier. It gets funnier. In my mind it appeared in a very coarse fashion as a wall of steel or iron that I could raise or lower like a drawbridge. Because I'd thought of iron, and because of the way it moved, I ended up christening it – The Ironing Board.

I could raise this barrier up in my mind, and I could actually feel a degree of solace I thought, although this was really a joke too, as I could also sense the presence of my mother and my guide behind this wall.

I had a vision of my mother leaning against it with her back, smoking a cigarette or something, and waiting for me to go through all the silly things I would have to go through. There was a sense of amusement and a great deal of understanding and compassion coming from her. The Ironing Board. This lasted longer than the other ideas, but still only about three days.

What happens after this blowing-out phase? My mind was blown all right.

My new spirit friends were doing their best to make me feel as comfortable as possible, and the entire universe itself was helping – all I had to do was keep breathing, keep breathing deep breaths. And eat.

Day Four

I made it through one day at work, so I can make it through another, right?

My body started to work, and after an hour or so I heard the computer chime ta-daa! – to let me know a message had come in, it was from Gordon – hope this finds you well, that was some meeting we had there!

You're not kidding! I thought, but I only had time to write a somewhat cryptic reply – the meeting hasn't ended. I was just so busy and I didn't know what else to say anyway. Hopefully that would get some kind of message across.

A familiar customer came in and was standing at the counter with his photographs to be copied. I knew this man, I knew his dog Ember, who had just passed over recently, and this customer liked me, he brought me chocolates at Christmastime.

He handed over the photographs which were large, about ten by twelve inches. They were photographs of his wedding day many years ago in Scotland, and they were taken outdoors at a castle where the ceremony had taken place. He was about to go back there and renew his vows. I took them to my machine and as usual, examined them before putting them on the platen.

At the sight of this castle in Scotland, I started to audibly moan at the feelings rushing through me from these images. England, Britain, Scotland, Wales, Ireland. My Island! Oh Britain, Oh England, Oh home. I was almost in tears, not so unusual as you know by now, but I'd been managing to keep it to myself and now it was getting away from me.

My customer looked up with an inquiring look on his face – was I okay? Was I asking a question? I mumbled something about being English and how much I loved castles and how beautiful the photographs were. Luckily, this sent him off into his own dreams of getting married thirty years ago in this sacred place. I knew it was sacred, I could tell just by looking at it, but I suspect all places like that are sacred so it didn't seem such a feat. I finished the job, handed the work over, and as he was paying I knew he hadn't come in by "accident." Nothing was by accident.

I must find some castles to add to my screensaver, which consisted of scrolling photographs and images I'd gathered. There was my school in England, Holy Trinity Church, and a photograph of my mother and her sister Vera, but other than that, it was animals, especially animals nuzzling each other and demonstrating what they knew it was time for us all to learn – and these were different *species* of animals. There is only one species of human being (ever wonder about that?) and we still can't get it together. Animals know how to love unconditionally.

I'd been staring at these photographs for months with joy and an expanding heart.

As I looked at the computer, I saw Gordon's smiling face go by, and I had to shake my head and laugh as I remembered plucking it from his new website on Friday.

There you are! You just changed my life forever – thank you.

Five o'clock came from nowhere so I locked the doors, shut up shop, grabbed my knapsack and headed for the back door.

Riding my bicycle was by now a mystical and sacred experience in itself. I didn't just feel the wind – the wind was caressing me – and the fact that my physical body could balance itself, or himself, on this contraption and send me off into rapture as well as get me home quickly, was wondrous. So wondrous, that on Sunday I was riding along, and I just passed out cold. I closed my eyes for a moment as I usually do, just for a moment, and I literally conked out as I was riding and found myself up the curb on the grassy boulevard. It's okay everybody – I'm okay!

Holy crow! I just became unconscious while I was riding my bike. This is too much! Better get home quick.

This time I didn't pass out and I was halfway home now – hello Mr. Groundhog, I hope I see you soon! Miraculously, I had another evening to myself – the universe was being most gracious – and the tears welled up again. I'd better get everything under control before I get home.

are you okay?

Who's talking to me now? I laughed when I thought that because I've been thinking it for years, as my own mind seems to have so many layers of observance. Didn't everyone's? Still laughing, I thought, this is interesting because now I have to relearn, I have to recognise my own thoughts, my own ordinary thoughts, the way it used to be when that's all I seemed to hear, and that was only three days ago, because now my own thoughts were becoming mixed in. Especially with my mother, there was a particular sort of merging going on where our minds swam together in a particular now, and sometimes we had fun determining the originator of a thought as it flew by.

Anyone but she – and I might have been panicking.

Blood – what a connector. Now I saw all the similarities in facial features and mannerisms in families, to be the universe attempting once again to show us how connected we are. In my own family you look at a number of people, and your own eyes are looking back at you. That is supposed to make us think. Also, I realised now I was in my fifties that a person has at least three completely different faces in their life, depending on how long they live. I'm on my third face now definitely, and it seemed obvious to me how this is our way of trying to understand reincarnation and other forms, other bodies, other faces, in even just one incarnation. The only constant is change, and I'm not the same person I was when I look in the mirror now, but I know all the other mes, the ten year old me, the twenty year old me, the thirty year old me etc., are all inside aend are part of me, the way all my incarnations will be when this cycle is complete.

When it came to this particular person, my mother, I'd been inside her physical body – I came out of her, even though there is no outside – what a trick. We were already one. Communicating with her already felt different from anyone else, although trying to remember exactly what her physical voice sounded like was difficult, and unsettling. The problem with my mother was that she sounded like me, because we are so connected in this life and many, many others. This doesn't help when you're still trying to learn the difference between thinking and listening.

She tried different voices in an attempt to make herself more recognisable, but in the end or should I say very soon, I just knew it was *her,* no matter what she sounded like. There was/is a feeling of home, something that goes so far beyond familiarity, but that would be a good place to start to get some idea of the feeling.

It was like falling backwards with your eyes closed, without a worry in the world. Whatever happened, it would be all right, everything would be all right – it'll all come out in the wash. It felt like my mother! My biggest fan! I'm where I'm supposed to be, doing what I'm supposed to be doing, feeling what I'm supposed to be feeling at this moment, talking to who I'm supposed to be talking to, I'm who I'm supposed to be, who I'm supposed to be-coming. Content – sigh – at last.

I was standing in the bedroom after work, and now I was starting to have serious concerns about how open I felt, and I understood that just sitting down and imagining the Lotus Flower closing would've been a bit laughable. Plus, I remembered the intent, and the deal. This had to be made permanent. We, they – were going to try to make this permanent.

"Day thirteen."

What happens on day thirteen mother?
I've always been infatuated by numbers so this didn't surprise me, and although eleven and twenty-two are master numbers in numerology, thirteen has always been a good number to me.

"Hold on until day thirteen."

Well I'll certainly do my best mum – I thought, but I feel delirious, euphoric, strange, otherworldly. I felt like being naked outside, although I didn't think that would go down well in this neighbourhood somehow. Holy men have gone naked forever. Did I actually feel like I was a holy man?

go into your room and sit down

The voice from everywhere, or maybe that's my guide's voice actually, maybe his voice sounds like it comes from everywhere. If ever I was not going to ignore something, I was not going to ignore this.

I went into my room and sat down. I did another visualisation/meditation and I saw the universe, and once again it was amazing how easy it was to envision anything and everything, and it felt like I'd been meditating for years when in reality, it was always something I'd kind of avoided, kind of thought unnecessary I suppose. I seemed to be in a dream most of the time anyway before this had happened, and was always drifting off into somewhere or other as I mentioned. Then it hit me, music was my meditation! Ever since I was accomplished enough to play without thinking about it, I would close my eyes and go somewhere else. The music would just flow, and if I was in the right place, a song would practically write itself. Those were always the best ones, and I would return from that place of inspiration feeling disoriented.

Firming. The firming. This was another firming meditation. I liked this name and I liked this idea, as though I was already the way I was supposed to be, and it was simply a matter of tempering. The energy flowed from the universe to me and back, in and out, within and without until there was no out. It was funny when I knew I'd done enough and once again said "out." Maybe I should change that to – enough.

"A slow, sacred bath."

That's a good idea. I'll just make my way back to the bedroom and I think I'll sit here for a minute.

Well mum, you know a lot now don't you? Not that you didn't before – I'm not implying that – but you're a lot more than you were the last time we were together in the same dimension, aren't you? You are a lot more.

That Buddha statue – where did that come from? Was it because of me? Suddenly there was a Buddha in the house, and you were painting it! How did that happen? You were Christian weren't you? Then again, you certainly let me choose my own path the day I came to you and said I could no longer attend confirmation classes. I think I'd been there twice and that was enough. I was fifteen I think – thanks for that.

It dawned on me that she had believed my ramblings. She'd listened to everything I'd said, mulled it over, and actually *believed* me! An open mind is sometimes a hard thing to find, and I was blessed by a mother with one.

Wait a minute. She was here first. I had a feeling that maybe things were actually the other way around. Maybe I had an open mind because of her?

She was born in 1921, shortly after the First World War and destined to live through the second one. I could hardly imagine being eighteen years old and the Second World War being declared. That would throw you off your game, would it not? Then again, maybe that would really get you wondering about the meaning of life and death, and what the hell was going on. Whatever the reason, I now felt some serious soul-searching had gone on, and she'd just kept quiet about certain things. Sometimes that's a good idea.

Things were fitting together in a certain kind of way, I couldn't put my finger on it exactly but I knew there was a word. The perfect word. It was like a jigsaw puzzle, a multi-dimensional jigsaw puzzle, and the puzzle was my life, and everyone's life, and well... just everything. Absolutely everything.

Everything has consciousness, and now I thought of nature spirits – faeries – beings who work with the matrices of plant life mostly. I tended to think of them as plant angels. There was a small statuette of a faerie in my bedroom, cherry blossom her name, and I wouldn't have been surprised to see her fly around the room, or at least move – I was ready for anything. I gave her an offering of an acorn broken in two, the cup in her hand, and the nut/seed at her feet. It seemed appropriate.

The point is, I couldn't stop thinking about faeries, and I couldn't stop thinking about us all being created from the same energy, and us all being part of the same web. The World Wide Web, I mused, is an external materialization of the inner communication going on within all things.

"The bath."

Right you are – how long have I been standing like a statue? I thought I was sitting down.

I climbed in and thought of heaven and the perfect word.

Day Five

How am I going to work? Is it Wednesday? Divine mystery!

Normality amidst the taking apart and reassembly of an earth-soul was the order of the day. The jiva soul, the personal one in Hindu terms, not my higher-self who I'm sure was quite secure in his love of the unknown, and was probably laughing his head off! Oh look at Peter, I remember that – of course it was a little different when I did it, but the same. Spirituality and paradoxes go hand in hand – it's part of the fun.

There was not much reference left, my familiar mind was no more – I just seemed to love everything. So when I received a note from Gordon about taking in the light/love through your crown chakra, and then sending it out through the heart chakra, it seemed like I was spontaneously there already.

My body was a great help, god love him, somehow managing to steer without a rudder. Time seemed to be coming apart in pieces, stretching and contracting. Soon a strange kind of looping would begin. After-the-fact déjà vu. It would hit me as a familiar scene in retrospect – space and time were playing hop-scotch.

Mostly, it all seemed like a dream. No, the dream became more obvious. That's it. That's what was happening, and the synchronicities were almost beyond belief. The world was finishing my sentences for me, metaphorically and literally.

Roxy, the boss's beautiful Poodle who spent a great deal of her time at work and with me, sensed the change and was even more eager to be close. This was more than just the usual result from my constant attentions, so I decided to call her in my mind and see if she would turn and look at me. She did! Did you see that? Roxy just...

Who are you kidding Neli? She heard a noise or something, she's always flitting her head around.

Oh man I know she heard me! Didn't you see? At that moment when...

But you'll never know will you?

No, I'm pretty sure that...

Well, I guess "pretty sure" is better than nothing. You'll never *know*, though.

You're wrong, I *do* know.

How?

I know because...

Oh, sorry to interrupt – but it has just come to my attention that you have already chosen your side, and therefore this conversation is redundant.

My side?

Yes, I know it was a long time ago, and you may have forgotten, but here it is, plain as day in *your* hand. You've been signing and choosing for longer than you know.

What did I choose?

Well, I believe it was your friend Seth who asked you to choose sides. Something about accidental and meaningless, or magical and meaningful beyond your wildest... Anyway, you decided to live in the magic – sorry, I should have checked – of course the dog heard you.

Just like that?

Yes. Once again, pardon the oversight, just didn't know you had *faith*.

Faith. Well, I found out something about faith. It's the same thing I found out about everything else, it comes from within, and surrounding yourself with people of a certain belief will not make your own beliefs any stronger. Faith is between you, and you. Because of this, when you have faith, there is no doubt. If there is doubt, there is no one else to blame. No one else to blame, and no one else to rely on – just you.

It also didn't surprise me that the words "faith" and "fate" look remarkably similar. Maybe – Your Faith is your Fate – I thought.

I had faith I could keep on working, in general for now, and today specifically, and somehow the dream transported me through the work-day and home.

One other thing, shortly before leaving, I discovered a photograph on my newly acquired camera that I put up on the computer. It was otherworldly. In the photograph, three of my cats, Sidney, Seren and Zachariah are looking directly at you, and each of their eyes are glowing a different colour: red, amber and green. Stop-Caution-go, I thought. It was incredible.

I didn't notice the date it had been taken on, and in fact didn't remember taking the photo at all. This would be significant later, as would this moment for being the inauguration of many fascinating photographs, but I had no idea of this at the time.

I rode home, put my bike away and closed my eyes. I could stand in this garden forever, breathing in the summer. I want it to rain on me.

Once inside, I started to sense the pattern of my own development, my education as my guide had put it, and my own past was yesterday, it was right beside me.

I remembered being in England and my father saying to me "mind over matter," and explaining to me what it meant to the best of his ability, which was good enough for me. He got the point across, and it was an idea I never stopped thinking about in my early life. It made sense the way things do when they make sense.

We came to Canada in 1964 when I was ten years old, and I remember being quite young when he told me this, probably seven or so. This was now *shown* to me as a turning point, or a touchstone or a stepping-stone or an activator. In a dream when you realise you're dreaming and become lucid, you twig to the fact that you're dreaming. You catch yourself and there's a realisation, there's a revelation – well something twigged in me when my father told me about "mind over matter." We were going back to the beginning of this life. Oh, this is so unbelievable!

Then we moved on – a few years later. This stood out powerfully in my life because we were moving to Canada. The house had been sold, and we had to move out before it was time to board the ship and depart for Canada. I didn't know or understand the details at the time, but I suppose now looking at it, the house must have been sold as close as possible to departure date but we still had a week to spare. All I knew was that we had to live for a week at my grandma and granddad's house before we left for our new lives. I had to sleep with my granddad for a week and this was a strange and new experience. I know I tried sleeping on the floor. I remember the cars on Manchester Road swishing past, but I guess I'd been uncomfortable, so now I was sleeping with my granddad. I suppose grandma ended up sleeping on her own in the other room. Here's where I was now *shown* another critical step in my personal development, and it was just too wonderful – me in bed with my granddad. I believe I love this universe! It went like this:

"Do you say your prayers P?"

He always called me P. I knew it was because he had a brother called Peter whom he also called P, and I liked that.

"Yes Granddad."
"All right, let's say them now then."
"Okay."

There were a number of prayers I could have said, my sister and I had a picture book and we had our favourites. I defaulted to the original, the foundation, the Lord's Prayer. Somehow, because I was with my grandfather, I didn't think, "there are four corners to my bed, there are four angels at my head…" would have been appropriate. Maybe just a little too childish I thought. Or at least writing this, that's what I think I thought. I began…

"Our Father Who Art in Heaven…"
"No."

He stopped me dead in my tracks.

"What's that Granddad?"
"You don't have to say it out loud."
"You don't?"

Come to think of it, he hadn't made a sound.

"God can hear you in your mind."
"He can?"

From this I knew he meant, God can hear your mind, or hear your thoughts, but that's what he said.

"Yes, just say it to yourself P."
"Oh, okay."

So I said the Lord's Prayer in my mind for the first time in my life.
Talking to God in my mind. Does everyone know about this? I remembered at the time being so intrigued and pleased by this, and I've al-

ways remembered it as being of significance in my life, and now I was being assured of this with no mistake. This was beginning to look like it was meant to be, in every way.

remembering is not remembering – it's being there again

Okay, this made sense. All is now – the Spacious Present as Seth said.

Is this really happening? Can this really be happening? I was reassured again by quotes from movies and books, images and scenes from all the things I've read and seen that have impressed me. Science fiction is an enormous asset as many ideas are presented in such a setting that would otherwise have no acceptable outlet. The authors can let their minds sail.

I kept hearing Spock. "Is this all that I am?" "Is there nothing more?"

That's the question isn't it? I was seeing this scene from the first Star Trek movie, where, lo and behold, evolution is the theme. Also, I recalled, the story is about the *need* to evolve, "Captain, V'ger *must* evolve." It crossed my mind that if there was ever a time for us – this was probably it. You don't have to look too far to see how much trouble we are in as a species being disconnected for so long, and maybe it's all come down to right here, right now. There is much to remember.

God is before you, and has many faces. One of them is yours.

Pop culture in general was a huge reservoir of available emotional effectors, and I began to see that my mother had a refined ability for finding the appropriate scene or line with the perfect inflection to reassure me. This was fun, and it was working! I was *not* crazy for a stretch again.

She'd said to Gordon that she wanted to mother me, she wanted to feed me. Well now she was getting her chance and I was ready to accept that help. It was less than two weeks ago I'd said in a note to Susan – I need my mummy badly. That was word for word what I'd said, and I meant it.

I'd reached a level of suffering recently that was a signal in itself that I was close to the end. Calling for help to the universe, screaming in my mind, calling my mother's name – I must've looked like a parody of every tragedy in literature. I could see myself with my mouth twisted out of shape and the tears rolling down, holding on to the door-jamb. I was a mess – and this was only a few days ago.

How quickly things can change! Never lose hope! My mother had come as fast as she could – she had *urged* me to call Gordon I now could see.

My mother and my guide were just quietly there now, and I was really scared for some reason. It was as though they were staying out of the way, and that scared me even more. I had a feeling that something was happening, that something was going to happen, that something was brewing, that something was stretching and waiting in the wings. I should be panicking, but even though I was feeling such trepidation, I couldn't seem to panic anymore than I could feel that old debilitating nervousness I used to feel.

This was better anyway, terror of a sort, but still a degree of functionality. Hooray for small mercies! I'd been fortunate so far. I hadn't really felt fear yet – just a little when I was dealing with the mask – but this was palpable and I felt a little sick. That feeling made me realise I hadn't been sick yet either and that surprised me.

use it as a reset button

Fear as a reset button, or fear is a reset button? This was the advice I was given and it made sense to me, I could use this. Now I imagined fear as a bucket of freezing cold water thrown over me, and I could imagine it clearly after the recent shower experience. I could use it to snap every nerve to high alert. I imagined shaking the water out of my hair and wiping my eyes, spreading my feet apart and wiping my hands on my thighs – bending forward – power stance. I'm ready, I think.

Ready for what?

Ready for my mother now appearing in my mind with three friends in tow, 1-2-3, three people I know, three in a row. This wasn't scary. I knew she was giving them definite instructions relating to how much time they had. She gave them about fifteen seconds each as it turned out, and I could see her usher-in my first guest.

Sherrie. Of course, I thought – I have friends who have just died, of course I do, how silly of me. Sherrie came through loud and clear. Is that the lingo, came through? I'm turning into something fast, I thought.

"Cutie patootie, you did it, you did it!
"Remember when I said you were the coolest guy I'd ever met? Well, imagine how cool I think you are now!"

That was it, quick and to the point, with a palpable love pulling on my heart.

I thought of the gift she'd bought – lightning in a light-bulb (lightning again!) – I'd taken it out of the walk-in closet and plugged it in a few days before finding out about her leaving us.

I know I did this on the day she died. I know.

Sherrie your funeral was a mess! Did you see and laugh yourself to bits?

No, sorry, not with Edna around. It was time for our next mystery guest.

"Peteski."

Peteski? There's only one person who calls me that – Steaven.

"How are you kid, it's me!"

Steaven! I have your – The Teaching of Buddha – book. There was more to *you* than meets the eye too wasn't there?! Are you okay? Was I one of your crossing guards?

I'd told him I thought I would probably be one of the people to help him, when the time came and the cancer had finished its job. How arrogant! Was that over two years ago now? Did I believe what I was saying when I told him that? Everything is a feeling – I *feel* as well as hear him saying I was – I was.

I'll talk to you again Steaven! – I just had a chance to shout as Edna came along with the pole and hook.

There wasn't a moment to catch a breath when there she was – Mum B.

"Hello Peter."

Somehow, contained in this was – this is my old voice, the voice you know, I don't need to sound like this anymore.

"I know your mother now, and I know what's happening with you. Try not to worry about anything, we're all with you.
Tell Joy and Colin I love them and I'm here!"

She somehow managed to impart something else once again – "when and if you can."

I could hardly wait to tell them – Joy and Colin are her children. I had visions of happiness and tears and embracing and laughter and dancing in circles and relief....
How interesting I was in the middle of evolution and dimensions of being I could hardly contain, and as naive as a child.
I was reborn, but the world hadn't been – yet, and I was to find out how these things can change the expression on many a face to one of perplexed concern. I had no idea the Middle Ages were still breathing, but I would find out soon.

Bye Mum B, I hope we can talk longer next time. Did you see me looking around your hospital room when you died? I was looking for you.

Mum B! We'd known each other for twenty-five years, one way or another, and shortly before she died we talked about life, death, the universe etc., and she told me about seeing a ghost when she was a youngster! Boy, you could almost think we'd been laying the groundwork for this couldn't you?
Oh, the never ending tears. Cry me a river wasn't just a metaphor anymore.
What is going on really? Is there a name for this? Awakening was all I could think of. A psychic awakening – spiritual awakening? They're the same thing anyway. I needed to do some research.

Day five was turning into some kind of day. That's the way I was thinking of the days now, and day one was mythical. This me didn't die in that coffee shop, but I am definitely in a different world, that's for sure. I closed my eyes and shook my head – this can't be happening!
Too late. Shouldn't have said that. Just before it came, I knew what my mother was going to send my way. Corporal Hudson from "Aliens."

"This ain't happenin' man – this can't be happenin' man – this isn't happenin'!"

Pretty funny mum – keep the humour coming. I still feel scared for some reason though, and the way you zoomed those people in and out like that told me how delicate you think I am.

I'm still in trouble aren't I? It was only five days ago you told me I was close to death, and now all this on top of it. Am I going to make it through this? No, seriously, am I going to get through whatever it is that's actually going on here? This was one of those serious moments, like at the board table with the agreements, and there was a small silence....

All right, well at least all of the cards were on the table, and no one was bluffing.

Am I actually this daring? There's no going back – I don't want to go back.

"You're a funnyocity!"

Thank you mum! That certainly isn't the first time you've called me that!

Now I had visions of a silver rose. Many years ago, I'd given my mother a silver rose on a silver necklace, and this is now what I saw. My mother was thinking about a story that amused her regarding this necklace. She'd been visiting me in Toronto.

"Hi mum, it's good to see you. Oh I really like your necklace."
"Do you?" Coy look – fiddling with the rose. "Well, you bought it for me!"

My lord, we are in two different dimensions and she still won't let me forget it!

Silver rose. The Tudor rose. The Lancashire rose. The Yorkshire rose. This is what I thought about now, and I went back to the story of the Tudor rose.

The House of Lancaster's heraldic emblem, or badge, was a red rose, while the House of York's was a white rose. When the War of the Roses was over and done with, the two were combined to create the Tudor rose – it was as simple as that.

Now I thought of the masculine and feminine again, and the two roses took on *that* meaning for me. The Tudor rose being the balancing of the two energies.

Another image filled my mind now and – of course!

I travelled back to a night many years ago at one of my mother's family parties. It was an anniversary or something, and my mother had managed to get me to dance a nice slow number with her. We were in each other's arms with that silver rose around her neck between us, and I remembered my thoughts at the time. I actually remembered my exact thoughts.

I thought – this is important, this is really important right now, I'm not a kid anymore, I'm a man and I'm dancing with my mother. Remember this Nelson, remember this moment – it means something special for both of us.

Holy crow!

More connections came tumbling into my head.

In England, we lived at 17 Rosehill Street, and our first address in Canada was on Blackthorn Avenue. Two of the streets around us were Rosethorn and Silverthorn.

I remembered my mother had joked through Gordon, "I even talk to people in Yorkshire now!"

There were rose allusions everywhere, and how interesting my warrior monster man John was there, in the 1400s.

I saw my father planting his roses in the garden and then everything spiralled back to this moment and I stared at nothing....

I knew my mother was the linchpin in my personal realm of experience, and I knew we'd been together many times, or all times. Gordon said we'd been sisters, and I knew we had more than once. He also said this mother-son life was unusual. It was like a bit of an experiment – I thought. One weird one for the road.

I now felt we'd done it differently because it was *this* life, the potentially waking up life, the figuring it out somewhat life. Mothers and sons don't generally get as much time together as siblings, or friends of the same generation. We chose to have less time together with this one, and I knew why.

One of us here – and one of us there.

That was the deal, that was the arrangement, and that was now going to happen with conscious interaction. *You* are there, and *I* am here, and the conversation is never further away than a single thought.

It took me fifty-three years to get here mum, and god knows how many lifetimes. I'm eating too.

The universe was allowing me to have this entire evening to myself again, and I was very glad for that. I had just walked downstairs, and as I was crossing the living room floor I felt a wizard's cloak descend onto my shoulders! Merlin and England and magic wrapped themselves around me. I could feel the weight of it on my shoulders, thick black velvet with animals and stars and moons on it, as you would generally think such a cloak would have.

Okay, so where's the hat? – I thought, trying to take it all in stride by now, but I was definitely scared a little. I was agog with absolute wonder and amazement, but still that fear of losing my mind. Was this why I had such an ominous feeling this evening?

I have worn something like this, or one of me, or part of me, or whatever you want to say. This is *in* me, and what was going on? I have a Hindu guide, and now Merlin is in the air. I'm living a book, and it's the most fascinating thing I've ever read, just the way I would create it if I was making it all up. Oh my.

Well, this ties in with Stonehenge, I thought, because I couldn't get Stonehenge out of my mind, and if I could have walked to England I would've put my shoes on and started walking. I also knew now why I had to go out last month and buy "Taxi" by Harry Chapin, because there was a line I couldn't get out of my head – "There's a wild man wizard – he's hiding in me – illuminating my mind." I was stunned.

I went back upstairs and got ready for the famous bath. I was trying to be really good to myself now. If there's such a thing as handling *yourself* with kid gloves, I had the feeling I should.

Once in the bath, I washed carefully and thought about my guide. I could see the mystery man again in the house on Rosehill Street in England, but I couldn't see his face clearly. I felt I probably would soon. We were sitting together in that room, just getting used to being together, and it was a comfortable feeling. I liked this man, guide or not. There were so many things to sort out.

Then I thought of John, the monster, and – I guess I'm going to have to integrate you carefully aren't I? You're a sobering presence and I know you'll be tear control. That's the first thing I would like to use some of your energy for, I doubt you ever cried over anything. You scare me though, too much of a concentration in you, and I know my fear of knives is because of you, and the way they *feel*... I'm going to...

And there he was, with great surprise and strength, or power, but only to make a point. I knew it was a statement about his own personal integrity, and it wasn't a battle.

However, his demonstration manifested itself as a push – a very hard push.

I was sitting in the bath leaning on my left hand, with my legs out to the right, when I was pushed front first to the side of the bath, and *held*, for just a moment. I could feel the push on my back, and I mention this here, because I was to be physically moved in a different manner at a later time.

I was okay, the pressure on my back disappeared.

Kneeling now, I splashed my face. I was absolutely astounded, and hoped I would make it through all of this while still feeling so frail.

So many things were happening. Any one of them could be responsible for feelings of trepidation or fear couldn't they? Especially when I think of this John character and what just happened, right?

I felt good this last experience had been more amazing than scary really, or at least half and half, and I'd always wanted to experience events like this so what was this feeling?

There was something else underlying everything, some kind of pressure that wasn't being washed away by the experiences so far. It was as though the universe would warn me if it would do any good, but how does he prepare for that, anyway? Well, maybe a deep breath when the time comes might help him out, so we'd better let him feel *expectant.*

As it turned out, things were just warming up. Let him have his bath, give him an experience in there, let him get nice and clean, and put on his clean clean clothes, and then we'll really turn it up. I barely had time to get out of the bath, dry off, get dressed, and make it to the sink before it began.

I'm fortunate, I seem to have lived a fairly virtuous life – but there was a spider, there were some ants, there was the time I hit my cat, and there was the time I pretended to throw my dog when I was a teenager. He whimpered, and I have died in my heart every time I thought about this for the rest of my life so far.

Rex, I'm so sorry! But he was here now, he was explaining to me that it was okay, in his life it was nothing – I was just a kid. He was my dog, and he is my dog, and he would always be my dog. I had my head in the sink and I could've filled it all by myself. I opened the tap and washed my face with cold water and they kept on coming, the tears and the pieces of my life. This is a life review and I'm not even dead yet!

Mintski. Oh lord, I hit my cat because she just would not shut up. I threw a bit of water on her and I scared her. People who don't know about animals will never understand, until they do. My heart had been damaged by this, and now she was here in all her Siamese power, and if we had but one tenth of the grace....

She said not to worry, I hadn't gotten used to her voice yet, and it had scared me.

She was right. The first time as it came out of nowhere in the dark, I thought the gates of hell had opened wide. Somehow without the need for words, I told her this wasn't quite good enough for me, and.... No, it wasn't like that. It was condensed, like sentences collapsing into one word – words collapsing into one letter. A story contained in the full-stop, a universe in a dot.

The closest thing would be the phrase – unfinished business. I'm sorry – just didn't seem good enough for me.

Mintski had been kind enough to come when my rabbit Roger had died and I'd arranged to meet him in a lucid dream. Rex was about to walk into the room also, but I couldn't stop myself from waking up. Annoying!

I'll see you again Mintski.

Now it was time for the insects. There were ants I had killed with the sun and a magnifying glass, and there was a spider I had killed with household poison spray, two situations I have been profoundly unhappy about ever since, and that is why they were here now.

I spoke to all of the ants by speaking to one, a queen, and I apologised for the purity of my ignorance. I was forgiven as I forgave myself, and continued, demonstrated reverence for these and all creatures, was promised from the soul.

Thank you for letting me do this.

My spider, who may have died physically, but has lived within me as sorrow ever since, now walked forward for a talk.
Forgive me! We were all so proud of our spray-can! Just a couple of squirts and no more pests! That's what the TV said everyone should do! I'm sorry!
My spider was kind enough to tell me his dying was just like going to sleep and not to worry. Once again with the not-to-worry. Do we deserve friends like this?
I was gasping. It wasn't like going to sleep. I felt it. I needed to feel it. Oh god!

I had vague thoughts of percentages. There must be an actual number the universe knows. It's a fact, some people awaken to the universe, or God, and it kills them. Death by enlightenment I thought and I laughed. I can laugh!

Does everyone know what a gift from God laughter is?
Does everyone know it only takes one letter to change slaughter to laughter?

This spirituality had snaked through all of my lives like a lit fuse, slowly burning down from one life to the next, sometimes sparking brightly and other times almost accidentally being trodden out, and now it was about to find its source. The umbilical cord had almost led to the mother of the universe. I was about to meet God.

༄ ༄ ༄ ༄ ༄ ༄

This was the day – this was my own longest day, a day of condensed knowledge, the Summer Solstice of all of my incarnations, and in the regular world that was fifteen days away – not bad timing for an experience like this. Lots of light/energy coming in at this time and hopefully it might be able to keep me on my feet.
I felt buffeted.
I didn't really have time for that sentence. It was one thing after another since my dad and my granddad and those visions, and my head and my world were swimming.

My mum had brought three people, three dead people and my god I could talk to them, and I was seeing roses, and John had pushed me in the bath, the bastard, and I have a wizard cloak, and I just apologised to the animal kingdom, and I feel really quite scared right now I...

prepare!

Prepare, but you can't so good luck. Maybe that deep breath would be a good idea right about now.
I didn't have to, it took my breath away. If every cell of my body had breath, it was all taken away.

The energy came from inside, from the earth, from All That Is, from below, from above, from the Goddess... and felt like I was standing on liquid lighting.
Well, you wanted me to act the fool more mum, and now I'm panting to beat the band and I'm jumping from foot to foot as though I'm trying to stand on a million volts. That must look pretty good.
It came from my core. The core of my body and the core of my soul and the centre of the circle.
A message from home.
The message.

It started to rise up like boiling spirit, and breath was everything, breath is everything, I am my breath, I am breath, I'm breathing, I breathe, I'm moaning, I'm dying.
It wouldn't stop, it wasn't going to stop, it would never stop, and I cried out as though I might have some control, as though anyone might have control, as if maybe God wasn't sure how much I could take and needed an idea. I was genuinely frightened now. Hello to the reason for all tonight's apprehension.

"Three times too much, three times too much!"

Was that my voice? What's a voice?

Worried about physical survival now are we? Don't worry, you were going to be dead in the old world anyway weren't you? Forget it Nelson, it's too late, the train has left the station, there's no turning that amp down, it's on eleven, you asked for it and this chord is for you.

"Holy cow I can't... I don't know if..."

The unknown thing called a voice was a squeal.
And then I died.

And then I was terrified, someone was more terrified than I have ever been in my entire old life.
Where did I go? Someone looked at the bedroom window and thought – if that was a cliff, I would jump off it right now!
Would I? This is panic! This is because...
This is because I don't have an "I" anymore. My ego has dispersed. It's been dispensed with and I'm deeply scared now because I have nowhere to gather. I don't even have somewhere to gather my terror, and that is the most frightening of all. So, who's talking?

"God help me!"

This *is* God Neli.

What did the dead person agree to?
This is why certain people do drugs, to get here – or try to.

What happened next is going to sound funny, but regardless, I now felt my brain move, or my head, or both. It was a sensation inside I have never had before, and I will never forget for as long as I live. Actually, "for as long as I live" doesn't make sense anymore – it hasn't for a while.
I was still standing beside the counter, in relatively the same place I'd been since having my head in the sink and then washing my face after the beautiful creatures came.
Now, suddenly, but it wasn't abrupt, I was somehow in the bedroom facing the window on the far wall, although it wasn't the window anymore – I couldn't see the window or the wall now, it was... space.
Outer space. The galaxy? The cosmos?

I wasn't sure what I was seeing as a location, it could have been our solar system or it could have been every galaxy everywhere, all of it. It was just, here...

The Universe was in my bedroom, and it was moving fast. It was a fast forward through time, but it wasn't fast or moving forward through anything, it was unfolding from the inside out, just like me, but I could still see my notes and pen on the bed!

Who can see these things? Is that excitement now and not fear?
Am I/you glad there was no cliff?
There is no familiar me to experience anything, but somehow "I" seem to have a kind of cohesive coherence.
I seem to "be" something, even now.
All I have is this thought.
All I have of me, of someone – is this thought.
I seem to *be* something.
All...
Concussion...

Concussion without a visible explosion, but I felt it in his bones, and all the stars and planets and "space" itself, became particalised – every firework in creation had gone off at once in great majestic rings like sacred smoke, all ancient and all new and all forever and the colours are feelings of aching and dreaming, and it blew right at me and through me and I am very far away and we are right here and I am the pen and we are space and I am the sun and we are the one thinking and I am the thought and we are the context and I am the point and we overlook the onlooker and we and we...

Now it was my turn to join the dance, or my bodies' turn, as I too fragmented, reduced to the essence of essence while understanding that all of these visions of explosions are implosions. The only true direction is within.

Was there a moment or a thought or an identity to acknowledge – this is it?

People are living art.

I Am All... I Am Everything...
No, that's not right – Everything Is Me.
That's better, that's friendlier.

Everything Is Me.
Everything has Consciousness.
Everything is Alive.
This is how God feels.
How can I feel what God feels unless...
I Am God.
Everything Is God.
I knew that. I did not know that. I believed that.
I know now.
I Know.
Of course.

This is why the word *elegant*, was created.
This is the word I've been looking for!

Look at the words tumbling by in the air! There they go! Words have geometry!
I'm in a book. I'm euphoric. I'm delirious.
Didn't I dream this – years ago?
This I is more.
Words have a physical presence/impact, a powerful psychic structure, like an event, or an object. A word can change the atmosphere in a room quicker than opening a window on a winter's day.
Words are spells. Spells – spelling – we spell words.
I am words, I am events, I am objects. So is everyone, everyone, everything, everyone, everything, every-one, one, one...

ONE

The centre of the circle is everywhere.
The whole is within all of its parts and is ever changing and growing, just like us.
There goes God being my cat Henry. Hi Henry – hey God!
I'll be talking to you maybe? I think I will.
This night will not end. I hope this night never ends. I am this night.

There's information everywhere all around me, it flows like water, like energy, all you want to know is there, is here, is part of us, it's always been part of us, knowledge is the same as a flower or anything else, it merges with you, it is you, the truth is alive. The truth is energy. The truth is you.

Energy – and it feels like Love.
It is Love.
That is what Love is. The original Energy behind everything there is.
The only idea there is.
When you go as far as you can go, it comes down to being or not being.
Why "be" at all?
For Love.
To be it, and create it, and give it.

There are so many things to love, to help, to learn from, to teach, and we have but some small idea of what all this is.
The more you see, the further away scuttles the horizon, holding up her petticoats just to tease. Never an end – never no more to do, or no more to discover, or nothing else to create, or no more to *be*, and divine mystery thrown in for good measure!

I think I was still actually standing on the floor, I think I can feel my body, and after getting big picture information, now I was receiving personal information regarding another of my mother's lives – but first I heard this:

"This is what is meant to be
I am I
and you are you
I am you
and you are me
sort of –
consequently."

Nice mum, the last two lines are interesting!

Edna and I have known each other many, many times before, to come, always. Silver Rose – Rosalie. She's called Rosalie somewhere as well. Somewhere and somewhen is as far away as your focussing abilities and your faith, your *knowing*, I would learn.

Rosalie – and it was Wild West times, mid to late 1800s – it must be the U.S.

No one could spell worth a hill o' beans, but they sure knew how to spell "lie"– so her name was easy. Look, here come the Can-Can dancers, and man I would be a bit on the scared side living here, pretty rough stuff and one of those dancers look familiar, but I've never ever seen her before and I know her.

Well well, here's a life where the dancing came out mum! Holy cow, one hell of a place to be dancing in though – and was there an echo of that other life behind the scenes here in this place?

I'm swept into another vision: music and octaves and frequencies and harmonics, overtones, partials, resonance, all of the names for tuned vibrations and they are going up! I can tell!

Somehow.

A "vision" about sound. The universe is pretty funny and this is really happening to me is this the same day?

I *am* in my body, and I *am* standing on the floor, and I *am* someone who can say, I.
Some – one.

We put the word "some" and the word "one" together and we use it to describe what? An individual? "Some" means – a number of – doesn't it?

Could it be we all know everyone is more than one person, and therefore "some," and could it be we all are one and also *the* "one", and therefore, one? Could it be so obvious that our very language has been trying to tell us something?

Some-one here in this body can still say I, but it's not the same. "It" will never be the same. What I assemble around me will never be the same.

Have I done this before?

No, not like this.

A strange little gasp from an obliterated ego whispers, "I've lost my mind for sure."

The new voices inside me sing:

you've found it!

Day Six

I could die now.

That would be okay – that's enough – I'm all right now. I could live with Edna, she would like me to, and these things are not automatic like you might think. People choose whether or not to live together, just as they do here, although there are other unique situations in that realm that are a little more profound at preventing such a desire from occurring. It all depends upon the level of your awareness.

Here, people inhabit different worlds depending on country, birth conditions, social status (all chosen), and spiritual growth. Certain types will never rub elbows with certain other types. There's a similar situation on the other side, based on frequency though, and how well you grasp the basic workings of the universe. You create your reality, your now, there in that "place" in a much more immediate manner, so the state of your mind is everything, just like now and here actually. How not surprising!

I thought about all the times over the past few years when I'd said, "Whatever's going to happen, it better happen now – I don't have much time left." Well, something had happened all right.

I thought about my school in England for the first six years of my formal education. My school was a church, a very beautiful old church – Holy Trinity. So many things were making sense to me now – I'd spent a lot of time in churches before I even got here, and that was a kind-of continuation. This is incredible!

There were so many things to think about, and I wondered how my mum was so sure I was hearing her now, after all these years of trying, and the answer came. A feed-back loop! She knew I knew, even if I didn't say anything or answer back right away, it was like feed-back. Old terms were being used in a new way, and they were the perfect ones to use for me. There were so many correlations to music.

Sometimes she would ask me to say her words out loud, just for fun or maybe just to be extra sure. Invariably at these times she would have me repeat something like...

"My mum is the most incredible mum in the universe," and we would both laugh our heads off. She is hilarious.

Just keep going to work, that's all you can do. I rode my bike to work on a rainbow, and thought about the night before.

Delusions of grandeur is an old term, but it came in handy last night when for a moment, I thought I must really be hot stuff now. I felt like I could solve every problem on earth single-handedly and I could feel it start to run away with me, until I realised the joke. When you realise all is one, then no one can be more important than anyone else.
This time, it's everyone. The second coming is the Christ energy inside all of us, your Buddha-self coming forth. We've had the external demonstrations and embodiments and now it's time for us individually to feel it, to know it, to be it.
Oh god, everyone's got to experience this!
At this point, I didn't know just how many people *were* experiencing somewhat similar experiences and events, in unprecedented numbers, or at least feeling something was definitely up. I still thought this was my own relatively singular journey, but soon I would start to see the pieces come together, and the picture would get larger and larger.
I arrived at work and saw a stack of documents full of staples over three feet tall waiting to be copied, and I thought of Leonard Cohen - "and all your work, it's right before your eyes." Now I was glad of this kind of work. This would take all day at least and more like it came in every day. My hands could do this, and I could think about the last three years. A lot of things had happened as I turned fifty.

I'd quit drinking. No matter how things had been in my life, I'd made a firm decision in my forties not to drink past fifty. I didn't know if I would be able to do it or not but that was the dream. If I didn't get serious by then, I probably never would, and I had the feeling anything magical that might potentially happen after fifty - when I'd been on the planet half a century - would depend on this. On Labour Day 2004, five months after my fiftieth birthday (but of course I'd given myself until my fifty-first birthday), I stopped for good and knew I would never go back. This was a huge victory in a life that didn't seem very victorious from the outside.

Henry came to me. He was born on January 20, but having six cats already we tried to give him away twice, only to have him become violently ill until the moment he was back in the house. Henry came for *me*, and it was very clear to me now that he and I made this arrangement before this lifetime began. By the time he was fully grown, I was the real me, and I would never have made it through the next few years without him on my shoulder. Henry is my familiar. Seren (Edna's favourite), Jesse, Scamp, Sidney, Fox and Zachariah also played their parts in keeping my soul together with their unwavering love and support.

On the downside, I basically stopped eating – living off chocolate and biscuits – more or less like my father towards the end of his life only his drinking hadn't stopped. I just didn't care anymore, life was too difficult and leading nowhere and I was in a vacuum of my own making. Any upset, and my appetite was gone, and I was upset and dying. Seven months earlier, the Red Cross had said no thanks to my blood.

I went further back and I *always* had a problem with eating. I never liked eating in front of people other than my family, it was too personal somehow. I couldn't eat in restaurants for years, and as I started to get over that, I still couldn't be anywhere near the window in case people would "see" me.

When I was with Gordon, this subject was a major one obviously, and he had mentioned two lives as a nun before my mother came along. I knew about one such life and the possible lasting effects of an oath of poverty, but he tied it in with the eating, and I had a flash.

The nun in the other life was mainly concerned with feeding the poor, and the most difficult thing every day was holding back the last of those bowls for myself. If I didn't, I wouldn't have the strength to feed them again tomorrow, but please don't let them see me eat this! I was almost ashamed to feed myself. With this my personal history was making sense. My feelings about eating had finally found a home, and I could deal with that later if I wanted to.

It's not a matter of one life affecting a later one, all lives occur in a vaster present and there's constant cross-communication between them. Each self is one note in the original song of your soul. Events spill-over, so what you do at this moment is really the issue.

Every thought changes not only the past and the future, but instantly affects everything everywhere.

Returning to the last few years, I had another flash. I realised it was also a fast. It was a three year fast before going to see the guru! Even something like that had been turned around into something positive! What a laugh.

I remembered something else during this time – my piano playing had noticeably improved without any extra practice on my part. I'd noticed this and was understandably pleased about it, but thought it was possibly just a result of having played for forty-five years now, and no longer having anything to prove. The other thing was a sudden reappearance of my English accent. Not as strong as it was originally of course, but noticeably more pronounced.

Thinking of both these things in the light of the recent incredible developments, I knew they resulted from my mother turning up the heat from the other side. She was trying everything in her power to get through to me in one way or another, to influence me, to help me.

Last night however, was something else altogether – I had touched the face of God. Isn't that what they say? I'd experienced something so profound there were barely words in the English language – or any known language – to contain it.

I'd already felt my mother and guide were astounded and somewhat shocked by what had happened on day one, starting with being able to actually see the image of the water and the lightning, and then beginning to hear the voices on the way home. They must have been overwhelmed totally by what had happened to me yesterday – I know I was. Or could they see the outline of that possibility?

Actually, that was the best word so far to describe the way I felt about absolutely everything – overwhelmed. I could barely take it all in. It was so fast and condensed – ten years in one week was turning out to be literal. I didn't have a prayer really, all I could do was go with the flow and make a prayer up as I went along.

My spiritual spark had gone up like a rocket and landed in the sacred fireworks factory. I was right off the old familiar rails and there wasn't a landmark in sight, but the sky was still above me and mother earth still kissed the soles of my feet and knew where I was. Nature and breathing were the anchors, and thank the Goddess I read all those books or I wouldn't have had a chance. Part of me still craved that cave.

Coming back to the present I decided to call Treaca. She'd been on a spiritual journey forever and was someone I'd known since high school – I had to let her know what was going on. Yes folks I'm calling Arizona on my work phone, if it's conspicuous when the bill comes in you can take it out of my paycheque.

I tried to tell her what was happening as tears hit the floor, and I vaguely noticed people were watching me but it didn't matter, this was bigger than any of that.

"Your time has come Neli – the river has risen – ride it like a wave."

I'll try.

Day Seven

It's Friday! I don't know if I've ever been more relieved about it being Friday in my life, and the universe is throwing herself at my feet! Every day is so new like it was when I was a child. I know inside this is the way it should be, this isn't odd or strange, this is the way people are supposed to feel. What happened to us?

Considering the length of time I was unable to take notes, it's a testament to the sheer power behind the events that I can put most of the days together at all. I felt rapture and devotion. A devotion to everything, to all of us, to this Earth of ours – the mother.

Mother Earth – Father Sky – Grandfather Sun – Sister Moon.

I needed to get my own family in order as well. I needed to find my missing relatives and talk to them – even if they thought I was crazy. I had to try.
I was putting the days and pieces together, but at the same time I was always transported back to now. There is only now – an incredible, fertile, NOW.
"The point of power is in the present," Seth had said a long time ago – indeed.

I couldn't stop thinking about music. My mum had said through Gordon that the sounds on the other side were incredible – she knew of course this would be one of my main concerns and interests. She also mentioned the unparalleled opportunities for learning with all of the schools and master teachers, as she put it. Now that really did sound like heaven to me.
I concentrated on my work. The synchronicities were flying off the documents I was working with and I tried to refrain from laughing out loud as I went about my business. Heaven was beginning to manifest right where I was. I dropped my staple remover and snorted a laugh – I just dropped God pretending to be a staple remover! Sorry about that!

An hour or so would go by focused on work, the machines relentlessly chugging along, and then I would send out one tendril of a thought, like a feeler – just to be sure I wasn't absolutely crazy.

"I'm right here."

I was going to take breaks now no matter what. I wasn't going to be a martyr anymore for one thing, and for another I needed to be outside. I needed nature. I needed the sun, the air, creatures buzzing around, the birds, the trees and the sky. Even if only for ten minutes – maybe I would see a squirrel. I needed to talk to my mum for a minute, and even after day five, this was still almost too much to comprehend.

I closed the back door and leaned my back on the wall by the shipping doors, letting the sun caress my face and my closed eyes. There was a slight breeze and it was alive.

For a moment I thought about music again, and what my mother had said through Gordon – specifically that your musical ability went up "five levels" and practicing was much "easier." She was doing a lot of piano playing and singing on the other side, and I remembered being little and always badgering her to play "Teddy Bear's Picnic" for me.

Now she added something else about music.

"It's as if music where you are is black and white – and here it's in full, vibrant colour."

Oh my. I wondered what I was doing here.

I slid through the day, and after getting home I went out to the store to buy a few things. The change I dropped as I was paying was exactly the amount I needed for the cashier – to the penny.

Astounded as I was, I left thinking – is this still the beginning of something really big, or was day five *it*, and everything's going to fizzle out now? How can you top that?

There I went with that idea again, despite the evidence, but I didn't think this was going to end somehow – we made a deal, remember? Stunned amazement was becoming the norm.

I was still having a hard time separating my own thoughts from the new ones, and Treaca had suggested maybe they could whistle or something as a signal when it was them in my mind. This was a great idea I thought, so we tried the whistle for a while, and then I changed that to the first five notes from "Autumn" by the Strawbs, and it seemed to work until it got rather annoying, and I thought it might actually be stunting the first lesson – the difference between thinking, and listening. I had to learn to tell the difference without any tricks or gimmicks, so we decided to let that go.

Back home, Jane, and friend Jane are singing and there's magic in the house, I can feel it. I need to have a bath now to wash the work week off me, and I need those clean clean clothes.

After the bath – and seeing faces in the bath bubbles – I was standing there, and my hands started to move by themselves. Up and down and all around a foot or two away from my body – rotating all the way to the top and then all the way down to the floor, front and sides and back, finishing with a circle around my feet. Aura smoothing! As far as my conscious mind knew, I'd never heard of that before, but it seemed to be a very natural thing to do, and this was the term that popped into my head as my hands finished their dance. It was like caressing my own energy field, and if nothing else, it was a tip of the hat – I know you're there, let me just smooth you out and say hello.

I'd better get dressed.

What's happening to me? Am I going to make it through this, really? I've been opened *so far*, now I'm actually starting to have a real concern about seemingly great ideas going slightly awry. I'm a radio with no off switch.

"Just hold on until day thirteen."

Again with day thirteen mum? Okay. I really wonder what happens on day thirteen.

Day Eight

Happy anniversary to me, it's been one week and I'm still alive! That's if I'm sure I'm not dead.

Today my friend Jane came for her piano lesson, and when I saw her on the driveway, time suspended. It wasn't Jane at all who I saw, but my Auntie Vera as a young girl! Times and realities were doing flip-flops. I don't know what Jane thought as I stood there and stared at her for what must have seemed like a very long time, but she rolled with it, and we had a great piano lesson.

Would I ever be able to tell her about Steaven? She'd been his girlfriend for a while, as had Officer Jane – when would I tell either of them? I thought of the two photographs I'd taken of Steaven and Officer Jane shortly before he died. They were candid black and white shots taken one right after the other, and if you quickly looked from one to the other – they moved. He and Jane and his dog Sirius moved like a two frame animation – it was otherworldly. They had a life of their own, and I spent a great deal of time looking at them after he had gone – now I knew why. Everything made sense and connected – we would have a future together *after* he'd died. No wonder I kept staring at them! I also knew why he'd added the "a" to his name on his last earthly signatures, he was already becoming the next version of himself.

Better keep it to myself for now though, everyone was at their own stage and I still had to come to my own terms with the depth of what was happening, but I could barely contain myself, this is so wonderful!

I wanted this feeling of rapture to stay with me forever, but at the same time I realised this was barely tenable. Who could possibly maintain this? Okay, well Jesus and Buddha could. I guess I also realised an ordinary person like me would never survive at this level, and so the magic had to become ordinary or commonplace to some extent or I just wouldn't be able to carry on. How sad! However, as we absorb the wonder, and understand it's actually the natural order of things, another plateau of normalcy descends, and we are once again in a comfortable position to accept another wave of awe – or to assume this is all just crazy, and the greed and fear-based insanity we see all around us is "reality."

If I had doubt as to the magic, the universe would begin a never ending stream of even more wonder, which had the interesting effect of making me doubt more, due to the sheer "unbelievable-ness." It was funny, I couldn't win, but I'd won everything – yes I had. I am blessed – I thought, but everyone has this in store. How am I going to tell people that all the wonder I believed to be true – I now *know* is true? How do you let people in on it? Some people still think death is an actual end!

I realised I'd been in my own world for so long, I just didn't know the general consensus anymore. Most of the people I knew were comrades on this journey, I didn't know what the man next door thought at all, but I knew one thing – all the religions of the world agree on one thing. The afterlife. Of course, it'd be a little difficult to threaten eternal damnation and torture to a population who didn't believe in the afterlife, kind of hard to keep them under control if death was really the end. Never mind – they agree on that if nothing else. That was something. I should expect to encounter a certain acceptance with the church-goers, right? We'll see.

Speaking of telling people, I guess I'll have to tell my Auntie Vera soon won't I? People get ostracized from their families over stuff like this – I wonder how it'll go? I'll find out soon enough no doubt (no doubt? – that's funny), but it won't be for a while yet, not until I'm a lot more stable and can assure her I'm not crazy. I knew all things would come in their own, perfect time – all I had to do was trust in myself and my two guides. That's all.

I was beginning to get used to eating everyday now, so I got something together and sat at the table.

I must have gone over the details of "the event" at the coffee shop a thousand times in my mind – why didn't I record it? I had my new digital recorder with me just in case something *did* happen, as I knew the extent to which Gordon's abilities had grown before-hand after a first look at his website the day before. The recorder had hours of available recording time, and it would've been so easy just to put it on the table instead of scrawling in my sketch book almost unable to see. Could I have forgotten something?

I knew why I hadn't used it, because then I would've turned into the recording engineer again, and become preoccupied with the recorder and – was it in the right position? Is it picking everything up? Is there too much noise? I thought about using it even in the middle of what was happening, but I knew it would be too much of a distraction, so my hand just kept writing and the pages just kept turning. Somehow this seemed more organic, and

I knew I would be left with something tangible. What if I'd relied on the recorder and gotten home to find nothing? Stranger things have happened. All right, so I was happy with this decision – I had to be now anyway.

I told my mother I'd always remained in contact with my sister Sandra – this had always been something of utmost importance to her. She'd brought it up countless times during her life, so I felt the need to tell her, even though I knew by her opening remark that she knew "everything."

"I visit Sandra and she senses me, but she's okay," she said. "It's *you* I'm worried about."

She went on to tell me how she merges with me, and that I was very weak and near death. "You'll go the same way I did."

I couldn't get over that. Having a stroke didn't scare me particularly, and it was a very fast way to go when you weren't going to survive it, but to *know* how I was going to die, and the six months to two years' time frame – it was phenomenal! If I'd have been in her shoes, I would've done and said exactly the same thing. She had the benefit of knowing my mind intimately, and knowing exactly how I would react – she had gauged things perfectly.

One other thing, I must have assumed I would go this way, and over the last few years whenever I felt a sharp head pain (unusual for me), I would whisper – not yet, not today....

She had finally reached me, knowing I had a meeting with Gordon, and she wasn't wasting any time with idle chit chat and wow isn't this amazing? There was no need to go into the mechanics of our communication, she knew how I felt and she knew what I knew. She was sitting across the table from me – it was as simple as that – my mother, my biggest fan. That's what I'd always called her.

Others would "listen" to my new songs when I had one to offer, but she would lie back on the bed with her eyes closed and she wouldn't miss a note. She'd always been behind me in everything I'd done – or not done – and she wasn't judging me now either, even when she'd added – "You still have a chance for this life to be a success."

I kept thinking about that as I grabbed the camera and went out for a walk. I felt badly my mum had been watching me all these years and feeling I wasn't doing a very good job this time around. I knew how proud she was of me as a person, as a musician, but she found it difficult to understand how I could have let myself suffer for so long and get to the state I was in. Loyalty? Cowardice? There was so much karma involved it made my head spin, and I was getting tired of thinking about *myself*.

I just wanted to be noble and steady in some way, but I'd ended up being untrue to myself and paralysed. I was so cerebral, and where I fell down was when it came time to act. I could think of many times in my life when I should've made a physical move, and I just froze. I'd always needed people to push me, but sometimes even that didn't work, and I was fortunate they hadn't just given up on me. It all comes down to fear, but how could I be afraid of anything now? I felt the support of the entire universe – we were one and the same.

I decided I wouldn't be afraid anymore.

After returning, I got ready for bed and had one last thought about it – well, no matter what happens now, after day five nobody can tell me this life isn't a success, right?

Day Nine

Anyway, I thought to myself, I always did want to talk to the...

beyond – beyond – beyond

A radio commercial, and as the word was sung it got higher and higher and higher. Do I have to say, the word about to come out of my mouth was – beyond? This was insane! I had to say thank you all the time, if there was one thing I was sure of, it was that saying thank you was a really great idea, and I felt it with all my heart and all my soul. Thank you. Just thank you.

This being Sunday, I had time to do some reflecting so I looked at the photographs I'd taken so far on my new camera. I hooked it up to the TV and found the first shots of myself taken in May.

I looked dead.

They were black and white, and that did well to suit the emotionless corpse looking back at me. Then I must have tested the movie making feature, and there was a ten-second clip in colour – it was truly frightening. I barely looked at the camera as my head turned, as though I really didn't care if it worked or what the results might be. This was just one month ago and they exuded *emptiness*. There was no energy coming from this person, it had all leaked away – this was a shell. How close I was to leaving this world behind was more than evident, and these would have been some of the last photographs of me. I doubt I would have taken many more after seeing these.

I immediately went for the delete button but something stopped me – that person wasn't me anymore. I didn't have to be afraid of *him*. I wasn't on that path now and there might come a time when I needed to look back. Maybe to remember how close I'd come – maybe if I decided to write a book about all this or something. I moved on quickly though, there was something unsettling about those pictures, you could tell that something was just... wrong.

All right, here was a little movie of Zachariah eating his treats and relishing every second of it. This was a creature full of life and light and he blew those images away with every crunch as I could hear myself chuckle on the clip. The cats always saved me every time.

I put the camera away and my thoughts went back to the coffee shop and the day of days. After the debriefing of my life there had been a time when it was up to me to talk and ask any questions I might have.

I told my mother I hadn't forgotten about the Salvation Army, and how she'd always drilled it into me to go to them if things went really bad. "It won't come to that," she laughed.

Well, considering how close I am to being dead, I guess it won't – I remembered thinking.

I went on to tell her she'd done the right thing by dying when she did, and it was a combination of relief and release for her – I could see it in Gordon. She'd been feeling guilty about this for twenty-three years our time, and now she knew beyond any doubt that I understood and agreed with her decision to leave. She must have known anyway, because there were many times alone at work in the piano store, shortly after she died, when I said out loud, "You did the right thing mum." This time however, she was here, and I'd brought it up before she even had a chance to. It was a pleasure to relieve her of that burden and let her know "for sure."

It was hard to focus on which questions to ask after all this time, and I knew I was wasting time by sitting there with my head hanging down, but I was reeling. I didn't know what was happening to me – I felt so strange. I didn't know where I was, and I seemed to be only vaguely aware of what I was doing, but something was going on, something was starting up that I would soon see (or hear) on the way home.

It seemed like Gordon had been commandeered (with his permission) and after a silence he or she spoke – any questions? "About a million," I managed to reply. Start with one – they said.

All I could think about was my dog Rex. He had been with me from five years old until I was twenty-one. I was allowed to pick him from Sheba's litter – I'd chosen the smallest of them all. I had chosen *my* dog.

"Is Rex with you?"

"Yes" came the immediate enthusiastic answer, and this is where Gordon told me that Treaca's dog was with her also. Later, I would understand that *his* people were all still alive, so he was biding his time with my mother and his friend Rex – of course.

"Brandy?" I could barely speak. Anything to do with animals and I'm a mess in the best of circumstances, but this was something else. "He was always so smart," I croaked.

"Smarter than that! – I don't just wag my tail now" came Brandy through Gordon – no doubt reading my memories – and the way Gordon spoke, you could just tell it was a dog speaking! There was a lilt to it – you could just tell.

"He's showing off his telepathy," added Gordon as himself.

Holy of the Holies! Do I *want* to make it through all this? My dog is waiting for me! This might all just backfire mum – I want to be with you and Rex!

They would be there though – there was no rush – and they knew I would finish what I came here to do, assuming I survived.

I tried to think of another question out of the million things I'd always wanted to know, and as we were on the subject of animals – I remembered the squirrel.

On the day of my mother's funeral in Brampton, Lindh and I were across the street in Gage Park shortly before the service. It was a beautiful August day, and it was a strange juxtaposition with so much summer life in the park and my mother's death just across the road in that cold building.

My father and sister decided they would like to view the body before it began, and was I interested? There was a certain odd pressure because this would be the last time to see her body, and there were only three of us left now so shouldn't we do this together?

I remembered the first time I'd seen a dead body when I was twelve years old and the subsequent bad dreams I'd experienced for two weeks afterwards as a result. Maybe they weren't on the level of nightmares particularly, but very unsettling to say the least. My friend – thirteen year old Sandra Douglas – was not in that coffin. If there was anything I was sure of at that time and at that age, it was that she was not there. What was there looked like a puppet or a doll.

It had a profound effect on me and I remembered very well the conversations I'd had with my mother about open or closed caskets after that. I knew she'd said she wouldn't want me to see her when she was dead, but with my father and sister either forgetting or simply deciding otherwise, it threw me off.

Did she really say that, or was I just wishing she had? I stood firm and declined the offer, hoping I wasn't offending my dad and Sandra as they turned to wait for a gap in the traffic, and then crossed to enter the building.

I turned to Lindh, "I really don't think she wants me to see her – I just don't think she does."

At that moment, a squirrel in the tree directly in front of us started talking. Actually, this squirrel wasn't talking to us, she was shouting at us – loudly! She was looking down from her branch, and it almost seemed like she had her little fists on her haunches and was letting us have it.

I knew immediately it was my mum. I knew she had managed to obtain the assistance of this little spirit to assuage any doubts I may have had. I was sure, I was positive and Lindh agreed. The raucous sounds continued for another minute or so, and now it was funny. My mother was here, and she was using whatever resources she had at her disposal to get her point across, and this four legged angel seemed only too happy to pass the message along. I had no doubts about my decision now, not even when my dad and Sandra came back to report how beautiful she looked. I knew she was here merging temporarily with this squirrel – how beautiful is that?

So now I had the chance to verify this after all these years.

"Mum, on the day of your funeral – were you that squirrel?"

"Yes."

That was all she needed to say, and that was all I needed to hear, and this was the chance of a lifetime, or so I thought, not knowing it was only the beginning.

I went back just a little further to the day she actually died. I remembered that morning all too well, and it was an hour or so before the dreadful phone call from my father that is forever branded on my heart.

I was asleep. I was very soundly asleep, and then I was wide awake. There seemed to be no transition from sleep to wakefulness, and I felt I'd been woken up. I looked around the room because it was the same feeling you would have if someone was beside you, waking you – perhaps gently shaking your shoulders. I wasn't able to fit the feeling into a neat slot. There was something different and unusual about this sensation and after a few minutes I'd decided to get up. I was fully dressed and ready for the day (I thought) when that phone call came and changed my world forever. However, after hanging up the phone and still being in the prime shock of the moment, I said out loud, "She woke me up!"

This was something else I could check now – twenty-three years later.

"On the day you died." I could barely talk, but I got the words out by gritting my teeth. "Did you wake me up?"

"Yes."

Oh god, I knew it I knew it, and then Gordon passed an additional piece of information to me in the third person.

"She found herself out of her body, and you were the first person she went to."

Oh my. Did all of that just happen to me eight days ago?

Later that evening I was asked to go into my room for another meditation/visualisation in which I was between the earth and the universe, and the energy flowed back and forth through me. I am the Earth, and I am the Universe, and somehow, I'm me as well. So is everyone, I thought – I don't have any claim on this, I just... found out. How could we have ended up feeling so small and weak and helpless? How could we have agreed to forget our divinity?

The firming continued.

So did the feeling of having been opened wide – and held there. The voices never stopped – my mother, my guide, the chorus.

it's okay you're all right you'll be okay don't worry this is magnificent we will look after you we love you

I needed that.

Sometimes I still felt a little queasy with all this energy flowing in and around me and my mum would say...

"Thirty seconds."

Sure enough, within thirty seconds the feeling would dissipate, and I would be just fine after that. Fixing my tummy from heaven mum? This is too much – but I want more! And more I got. I found I could ask her to "run a diagnostic" on me, and she would give me a rundown of my present condition.

I also noticed that a lot of events would take place at midnight. There really is something about the midnight hour – I thought. The witching hour is midnight or twelve to three in the morning isn't it? Or was it just that everyone was asleep except for me? No, there really is something about that time, and so I thought of twelve and numbers again. I was born on the twelfth, my sister was born on the twelfth, my mum and dad got married on December 12 – the twelfth of the twelfth.

There's a real power in numbers. What was one of my first feelings when all this started to happen? This is day one – and start counting.

Day Ten

Well, that was the weekend, and so it's back to work again and if I managed to do it last week – I can do it this week.

It's summer, it's beautiful and paradise is right before us. Winter is my season though, and it'll be coming soon – look out. Snow! Magic faerie dust from the sky. My god, I don't know if I'll be able to take it when I see snow – that's my ultimate.

Just go to work and try not to let that smile look too ridiculous.

I feel like I have a secret identity! Hi Mr. Groundhog!

Okay so my machine broke down – well not everything's perfect quite yet. Shall we say malfunctioned so it seems a little more streamlined than a toaster? These were high-tech machines and I had to call a high-tech machine repairman.

The Canon technician arrived and I liked him immediately – not just because he had long hair and seemed to be about my age, but because hippie-time was a very important time to me, and the world, I believe. It was the start of a lot of the right ideas, if you think about it. All You Need is Love – is about all the philosophy you will ever need.

I wondered what it is that makes us like people who we think are *the same*. I wondered what was going to happen now he was close to me. We started to chat, and talk about the machine and our various histories in the business.

The topic switched to the car he was working on and how much he enjoyed what he was doing with it. I don't like cars, and I've only had one of them in my life, an MGB for three years, so when he said it was an MGB, I found myself laughing a little too loudly and saying – of course it is, of course it is.

He looked at me strangely but I didn't care, I only seemed to be making people feel better than they felt before. He mentioned he didn't have any children, and I said, well, you can't have kids in *every* life, and felt perfectly comfortable saying that to him. He looked at me again, but didn't say anything. I figured I didn't have anything to lose, and I didn't really care if he thought I was strange, odd, a little peculiar, or whatever. I hoped I was interesting. Screwdrivers on the floor, test copies, and the repair went on.

Soon we were showing each other photographs we both happened to have available. I showed him the Stop-Caution-Go cats. This was when I noticed the date – thank heavens for digital embedded info – and I saw it was taken on the very morning before I set out to see Gordon! Holy crow!

As I was having this revelation, he was looking at those red, amber and green eyes staring right at you, and I could tell it had a definite impact on him. It's a freaky one.

Now it was his turn – there were photographs of his MGB from various angles, and then a photograph of a beautiful table made in the shape of a guitar. He mentioned having made it, and I thought – he likes to work with wood as well, this just gets better and better. I thought of the boxes and bookcases I'd made.

It turned out the shape of the table was because he was a musician! He played the bass guitar with some guys and they were always looking for a keyboard player, he mentioned casually. Well, you're looking at one, man!

Now, my behaviour was startling even to me. Upon hearing – I'm a bass player – I found myself spinning around in circles saying, of course you are, of course you are, in a kind of singsong voice.

It was a little scary.

I know you're excited Nelson, but pull it in a bit will you? You're really starting to look a little bit strange from the outside now, take a breath.

He repaired the machine, and afterwards fumbled for one of his cards and said – if you ever feel like playing keyboards and need some people to play with, like I said, we're always looking for someone.

He gave me his personal card, and when I looked at the name, once again I was floored. Would this just not stop? His last name was Butt, and that was close enough to Butts for me. Robert Butts was Jane Roberts' husband, and without him, there would have been no Seth material. He was integral in every way to that situation – it was the three of them.

I felt like singing at the top of my lungs! How many synchronicities can you bundle together anyway? They were folding inside one another.

This creating your own reality thing.... I guess I'd always thought it was broad strokes with a coarse brush, but now I realised how intimate it was, it was the dot on the I, it was the whisker on the altar, it was precise, *and* all encompassing, and it was becoming more and more immediate. The Quickening, I thought. More movie allusions – "Highlander." This film would be important. We shook hands, he left and all I could think was – this is a dream.

Is that the phone ringing? I must still be at work. Answer the phone, add a couple of things to the calendar and it's time to go home.

I don't watch TV much anymore, I like actual films but regular TV is over and that's enough. On the rare occasion I did turn it on it was usually late, and so I'd gotten into the habit of clicking on the captions so I wouldn't disturb anyone with the audio. How fortuitous it turns out, if you believe in fortune.

The TV captions now began to talk to me! Yes, you heard me right. I was talking to my mother, channel D was wide open, and when I looked at the TV screen – there was the word – "Mama." That's what I used to call my mum just for a joke, so it jumped right out. Then I thought to myself, okay that's interesting, are you going to play with the TV now? I could feel that sense of fun, my mum again, and she'd be just the one to try something like this, not to mention that spirits have been affecting electronic equipment for a long time trying to get our attention. They've been trying *everything* to get our attention – wouldn't you? I was thinking of all this when I looked up at the TV again, and what I saw was –

"She's dead, so what's she saying?"

I just had to laugh. Under what possible context could someone be saying that line I just didn't know, but it all fit somehow and I laughed with abandon, noticing as I did so how I could feel my mother's spirit expand with joy. It was amazing – you can feel another person's joy inside.

This was hilarious and just the beginning of what we would end up calling – spin the remote. Pick a channel – step right up! But it's time to turn it off now children – click. We'll check into this again, that's for sure.

Later – staring at nothing, thinking of what I was becoming...

"You could affect people's behaviour with this ability."

Affect their behaviour mum, what do you mean – control them? You've got to be kidding!

"I am kidding – you just passed another test."

Day Eleven

There are too many things going on in my head.

My mind seems to be everywhere – literally. Linear thought is difficult. Playing an instrument and singing at the same time is *one* thing, but this was more like being every instrument in the orchestra.

Focus Nelson, it's all about focus – until you can *hold* more.

There's so much. If it wasn't for all the reassurance, all the gentleness, all the understanding, and all the love I felt, I just don't know how it might have gone.

I believe today is Tuesday, but every day is just brand new and has never existed before, no matter what you may want to call it. That's one thing I *do* know.

We cruise through the work day, and at break Edna and I play a game, seeing how far ahead we can go knowing what each of us is going to say next. It's a good exercise, but we soon decide it's more fun to talk in the old fashioned way. The art of conversation now contained this new kind of etiquette. You don't cut someone off and say you're welcome, *before* they have a chance to say thank you. Even so, sometimes the words just seemed to catch up after the message had been passed. It was a taste of communicating in a non-linear way, without even words. My mind of only ten days ago was becoming something of the distant past.

I biked home and once again the universe made sure I was alone. Well, not alone exactly, not the way it used to be, not the way it would ever be again. Just alone physically, except for my seven cats – the babies! I was standing staring at nothing – indeed, from the outside it would probably have looked like I was frozen, and this was another state I seemed to spontaneously go into now. Instant meditation/trance.

"Let's go to your room and write some music."

Am I hearing this right? Are you serious? I'm in heaven – no, you are – never mind... let's go!

Oh, this just gets better and better I can't believe this I just can't believe this really can't be happening I'm walking to my room now and I'm going to go in there and my dead mother is going to write some music through me of course she is that's what she's going to do why wouldn't she we're both musicians we both play apparently she's been playing a lot lately okay let's turn on the piano that's right it's the twenty-first century we have to turn the piano on okay here we are what do I do just sit down and start playing okay no problem let's sit down here we go…

The piece came with a nicely tailored fit and I think I may have installed a zip and a button-hole or two.

I'd thought, D minor, there's a good place to start, and I didn't do much else – consciously. The first two or three chords could have been something I would have gone to, but then it took a leap! Definitely a couple of things here I wouldn't normally think of – and I like it! I like it a lot! This is beautiful, and it's finished. What was that, half an hour? Words mum? It's so nice just the way it is as an instrumental – I would probably just leave it. I can't believe this – this is insa...

"Fun."

She cut me right off, and offered me a suggestion for when I was going to say the word "insane" – simply replace it with the word fun. This was a very simple practical idea, and I'd many occasions to do just that. Elated and amazed at everything, I looked at the keyboard before going back into the bedroom. It seemed to be set on one of the internal songs, and the display showed me its title –"Against All Odds." That's funny.

We recorded it into the internal keyboard memory. I'd only owned this instrument for sixteen days – how not surprising.

"Oh man, this is insa... fun."

"See? See? You're okay."

You're okay too mum – you're something else. And that took me back to the coffee shop again and hearing her words for the first time in almost a quarter of a century.

"You'll always be my boy," she had said, and "You're never alone."

No matter what other lives we have shared together, in *this* one I was her son and she was my mother, and there was something wonderful hearing her say that. I was in a trance, sitting in front of the keyboard with my body, and back in The Second Cup in my mind.

Gordon had also told me she was with an Aunt, but I didn't know who exactly, as there were a few who could fit the bill and there wasn't time or enough coherence on my part to go into everything. I had one Aunt on the other side, but my mother had a lot – my grandmother had quite a few sisters. She was talking point-form. Who knew how long this would last or how close we were to Gordon having to stop and leave? No time for great details – I understood that. This was before question period – but who was the Aunt?

Gordon went on about my mother, "She lives in Lancashire – the *template* for Lancashire."

That made so much sense to me. What we have here is the three dimensional version of the original place, and this is where she'd made her joke about talking to people in Yorkshire now, due to the War of the Roses having been between Lancashire and Yorkshire.

My thoughts skipped to the end of the meeting, just before my last question about maybe talking again in the future – I had to laugh every time I thought about that now. I'd summed everything up into one final statement:

"You were the best mum." Were? Another thought had crept in – just look at this!

"You were the best mum ever – I love you."

You could see the elation as Gordon beamed and puffed up like a peacock as her feelings entered him as a result of that statement. "You won't believe the happiness she feels." Oh yes I would Gordon – I can see it.

I came to what was left of my senses and I was still sitting in front of the keyboard. I pushed play just to see if the music was indeed real, and the emotions I felt during the two minute piece as it filled the room, were beyond anything I could have imagined. I was being obliterated with ecstasy. Where did this come from? Heaven?

I stumbled back into the bedroom, and the TV was on with the captions and no volume.

"Look at the captions – now!"

Holy cow mum, you don't have to shout.

I looked at the TV captions to read a stunner – "So I wrote the song."

This is too much altogether, and very funny, but I might just explode. How many people could handle this and not think they were in a dream, or crazy, or dead? I never ever once thought I was hallucinating though.

I turned off the TV and stood there in a shock/trance. That was enough. No doubt to lighten things up a little, and give me the release I needed, Edna placed one last thing in my head – it was perfect:
"The power pouring through that mind-meld must have been staggering" – I heard. Thank you Dr. McCoy – I thought, and laughed and cried until I was spent.
What would we do without Star Trek mum?

Day Twelve

I am glad it's summer, I thought to myself as I rode to work, I need to be outside – I *need* nature.

I was having thoughts of the long bow, John probably used one centuries ago – I wonder if he was a good shot? I had vague thoughts of learning to shoot one, as Treaca had suggested this might be a good way of connecting with this incarnation, but after looking into it, I realised being in a gymnasium somewhere was not for me, and this seemed to be the only way available in this city.

I need some of his toughness though, that's for sure, but now I was beginning to realise something else, I think he needs me more than I need him at this point. No, that's not quite it. I think I can be of more value to him. In fact, I have a feeling all my incarnations are coming with me in some way. I feel they can ride on my coat-tails, and I welcome them aboard. It all comes together *here*, in this lifetime somehow. I hoped I wasn't being too self-important, but it felt right, regardless of how unusual it was to feel *central*.

I parked my bike, took one last deep breath of the brilliant day, and went in the back door to open up the shop.

I was half-way through the second week at work, and I was doing all right so far. There were still some side-ways glances and tears I couldn't hold off until I got home, but all in all things were going okay. The calendar was getting a bit strange looking, but there was no way they could have determined I was talking to dead people by looking at that. I made a point of being vague and cryptic to the calendar-reader, but clear enough for me to keep some record of what was happening. Part of me actually wanted them to ask me about it, but they never did.

I was still being told to not break the spell with copious notes, but it was difficult to resist filling in those two inch squares at work, and jotting down enough at home to hopefully bring it all back when things calmed down a little. It was impossible not to start a journal of some sort, even if it was only a few key words per day. Once things cooled off, I could write myself into a stupor, but I knew the advice was sound, and if I spoiled the experiences as they were happening I wouldn't have anything to write about anyway.

I was regularly taking the formerly nonexistent breaks, and at the nonexistent lunchtime I was going out and getting those milkshakes, with or without the chips. A healthy diet didn't matter. Prior to this I'd had almost no diet at all, and on day one through Gordon my mum had said, "Eat anything, junk food, anything!" When my guide had come through, his contribution to keeping me alive and fattening me up was, "Eat the rind of the pork!" I thought this was pretty funny, but a bit odd – didn't he know I'd been a vegetarian for twenty-nine years? Of course he did, but I figured he was *that* worried, he'd gone back to his own time and what they would have fed someone *then* who was skin and bones. I got the point. "Not you Gord!" he'd added, and Gordon and I laughed in this world while "they" laughed in theirs. I remembered thinking that humour was universal, and there was the added bonus of calming me down a bit.

Gordon seemed a little surprised when this guide arrived because my mother had already been talking for a while, and that in itself would have been enough. Then another moment of surprise as Gordon added, "Oh... they *know* each other!" That made so much sense to me though, and wasn't a surprise at all. Later on it made even more sense as I learned my mother was an apprentice of his, and was interested in being a guide in general, even before the breakthrough with me. Nice of him to let her have her say first.

I splashed water on my face and then went outside for ten minutes. I couldn't stop thinking about his opening remark to me, "It's time to round-out your education."

There was so much inside that simple sentence. It implied this was the end, the culmination, the finishing-off, and I felt good about that. I felt *proud* of myself. I might have been on this earth many times – I felt I had – but I'd done it, I'd gotten somewhere, I'd figured a few things out. It seemed ironic that it was *this* time period, the one where the slogan "God is dead" was popular a while back, the one so far removed from anything... sane.

I stood outside, marvelling at the illusion, and continued to think about what my guide had told me on day one. "You haven't had enough warrior lives – they have great self-expression."

Well, I guess that ties in with the 70% to 30% imbalance, in favour of the feminine. I would have to work on that, and I knew it would involve more action on my part somehow. Action – self-expression. Okay, I was beginning to see. I had to remember that being a warrior also meant being noble and honourable for the most part, and not necessarily being a brute like John.

He also mentioned using music from what warrior lives I *did* have, as a way of connecting with that energy. Clever man. Drums might be good for this, I thought.

All in all, if I had to be too far one way or another, I was glad it was *this* way. I also thought – I have far more lives as a female than as a man, and this was a big part of it also.

Do I know what I'm talking about? It feels right Neli – it *feels* right.

"All souls go through this" was another statement he made that had the effect of making me feel okay about things in general, and I was sure that was the idea. It was time to pull all aspects of myself together into one nice cozy stable whole. No problem! I hope.

At least I knew what was required, and it was going to happen one way or another – it had to. Better to know what was going on than to be working in the dark.

I liked the way he said riding my bike and playing music would be conducive to talking with him – meditative states. This was before all the subsequent events however, the universe had shifted now and so many more things were possible, assuming I survived. Would I ever get this man's name?

I had a vision of all the souls on earth being cups of water drawn from the same source. They look the same, but pour them onto a flat surface and every shape would be different.

Then I thought of snow (just like me to think of snow on a hot summer day), and how every single flake was unique and never duplicated – just like us – but of course from a distance they all look the same. This had always amazed me, and made snow even more magical, if that was at all possible. And snow is water, and again from the same source – the same ocean.

The tears were coming again and I had to go back inside, so I wiped my face with my finger-tips and pulled myself together. I fought the urge to raise my arms to the sky and to start chanting something. I could see Native North Americans dancing – always one foot on the ground and one knee in the air – my god! There's symbolism in everything! One foot on the earth and one hand in the sky! That's how I felt.

I grabbed the door handle to go back inside, and let the cool steel bring me back to the "real" world. Whatever happens now – thank you for this life, this experience, this miracle, and this silly job.

At home I turned the TV on with no sound, and we played spin the remote. I looked at the TV – "Vulcan mind-meld." That's pretty good mum, considering the line you put in my mind last night from Star Trek – The Motion Picture. This just becomes more and more incredible.

What's happening to me is startling and amazing, but *I'm* not amazing, *we* are amazing. This is inside all of us – this will be discovered by all of us, each of us in our own way discovering our own comfortable truth. The basics will be the same.

I looked at the TV one more time before I turned it off – "Everyone helps everyone, there are no favourites." I couldn't have said it better myself. I was floored.

Everyone was asleep except for me and I looked at the dim light coming in the bedroom door – something was happening there, something was attracting my attention. It was as though the air was getting thicker, and it continued to do so until I was looking at my first apparition. She'd somehow made the darkness itself a little denser and impressed herself upon it – it was a dark oval shape and there was a feeling that went along with it.

Hi mum! I bet that's not easy – pulling that one off, and look at that, there's no fear at all. Who would be gentler than your mother? And it's a dark shape too – with no negative connotations whatsoever!

I noticed myself thinking, my god, I've always wanted to see a ghost and there it is, everything is happening at once, it's like a dam has burst, I've really gotten myself into something here.

I slid into bed and assumed the position, we've all got one, the perfect way to arrange yourself for sleep, and in my mind I tried to arrange my new life into some sort of order as well. New life – was this my life now? It's all I've ever been aiming for, but I can barely keep up with this.

It was at this moment I felt my mother squeeze my right shoulder, as I was on my left side. The house was asleep, there was only me. It was physical – it felt physical, and that would be another pretty difficult feat I thought, and as I said thank you and cheated by jotting a note.

I had one other thought as I drifted away.

She's powerful.

Day Thirteen

It's day thirteen today, and that was the first thing in my mind the second I woke up – it's day thirteen and I wonder what's going to happen? The second thing –

"Hi mum."

"Good morning love."

Okay, it's all still real and it's day thirteen and it's Thursday and I have to go to work and be normal. I burst out laughing – joy at what the day would bring type of laughter – my face was getting used to smiling again, it had been a while. This is unreal. This is so real.

"I'm right here."

I know mum, and this is excitement on a grand and unique level isn't it? Let's go to work!

I drifted through the day wondering when the real work would begin. This had to lead somewhere didn't it? There absolutely has to be some kind of an overall game plan that goes far beyond what I... what? Had hoped for? I could never have hoped for anything on a level like this. What has happened to me? – was becoming a mantra, along with what *is* happening to me, and let's not forget the still ever popular – am I going to make it through this? Mix this with bliss, and I guess I never knew what bliss was, because at any particular moment I could just die, with a smile on my face. That's if I'm not already dead – sometimes I still wondered....

No, not dying now, not if I can just make it through this part, it has to calm down eventually doesn't it? I'll keep eating and... oh god listen to me!

And... Oh God, listen to me, I need to make it through for some reason. This is so much bigger than me... bigger than the old me anyway, this is...

Who are you praying to Neli, yourself? Aren't you God now? This gets complicated, yes sir – I need to sort things out, that's what I have to do, just sort things out... there's the phone.

We made it through another day – me and the voices. We rode home together and we praised the air I breathed. No need for breathing where you are mum, but I'm sure you do it anyway, that must be a hard habit to break. I walked in the back door, went upstairs and fought the urge to just lie down on the floor right where I was, I was that exhausted. My body was exhausted, that was it, but my spirit was elated and that elation was causing my body to be even more exhausted. I really must eat something – everyday would be a good idea. I will I will I will live well I will.

I sat on the bed and thought about who I was. The old me had some semblance of a shielded, single mind – I seemed to remember that – but the new me was still getting used to the new voices, and now it was to the point where I needed to re-familiarise myself with what my own thoughts sounded like. I felt like I was starting to forget. Ever accommodating, my new friends spoke to me in exaggerated ridiculous accents and then gave me time to think for myself, so I could remember what *I* actually sounded like!

All right, *there* I am – oh my, I'm having some very interesting times.

I got my tabla drums from the walk-in closet and made it back as far as the bed before I was engulfed in a powerful wave of emotion that sent me gasping on to it. I clutched the Dayan close to my chest – the smaller true tabla drum – and I sailed again on this new bottomless ocean of emotion. I passed-out – I slept – I wept.

"If this is love you got to give me more..." Oh John Lennon, I don't know if I can take any more... I want more.

The Beatles, that's a good idea, that's what I'll do – Sergeant Pepper and my drums. I'll gather myself together in front of the music system and I'll let myself go, if I could possibly go any further. "Within You Without You" and "A Day in the Life," that's the ticket – that's the ticket to ride.

I got myself organized and marvelled again at the opportunity before me to play the music loud – once more I was alone in the house and the universe loves me. That's good, everything was in slow motion or maybe underwater is a better description. I found the remote and got comfortable on the floor. I've played these drums before – I don't mean in the last six months, since I got them – I mean I've played these drums before, these types of drums, many times ago. In this life I don't know what I'm doing, but once I found the "home position" for my hands, there was a familiarity out of context. I found I could create many different types of sounds, which is what the drums are famous for, but this felt easy and comfortable. I've been here before.

Time was coming together – I thought of my monk's robe and my mediaeval shoes next to these drums in my closet.

On the Bayan, the larger of the two drums, I found modulation – to produce the "whooping" sound – was something I could do right away, whereas my book said it was a very difficult art to master, one which may take many years. I'm sure my technique was terrible and the purity of my tone debatable, but I could do it anyway.

These two little drums joined the ranks of many magical things that had kept me alive in the last three years, Henry on the top of that list with the tabla arriving in the last six months as reinforcements.

The Tanpura and Sitar began to drone and play on George's masterpiece, and then the tabla came in with the whooping sound, then the piece takes a breath, finds its stride, and begins its majestic journey as all the pieces come together to take your heart away.

"We were talking…"

Yeah, a lot of people seem to be talking lately George.

I'll never be able to play like that – I thought, but I started playing anyway. The Dayan was in tune to itself, but not to the recording – annoying, but not the end of the world – however, as I began to play, I noticed the pitch of the drum changing until it was in perfect tune with the recorded music!

Should I be expecting things like this now? No, but *you* should expect this thank you thank you from me. Do I deserve this? Did I earn these miracles somehow? Just keep playing Neli, see if you can keep up. See-if-you-can-keep-up.

I kept up with the music, but I could clearly see I certainly hadn't kept up with George – he was very awake all that time ago. "With our love we could save the world" – is a literal fact, so is – "and the time will come when you see we're all one."

The song ended, my wrists ached and I thought of George and another song of his I play frequently on the piano. "Isn't It A Pity," turns out to be a bit of an understatement. Tears streaming but not crying, I thought of everything we've been through as a species, as a race, not knowing the full extent of my ignorance to our true history, but knowing enough to know we've suffered a lot. I've been sometimes ashamed to be a human being, but now I was starting to think of us in the same light I shone on the animal kingdom, with a love and compassion that hurt. We're okay, you know?

I let the room remain quiet and thought of George and isn't it a pity, and when it came to the line of lines, what I consider to be one of the finest verses *ever* written, I was a mess, I was a wreck, I was experiencing an emotional rapture and I cried for all of us – his message was so clear:

> And because of all their tears
> Their eyes can't hope to see
> The beauty that surrounds them
> Isn't it a pity

We must stop crying and I can't – that's funny. However the real message was about helping people to see. To wake up, rub their eyes and see.

I wiped my face, my finger hit the button, and I moved on. "I read the news today oh boy," seemed to just sum up the current state of affairs didn't it? Or have things been this bad for this long? John was so far ahead anyway and god he was so close when I was a kid – Liverpool is so close to Bolton.

John carried on reading the paper, but then suddenly he'd love to turn me on (Paul wrote that part did he John?), and the music begins to climb in an unbridled, wild kind of way and it takes me straight up with it, just a taste of what's to come soon, then we have a smoke and we're in a dream, which is exactly where I am. I must pull myself together. Maybe I can use this John incarnation, the War of the Roses person, maybe I can integrate him a bit – that's the idea isn't it?

I formulate the idea to integrate some of the masculine energy from him, just as John would like to turn me on once again – and the piano thumps – the voices just grunts – and the swirling climb begins once more.

I'm beyond space and time, and as we reach the pinnacle and the music stops before the final climactic reality-shifting chord, I whisper, "just enough." I don't want *too* much of his energy.

The chord of E takes over with a numbing authority, and I slowly lie on my side on the floor. Yes, I think I could say things are beyond my conscious mind right now....

People came home and life flowed until everyone was asleep except for me and the seven cats. The night wasn't over – it was time for a bath.

I had a sensuous bath and thought about the miracle of water – just look at it!

I also thought about the constant whining in my ears and how loud it was and how I knew it was something that would not be going away in the near future – or at all.

I'd been experiencing this for many years and it was an in integral part of leaving my body as I could intensify it just by concentrating on it, and then... out I'd go. The "electrical feeling" I used to experience in my solar plexus had dwindled or wasn't there at all sometimes now, but this high-pitched whining sound was always present at those times.

I got out of the bath and began to dry myself off, sitting down as I did so. That's when Sidney came in, Sidney the young black cat. I looked at him and found myself thinking about Mintski, and about our recent encounter, I was thinking about it not being finished – the unfinished business.

The second I had that thought – Sidney, who'd come around the other side of me, decided to jump up on my leg and then aborted whatever it was he was attempting to do – taking off again and leaving deep scratches in my leg. Suddenly he wasn't Sidney anymore, but Mintski, and she spoke.

"Did that hurt?'
"Yes."
"We're even now."

I looked at my leg and I looked at the shape of the scratch that was now gently bleeding, a lot, it immediately reminded me of something – and then I knew what it was.

A crop circle – one of those crop circle pictograms that looked like a key. There was a line going horizontally about four inches long, and then four lines going vertically up from that, a couple of inches long. Under the main line were also two smaller lines going vertically down an inch, with another short horizontal line from the bottom of one of those.

I looked at it and wondered how it was possible such a shape could've been scratched from the way he/she had pushed-off me, and then I had another revelation. Earlier that day I'd trimmed the claws on the particular paw that had just scratched me, and there was one claw I'd been unable to cut – when Sidney's had enough, he's had enough. Somehow, the shape was partly due to that particular claw!

I also had a thought that I knew what crop circles were now – birthmarks.

By now so many things had happened, I didn't know if there was anything left to day thirteen or not. Then:

"Are you ready for your final gift?

I was sitting there naked, staring at the sky through the skylight, and I knew it would only be the last gift of *the day* the way things were going... but of course, yes I'm ready.

Once again it manifested as a knowing – I just knew now I could turn it off.

It was safe to shut down now, if I wanted to. The path had been deliberately, prematurely worn smooth, and it would never grow over now.

It became clear that thirteen days was the amount of time we'd chosen to make this connection unbreakable – at the same time trying not to put any more strain on me than necessary. There was no particular feeling of *having* to close down, just a relief of sorts that I could. I knew I could be alone if I wanted to be, I knew I could have privacy if I wanted to! It might just be an illusion of privacy but it was still a feeling you could have, and I was very happy about that, as it was a feeling I've enjoyed my entire life so far. I can still sit in a corner all alone and pretend to be miserable! My wonderful day thirteen, my wonderful number thirteen! This just felt perfect.

I was still at the etiquette stage though where "forgetting" about my mum for a moment or two would throw me into a panic. How rude! I'm so sorry. So this was weird.

I tentatively tried my new abilities. There was still some trepidation here, thinking – but what if I won't be able to open up again for some reason?

Surely not Neli, not after what you've been through for the past thirteen days to forge this link in forever.

I knew I was just at the beginning here, but I'd been doing the opposite to this for thirteen days running – keeping all systems go – it was a little odd to go the other way, and I was stalling a little.

"You turn off the radio, the signal and information are still there, it is established. Now you can turn off, be alone with only you and your thoughts if you wish – we are established."

Established – I liked the sound of that – thank you mum! It's just that I thought I might have lost what... the ability?

"You have lost nothing – how could it be otherwise?"

"Always more – never less."

I know mum, where have I heard that before? I guess you know I say that all the time.

All right, I'm a radio with an off switch now! Must try it. Don't go away though, okay?

"Never."

It was a feeling I hadn't had for almost two weeks and after a brief moment or two... that was enough. How odd! Where are my friends?

It wasn't so much learning how to turn it off at all, it was more a matter of becoming accustomed to the vaster expanse, and realising I could flow from one to the other. I knew the point all along was to *hold* both realities at the same time, it wasn't about one *or* the other – it was singing and playing the piano at the same time.

I can do it, I'm okay, I've lost nothing and I want you to come back now.

"Always."

"Holy cow mum." A flood of warmth ran through me as the universe came back.

Later on looking at my leg, my mum now suggested going into my room and taking photographs of the scratches. Any excuse to take a photograph – that's my mum.

As I did so, I thought about Mintski. I thought about how she rides in Sidney sometimes, and in a seal-point Siamese cat like her who lives up the street – Iffy. That's what they call it – riding in someone.

I saw myself writing a book one day and I thought about titles – Thirteen Days seemed pretty good. I thought about money and actually getting paid for doing something I love, that would be a dream for sure.

Carrying on with my new practice, I realised I could close everything down, shut everyone out so to speak, but they were always right there as soon as I thought about them again – one thought away. "One thought away" should be on my next T-shirt.

I was beyond exhausted but I'd taken the photographs, and Sidney jumped up on my drafting table which was high enough so he and I were eye to eye. He came over to me and I rubbed my face on his and stroked his sleek black back. As I did so, something happened – it seemed like he opened up and I tumbled head first *into* him... and I discovered he was bottomless. Cats are so old they are bottomless – that's what I learned from him at that moment. Cats are so very ancient.

Once again with the tears, but tears of joy this time. How many more things can I experience? How many more miracles can I accept? Being absolutely, completely and totally insane would also explain a lot of things, perhaps all of these things?

I made my way back to the bedroom and then smoked a cigarette. No one can understand smoking unless they do. Smoke is multidimensional, smoke is sacred, smoke has been with me many, many lives, and is very important to me right now – smoke is my friend. I like fire. In England as a child, the fire ran the house.

I turned off the light and headed for that other world where my mother and my guide and I would decide what to do next, and *they* would remember everything. Upon awakening, I would probably remember nothing. It must be funny to them when I wake up and disappear right before their very eyes... or is that still happening? I'm in both worlds at once now it seems.

By the way, am I *ever* going to find out this guy's name?

"Sleep baby."

"Goodnight mum."

New Moon
E-stands for Evolution

It's Friday and I ride to work testing my newfound ability. I can turn it off – I can turn it on. I can ignore them if I want to, and I don't want to, but I could. It was good to have an off switch and to know I had that kind of control, but shutting the voices out was now becoming a strange and somewhat synthetic idea. Why would I want to do that?

I have a spirit entourage – we all do, but to consciously work with these people – this is Shamanism. My mind drifted to the Mongols and I thought about my life-long fascination with Russia as I pulled up to the back door.

I've made it through a very important phase and I wonder if I'm home free now. I wonder if I'm going to *live* now. Work is work and that's all it is – it's just something to do while I think about what's really going on.

What will be, will be, and what won't be, will be somewhere else. That's the kind of thing I'm thinking about, and I'm thinking about writing that book again. I'm also concerned the whole thing might just collapse for some reason. Get passed it Nelson – dress rehearsal is over.

A few minutes on the computer to tell my friend Lorraine – Walking Wolf Woman – that something has happened to me, "I know, I could feel it in my heart," was the quick reply.

Of course she would know Nelson, you just found out a lot more about who *she* is. She's been waiting for you. Remember all those years ago when she told you about the crystal skulls?

I added some notes to the calendar, I wonder if they do read this when I go home? Good luck to them – I don't have anything to hide. Then again it wouldn't hurt to still be careful.

Once at home, I find Henry on the stairs, I lean in close to kiss him behind the ear, and I distinctly hear him saying, "I could fall into you." Stunned, I tell him I could fall into him also, as I knew exactly what he meant. I could lose myself in you. I realise that's the original meaning for *falling* in love – you merge with someone and lose yourself. Oh Henry, my beautiful cat – thank you for this gift! I'm going to have to use another word for miracle – I seem to be saying it a lot.

It was the weekend, and once again I didn't need to give a piano lesson, so the day was all mine – how exciting! There was singing in the house and I thought of my cousin Judith, what would she think of all this? I must talk to her.

The next day I found myself having another spontaneous visualisation/meditation. My friends and I circled the earth with held hands, and poured our hearts into the mother. This seems so natural, to do this.

Later, Colin came for a visit and I would've been nervous if it was still possible for me to feel nervous. Mum B watched and listened and understood I couldn't just blurt out to him at that moment that I had his dead mother on the line! I was beginning to learn it was all about watching for small openings, and then maybe sneaking something in that way.

Thinking of a friend who could possibly use a healing, I did my best to accommodate and sent energy her way – I hoped it did some good and I knew it had somehow. Things were different now, things were working and I had no doubt. Or maybe I had no doubt, so things were working.

I thought of everything so far, and drifted through my new mind – hi mum!

How am I doing? Am I going to make it? Will I ever stop crying?

"It was a huge risk and you didn't care – such is the power of despair."

"Was" a huge risk mum? Nice rhyme.

It was Monday, I was back at work, and it seemed very strange to still be there doing this particular job, and inside being connected to the entire universe. The crying and crying and crying at work and everywhere was a strange thing, but somehow I really just didn't care.

Now it came up there was a piano available for free if someone would just please take it away. Things like this just didn't surprise me at this particular point, and I had a feeling I would have an acoustic piano again soon. This lead to thoughts of orchestra conductors, and I decided they were casting magic spells with their batons.

Where are my thoughts going? I seem to be all over the place.

"You're in a bit of a tiz-woz."

I thought about Hindus, Druids, Wizards, Faeries, Angels, Wiccans, the Celts, the Egyptians and Native North Americans. Suddenly I realised the Native American was one of the main reasons why I came to Canada in this life! I knew a large part of it was to connect with this energy – to connect with these people. I thought maybe I'd spent too much time in England and Europe, whatever too much means.

And now a word is in my mind, just like that! I was thinking about the synchronicities, anachronisms and idiosyncrasies, and "syncretism" just came out of nowhere. I looked it up – a merging of different philosophical or religious beliefs or practices. Well, it's that time isn't it? When God is everything, what is there to disagree on?

I woke up on Tuesday with a nice morning greeting...

"You have the opportunity of the ages."

I know this is something special mum, I really do, but of the ages?

This was all to make a lot more sense very soon, but I still thought this was local – my own personal awakening experience, although the entire universe knew of course. Is there more going on here?

I see a Native North American in the shadows, waiting – his name is White Feather. He is just making his presence known to me. Our conversations will be in the future, but for now, just a nod of acknowledgement. This is incredible, and I knew from Lorraine that these master teachers have always been here to help. The "Indian Guide" is real, a bit of a cliché – *because they're real.* No problem – happy to know you! I've been collecting feathers forever and ever and... I feel you probably saw every single one I picked up – oh god my heart knows you!

Now a Druid, his name is Duncan – when you're ready – he says, we have to wait for you to become a little more, but I'll be back. I'm elated, my head swirls in England, in sacred sites, and the remains of the past that is really so close. I see robes and fire and – Duncan. I couldn't see his face clearly, but I couldn't see my guide's face clearly yet either, there was something about that – it was a measure.

I was beginning to feel I could venture onto the computer and do a little digging. I really needed to know a few things, for instance – everything! Sitting there, I realised I had to do something first though. I had to make a statement to the world, I had to come back from the dead, and I had to solidify my identity. I had to say I'm here, and I'm going to stay for a while, I think.

I acquired a personal e-mail account on a public server. This way I could check my mail on any computer, and right now that meant the computer at work and the computers at the library. All right! Then I went all the way, for me, and actually registered on Facebook. So very out of character for the old me, but I thought – I have somewhere to go now, I have something to say... and I was just following these impulses as they came along, knowing it was really the best thing to do. It had gotten me this far hadn't it?

I punched in – psychic awakening – spiritual awakening – religious awakening – things of this nature, and I let the information come to me. I knew I wouldn't have to dig, I knew I wouldn't have to search and strain and sweat, I knew that what I needed to know I would find, and I knew I would find it quickly too because I didn't have much time to do things like this at work.

It soon became evident I was having an explosive and profound Kundalini Awakening! Upon further research, I realised I had a good dose of the shamanistic version too. Both of these felt right – the Goddess Kundalini felt right, and I was beginning to understand some of what was happening to me.

Kundalini means "coiled one," and is usually represented as a serpent (sometimes a cobra) asleep at the base of the spine in three and one half coils. These serpent references are found all over the world.

In the Eastern traditions, she is the Goddess, the Divine Energy, and is within every person, just waiting to awaken. This is similar to the "Buddha Nature" in all of us. This awakening is the gift of gifts, the greatest prize of spirituality and is acknowledged in all cultures and all religions by various names that all really mean the same thing.

This is the peak experience of the mystics and prophets and seekers. This is when the walls come down, and the transformation of mind occurs instantly. This is when God comes knocking on your door.

The transformation of body begins also, and may not be quite as instant, but is fast and relentless and unstoppable. It is a cleansing, and a balancing and the most profound event in any life, or any cycle of lives. It is everything you've been waiting for, and beyond anything you've ever tried to imagine.

It is Love, in its purest form.

Every lesson in the universe, rolled up into one.

On one side, all the psychic/spiritual abilities are now set free and acknowledged, and on the other side, everything that has been repressed and not dealt with up until now – all the dis-eases of mind, body and spirit – will rise to the surface to be transformed and released. Depending on how much cleansing you have to do, there can be many dark nights of the soul to go through on this journey into the arms of the Goddess.

As they say, once you're in the jaws of the Tiger, there's no letting go.

Once begun, the primal energy will rise through all of the chakras (chakra means wheel, and they are vortices or centres of consciousness for the transmission and reception of energy), opening, balancing and cleansing away any and all blockages.

The endocrine system is particularly used and affected, as I myself can attest to by my own thyroid gland becoming extremely active. Fortunately at this point, I'd found out enough about my situation to be happy about the development, in fact ecstatic, and not to worry or run to a conventional doctor.

I also learned that spiritual learning can follow from one life and continue in another. Maybe that's why I felt I hadn't really done enough in this life to warrant this!

Maybe I came into this life with a spiritual account already fairly full.

I was reeling and beyond excitement as I stacked more paper into the printer.

The shamanic material disclosed information about – making agreements to be trained – spirit *companions* more than spirit guides – maybe surviving... or... maybe not.

It was all beginning to look quite familiar, and I just held myself at this point. I knew what was happening, and it was very, very old and well established and connected with people and places and things I've felt inside me my entire life.

Okay, print some of this off before anyone comes along, and I think I'll have a smoke outside and look at the sky.

Victory to the Great Goddess Kundalini! I have the girls on my side!

By now I was getting a solid name for my guide but of course and as usual I didn't want to accept it completely, so I thought I'd wait until I had some kind of a sign.

Sitting on the deck at home, I looked at a package for a gardening accessory and stared at the company's name – Gardena. The vowel sounds of the first two syllables brought me back to the name I'd had for a day or two, it had filtered in, but it just wasn't right somehow – now I had the notion the accent was wrong, and that was all!

The accent wasn't on the a (as I had been thinking) – it was on the i – the E sound.
Bhun-DAR-ee, became Bhun-da-REE.

We travelled from Africa to India with the changing of the accent, and the name took off at the end like a bird. And now the bird turned into notes, and I could hear a song as it flew into the air, it was a song I'd grown up with and had been one of my practice pieces on the piano. The "Singing Nun" of all people, do you remember her? "The Happy Wanderer" was the song, and the chorus went like this.

> Val-deri, Val-dera
> Val-deri,
> Val-dera-ha-ha-ha-ha-ha
> Val-deri, Val-dera
> My knapsack on my back

It was the Val-deri part I heard now as confirmation, loud and clear, and I knew at last how to pronounce his name beyond a doubt – I also knew something else, it was <u>Sri</u> Bhundari. Got you!

I was doing okay. It was warm summer and I was still going to work and I basically considered myself to be the luckiest person on the planet. It kept thinking about my Aunt Ciss, she was my mother's aunt and she was the one person in the family who I knew had some abilities or powers. Now it hit me, *this* was the aunt whom Gordon had been referring to. Of course! It was so obvious now I thought about it and remembered how much Edna loves this lady.

She used to read people's tea leaves, however she wouldn't do that until you were twenty-one years old and she was gone before I reached that age. I needed to go to Blackthorn Avenue, the place we lived first when we came here as I mentioned, what I didn't mention was that it was because of Aunt Ciss – that's where she lived.

Things like this were going through my mind at work, and numbers, lots of numbers, integers, and names, taking names and words apart, pulling them inside-out, doing things with them, so when I got home that night it didn't seem strange for my mother to suddenly say –

"The E in my name stands for evolution."

What's that mum? The E in your name stands for evolution? I said that out loud – I still like to do things like that. Evolution, there's that word again! I'd spent a lot of time believing in a major step up in evolution for us, I thought it might happen around the year 2000, but since then I kind of gave up. I thought – how could there possibly be something world-wide like that? It needs to be world-wide.

Okay, I thought, I'll bite – so what does the rest of it stand for?

Silence.

What does the rest of it stand for mum?

Amused silence.

Okay, I know you're there, and I know you're laughing, why won't you tell me? And then I thought about it for a second, and the penny dropped – my mother's name is Edna, the rest of her name is... DNA!

All right, this is the kind of thing I love this is more than incredible this is absolutely unbelievably incredible, Edna – Evolution – DNA. Holy Mongolia!

As if that wasn't enough, later on I was sitting there seemingly drifting in and out of about three different states of consciousness, and I was thinking about just how incredible all this was and how it was becoming more and more difficult to explain what was happening to the outside world, when I thought about my camera again.

I'd already discovered the "Stop-Caution-Go" cats photograph was taken on day one, and I knew that particular photograph had been the last herald I'd had about something big about to happen – once I'd noticed the date it was taken on – so I was thinking about things like this when –

"Take photographs in the closet in the dark."

In the night? In the dark? I thought about "The Haunting" again, and actually felt a fair amount of trepidation about going into the closet and sitting or standing there in the dark. At the same time, how could I resist an invitation such as this? I thought of my mother's old camera, which I still had, as I dutifully picked up my own, turned out all the lights so as not to shine under the door, went into the closet, closed the door and turned off the light. The only light now was from my camera so I turned off the LC display. Okay, I guess I'll take some photographs. I took eleven shots in the pitch black dark with no flash of course, and I was rather glad to come out of the closet. That's funny.

I also thought that whatever excitement I felt (what would possibly have been nervousness previously), could actually only be a positive type of energy, and might actually help things. You had to know that what she was after was something I might be able to see in a photograph – I was very excited!

I put the camera down and decided to have a cigarette and just think about things for a minute. I'm like this, even when I receive mail I know is fun, like a package or a letter from a friend, I like to just set it aside and think about it for a moment and pick the exact right second to open it or look at it.

It didn't take long before that moment came, and I looked at the photographs: first one, black and blank, the next nine were exactly the same, but when I got to the last one – there was something at the top in the centre that seemed to just appear at the last second as I looked. A tiny green shape. Okay now this was fun, now I was excited, now I was really excited, and I slowly zoomed it up on the small camera display. Oh my! It was that green yellow astral material, and it was in the shape of a sideways V.

I quickly got my patch cord so I could plug the camera into the TV set. Oh boy, oh boy I can hardly wait to see this and look at that my heart is really pounding this is really exciting!

"That's my nose job nose."

I just stared, it looked like a nose! My mum had a nose job a few years before she died, and that was what she was referring to now. I laughed and then I laughed about what I was laughing about – it was liberating. I realised at that moment the medium, the substructure of my life had changed. Somehow it seemed easy not to worry. Somehow everything would be okay. Somehow, I now had evidence of a sort, and if you knew me at all you would know the photograph was genuine, so at least I had *that* going for me when it came to showing it to my relatives and friends. I now had something – tangible.

༄ ༄ ༄ ༄ ༄ ༄

It's the solstice today and for me it's day twenty. The veil tends to get thinner on this day, and the way things were going for me, I didn't think I really needed it to be much thinner at the moment!

My bike and work were two things I could rely on, and the sun seemed to be still coming up each morning. I felt excited about whatever would happen next. I also had the feeling again that I could die at this particular moment and it would be all right – I could leave now. Although actually I wanted to stay here more than ever, I could leave now because somehow I had found out what I needed to know. I'd done what I came here to do, and whatever happened from here on, was extra, or maybe it was what I was *really* supposed to do? This we were going to find out.

I looked at my photographs on the work computer, and laughed imagining adding the one of my bare leg with the "crop circle" scratches to my screensaver – no.

I noticed one odd looking one and took a closer look. Three photographs had fused together into one to create a strange image. I suppose a computer glitch of some sort corrupted the files, and two photos taken through a mirror comprised most of the image, but right there, perfectly in the centre at the top, was "the nose." I couldn't believe my eyes. Even computer "problems" were turning into magic!

It also didn't escape me how I'd just acquired the newest and most sophisticated computer of all the ones here – it was more powerful than the boss's. Right on schedule, I thought – exactly what I needed when I needed it, until I get my own. It was all I could do not to raise my arms up to the sky – I'm in a world all of my own now and thankfully I can do this job on autopilot.

While I was there, I finally got around to finding photographs of castles for my ever expanding screensaver. Along with about ten of those, I added the Tudor Rose, an actual silver-yellow rose, the Lancashire countryside, and a map of England. This screensaver was getting interesting!

At home, Jonathon mentioned a dream to me where he was in a high tower, and in the tower/room there was a sink with black liquid spinning down the drain. I easily saw this as negativity going down the drain, and the high room suggesting a spiritual journey and a much wider vista. All right, I felt good about this dream.

"He's a strapping young lad."

I know mum, he's eighteen now.

Shortly before going to bed my mum suggested playing spin the remote as the TV was on with the captions. I grabbed the remote and "randomly" chose a channel and punched it in – it was a music video playing, the sound was low, and now the captions were delivering the words to the song and at that moment those words were –

"We're better together" – over and over and over, audibly, and on the screen.

Yes mum – we are. See you tomorrow.

Things were beyond better, but I couldn't help saying out loud to myself before I went to sleep – "I'm still shuddering."
Twenty pounds on my body would make this experience a lot more survivable.

First Quarter
Earth is Talking

It's been three weeks and the planet's talking to me. I already felt the universe was aware of everything, but now I felt the earth herself and all of her creatures knew about me too – I hoped so. I realised again I never once used the word hallucination at all – if you want to know about hallucinations, just look around.

Ebb and flow – flow and eddy. This is the way it goes.

My physical brain was trying to catch up to my mind now, and I hoped it caught up soon. Brain is mechanism, and mind is spirit. I had the feeling long dormant portions of my brain had been or were being activated. Something had begun with that moving feeling in my head.

I got some Zener cards, with the cross, circle, star, square and wavy lines (or water) on them. ESP cards they use to be called. Now I had some fun with these things, scoring much too high and revelling in it – this is just normal really.

I noticed a piece of jewellery on the counter featuring a real shark's tooth, and I thought about the ability some people have to hold onto an object and receive impressions – psychometry it's called, and I thought I'd give it a try.

I closed my hand around the tooth, and I closed my eyes. The first thing I experienced was a roaring, whooshing sound in my ears, and I knew it was the sound of the water as the shark would be racing through it. This was amazing! To a shark, the water is very loud, and I figured they must have very good hearing. I actually didn't know anything about sharks, but later I would find out that this was very true. This can give you some idea of how intense these feelings were, because I really didn't feel the need to verify anything at all at the time.

I had one more impression, and it involved the killing moment. Sometimes it's referred to as a frenzy. This was a surprise to me, because I've never been interested in this kind of thing and I'm probably one of the few people who never cared to see any of the "Jaws" movies. Anyway, the feeling I got from this, was that the moment was orgasmic for the shark – truly a climax of sensory input, and so it made sense those vibrations would be stored here. I put the tooth down, and said thank you to the shark. I was elated.

I began to find myself in the video store without any particular reason to be there, I just knew there was something there for me. In this way, I rediscovered "The Celestine Prophecy," and "What the Bleep Do We Know," which I'd seen, but now I had to own, and uncovered "Conversations with God" – which also led me to the author Neale Donald Walsh's other books.

Science finally catching on to the spiritual multi-dimensional realities is an interesting thing, and quantum physics has come along to bridge that gap for a lot of people – it's a blessing.

I discovered Neale's books and movie were about a man talking to God, a man who was in a very desperate state indeed leading up to this development, and it started to sound familiar, and I thought – thank you.

I wasn't exactly *talking* to God – yet, but I knew a few things now *about* me and God, oh... like we're the same.

See? People have been talking to everything forever Neli – perfectly natural.

Maybe, but I had to look into this man seriously and find out what was actually going on in his head. Any doubts rattling around in there Neale? You can tell me....

Wonderful books, and he has had his doubts just like everyone else.

It seemed to be an integral part of the dance. I had no idea how much time the Buddhists spent going on and on about doubts over and over and over. They did so much work for us discovering treasure after treasure about how people and the universe fit together, and then they wrote it all down. They wrote-it-all-down!

More visitors dropped by, Colin and Joy among them, and once again it was the strangest situation while Mum B waited and watched once again.

Don't worry Mum B, I won't give up. What's the worst thing that could happen? That they think I'm crazy?

Giddy was the word of the day. That's the way I felt and we were twenty-three days into this thing. I still could barely walk a straight line – all kinds of things were in my mind. I was thinking to myself, what is the meaning of linear time? Then I thought, well, it gives you time to learn. – ha ha. Then I thought – doom is just a mood – I was playing with words again, backward and forwards.

I was thinking about syncretism, I was thinking about predictions, I was thinking about my mum's Buddha in the hallway, I was thinking of England again and Lancashire and Yorkshire and Constantinople in the year 1625. I was thinking about the movie "Close Encounters" for some reason, and I was thinking about mystics and a lady of the night and I was thinking of a silver rose.

"Predictions are folly."

Yes, I'd have to agree, a waste of "time" actually, once you know a few things – like every variation of any event happens in its own time-line. There are trends though, there are *leanings*, (look at that word lean!). As I had *that* thought, I also thought this would not be a good time to make any kind of a prediction, as too many things were happening, there was something going on – just look at what was happening to *me* for god's sake! I actually do mean – for God's sake. Everything everyone does is for God's sake. Isn't it? We have to start thinking a bit differently around here.

Riding my bike, something caught my eye so I pulled over and picked it up, it was a very tiny clear crystal ball. A faerie bubble! Within the next few weeks, I found two more, one red and one smokey grey. You wouldn't have thought they would have been visible as I was whizzing by, but somehow they found me.

My bike was critical – a meditation on wheels. I could think clearly (as much as possible at this point), and "we" could talk without the usual distractions of home. My mum was a constant source of amusement and support, and whenever I thought – would she really do this or really say that? She would say:

"What would you do?"

And I realised I would do exactly the same thing. This was invaluable in many situations I found myself in. Her humour was the best medicine of all – when I would eat more or less properly, she would sometimes say:

"Good – I can't stomach it when you don't eat."

Another comment around this time about her current "living" conditions:

"It's so expansive here – not expensive."

I could hear the laughter, and I found that love and humour were everywhere on the other side. They could laugh with the abandon of eternal beings who knew they really had nothing to "worry about." We need to do that, but it's a bit different when you're in the trenches. However, there was always the complete understanding about our situation, and empathy – as only someone who has been here would know and feel. When I took it all way too seriously, which is my wont or downfall, I heard:

"Just play."

ઽ ઽ ઽ ઽ ઽ ઽ

It's day twenty-five, Tuesday, and I have to go to work, but for "some reason" I decide to play the TV caption game for a minute before I go.

I was thinking about Aunt Ciss again, and the night before I'd told Jane an amusing family story about her. I was about twelve years old and we still lived downstairs from her on Blackthorn Avenue. Her husband Billy had already died, so she lived upstairs alone when a male friend of hers from England decided to visit, and was staying with her for a week.

I remembered this man, he had a heck of a time driving on the right side of the road when he was here, and there were quite a few stories about this visit after he'd gone back home – one tale stood out above the rest however, and became family folklore.

One day he chased Aunt Ciss around the kitchen table! I guess he thought he'd try for a *really good* holiday, but Aunt Ciss was far too nimble, and I think he went (or was sent) home shortly after this. I'd always loved that story, and I enjoyed relaying it to Jane last night.

Now I clicked on the TV, and it was on the news/weather channel – I didn't change it and I looked at the captions which were already on. This is what I saw:

"No chasing around the table, she wants to be your mentor."

I'm not kidding, and I could hardly believe it either! This was getting more and more incredible as the days went by. I just couldn't believe my eyes, and again I wondered if anyone else would believe what I was now experiencing as a matter of course.

What was the context of this sentence? Should I try to contact the station and get a copy of this somehow? It didn't seem to matter – this was real.

Later on, thinking about how these spirit friends were just one thought away, she began her mentoring by telling me it was just like making a phone call in a way – people will answer, or not. They just might not be in the mood. Not that they wouldn't hear me, or care about me, they might not feel like talking is all. More and more I realised people were just, well, people – whether here or there, we are still just "us."

Thank you Aunt Ciss! That really helps me out – please pop in any time – I love you!

At work I now started printing material from the internet in earnest, being fully aware it was no accident I worked for a printing company and had full access to an assortment of amazing printers. This gave me the opportunity to print large documents about awakenings from many different points of view. The fact that I was also the only full-time employee and spent many hours in the store alone, also changed from sometimes being a stressful situation, to now being just perfect for this research.

What was so incredibly exciting, was reading about *myself* in these articles. Everything had changed – it wasn't theoretical now.

I'd been reading books on psychic/spiritual matters for years and years, but it was always about someone else, and I would read them with the feeling of – wow, isn't that amazing? Maybe someday....

I was reminded of one of my songs– "It Can Always Be That Way."

And so I read about it
Dream about it
Feel without it

But I know it can always be that way

Well, that day was here, and now I read with the attitude of – yes, that's right. And – no, it wasn't quite like that for me.

It was quite a sensation to have gone from being an outsider – wishing to one day experience something like that – to now being on the inside. I'd somehow become an authority of sorts, just by living through this – so far.

So I read everything I could find, and I found out there were mountains of material on transformations such as these. Lots of dire warnings too, but I felt safe with Edna and Sri Bhundari. I wasn't going at it alone, I had my people and I knew the three of us were an absolutely awesome team. If there was a weak link at all, it was me and the shackles of doubt. I would be like the Buddhists, I thought, and wear the armour of perseverance. For now, I rode home wearing a knapsack heavy with information.

Messages now came from everywhere and anywhere.

I went to the pet store to buy some cat food, and my eyes were drawn to a young girl walking by, and the T-shirt she was wearing: "I promise to teach with examples and not words" it said. What kind of T-shirt is that? Who cares! It was just for me. I put my hands together and closed my eyes for a moment – thank you again and thank you and I am in some other world now folks.

The store Treaca and I used to go to when we were younger, and that I couldn't remember the name of for years, now just popped in my mind. "Orientique."

That's the name! After all these years, there it was – I could see blockages were also being removed. Oh my lord, this is too exciting, I'm turning into – me! The me I've always wanted to be – that rhymes! Okay, calm down Nelson, calm down, go and get that cat food will you.

Already it's basically impossible to explain what has happened to me. I'm going to have to write a book just to give to my friends, as so much has happened so fast, there's no way I can keep it all together. Am I going to be able to write this story?

"We start on page one, and we see where the story leads us."

Sounds good mum, but I'm all over the place.

*"Everything will become **reliable**."*

You always seem to say the right thing... god, what's going to happen to me?

"What would be the point of life if you knew all the answers?"

"Life is a book you read one page at a time."

Yeah well, I guess now I have to write the book, don't I? Listen, while I'm riding home here, tell me what it's like where you are right now, if you can put it into a few words for our future literary audience.

"It's incredible, unlike and better than any kind of greatness you can imagine."

Oh my.

"You can merge with anyone or anything, you can experience anyone's world view – you've started to do that now."

Jane Roberts and Seth and world views – I love it when you bring them into the conversation. It sounds like heaven!

You can fly, Peter.

Oh you just had to rub that in didn't you? I know you can fly. I always knew about the flying – that's why I used to run down the street when I was little and jump as high as I could, knowing I should be able to fly. It was so frustrating.
I *could* fly, up until recently, up until being born inside this beautiful but dense body, and when I was small the memory of it was still fresh in my unclouded mind.
This is why the main super-power of just about every super-hero created in the "comic" world, can fly. We carry that in our hearts and souls and dreams, and it comes out as "inspiration" – the word coming from "spirit." I always loved anything to do with flying carpets too.
It sounds as incredible as it could possibly be.

"How could it be otherwise?"

I know mum. Always more – never less.

MOON TWO
I'm not seth

Mum B dropped by and told me I should be all right in the house for a while at least, even though things seemed so dicey. I should just concentrate on integrating and, what... surviving? She is such a warm presence and I thanked her with all my heart for any help she might bless me with. Without her, would this house have ever even been bought?

I'd always liked her so much, and it was good for me to know there could be no hypocrisy now, and she knew all of my feelings for her were and are genuine. It would be nice if that was the way it was here wouldn't it? Actually, just underneath the surface, we all *do* know how people really feel. Mind to mind however, is honesty on a level we would be well to emulate here. It's a very freeing feeling to know you can never be taken the "wrong way."

Steaven's ashes are in the bedroom in a beautiful wicker box, and I put my hands on the sides of it, and I thought of him. One thought was all it took once again, and I heard him clearly – "Peteski, you did it, you did it!" This made me think of Sherrie when she said the same thing on day five, and somehow it became clear that Steaven and Sherrie were friends now, somehow united because of all of this business with me, and for their own reasons of course.

Sherrie and I had a lot in common with our shared beliefs about psychics and the spirit world, and she would lend me books and tapes of her favourite material. Oh Sherrie, I bet you could tell me a few things now! I miss you so. The word bittersweet came to mind. You're right here but I can't hold you. Later on it would be Sherrie who would introduce me to what she called a "spirit hug," and I would feel it through my body and soul. Thank you for that gift sweetie – I just couldn't stop saying thank you.

So many things were beginning to make sense to me, and I thought of a cab ride I'd taken a couple of months ago. It was so interesting that it had stuck in my mind, and I thought of it now as I was thinking about how much I wanted to share all of this with people – how much I wanted to teach. Was I becoming a teacher?

We were zooming along across the Leaside bridge, and the driver turned right around to look at me (keep your eyes on the road!), and looking into my eyes he asked, "This life – what's it all about?" Without thinking, I came out with, "It's about power, energy – it's about learning how to deal with energy."

Did this man sense something about me? Did he ask the same question to every customer? I was beginning to consider that he didn't. How incredible is all this! What seemed odd or even bizarre at the time, was now making an intricate kind of logic. He knew something. Or he didn't, and I don't know what the hell I'm talking about. I thought my answer was a good one though, as I realised more all the time just how powerful we really are – and I'm just scratching the surface somehow. What did Seth say? "You are Gods in-the-making."

I had to play my favourite U2 song, how funny that it's called "Bad." Now the chorus took on an entirely different meaning, and I sang it as loud as I could:

> I'm wide awake
> I'm wide awake
> Wide awake
> I'm not sleeping

Holy cow, I can sing and cry at the same time – sort of. My emotions are on overload, and it *feels* good, it *feels* right. People are just feelings walking around. This is a masterpiece. Does he know? Is that why he's helping all those people with nothing but buckets full of despair in Africa? Service to others is the key. I think he really *is* awake. This is what it meant to me now, regardless of what the lyric actually referred to.

I thought of Peter Gabriel and "Solsbury Hill," another masterpiece, and I don't use that work lightly, it's one of the most moving songs ever – to me.

Listen to those words Neli – that Eagle *spoke* to him! Then what happened? He decided to keep his mouth shut, and why was that?

> To keep in silence I resigned

My friends would think I was a nut
Turning water into wine
Open doors would soon be shut

This is starting to sound a bit familiar isn't it? Then, the clincher:

Son, he said
Grab your things
I've come to take you home

Home. That's the word that does it for me. The other side of this veil is home, I always knew that. I knew the word had far too much power for an address on a street, and then I saw something else...

H OM E

Holy cow! Om has been smack dab in the middle of there all this time!

Om – The condensation of every Hindu mantra into one. The same way the Sri Yantra is the source of all the yantras (sacred geometrical figures), the mother of them all. Or, to put it another way, if there was only one chant or one mantra, OM would be it. It's considered to be the original sound, the fundamental vibration that created everything we know, and the first sound uttered by a human being in this reality – the mouth a circle.

I listened to the song in an ecstasy, and then turned the music system off. Silence was the only thing that could follow that. Then I thought of Peter Gabriel and his humanitarian work around the world. He was also very awake – you could just tell.

When you do finally awaken and see the glorious light, you know there are no divisions and we are all indeed one – or as Neale Donald Walsh and God put it – there's no one else in the room.

Oh me oh my, this is why I was born, to learn this – to *remember* this. I have to sit down for a minute.

I went outside and there was sister moon, full and looking brighter than ever. It seemed like the Moon was brand new with a different and more powerful kind of energy, and I raised up my arms and told her she was beautiful. "So are you," I heard, and it didn't seem so peculiar that the Moon was talking back – not any more. I felt like taking my clothes off again and bathing in the light of that silent mistress, but held myself back for now – a little too public around here but maybe one night I'll get away with it.

Everything is alive, and just waiting for you to realise that truth, just waiting to talk and welcome you back, and I could feel an excitement in the universe, something was going on here and the anticipation was building.

One month and I'm still alive, no... I'm alive at last, but could I still be making all of this up? Even after day five, it seemed like I could still have doubts, but how could that be? I figured my old life had a kind of inertia, or momentum and it might be a while before it ran down, but things would never, ever be the same again, that was for sure. There were enough signs now that made me fairly certain I hadn't died, so I went back inside and carried on with this new living.

I didn't actually die, did I mum?

"Not yet."

You're right about that?

"You bet your Jolly Roger!"

We both laughed at that. There were so many things to think about, but I really didn't have to think about any of them, things would unfold in their own way whether I thought about them or not. I was on some kind of ride here, and the main thing was holding on – holding on for dear life. Seth was right again, when you're sure about your divinity and the eternal nature of existence, it just makes this physical life even more precious. I went through a lot to get here, we all went through a lot – we deserve medals – not everyone does this three dimensional routine. What did Jane Roberts say? Life is sacred – all of it – or none of it. Not just people's lives or even worse, certain types of people or certain ages of people, or those with certain beliefs. We have had it so wrong for so long. Why wasn't I told that it was a violation to kill a flea? What went wrong?

Everything is so beautiful.

Well, we agreed to, didn't we? Like I mentioned earlier, we chose to do this, and what a decision that must have been. I thought of all the suicides, people who – in the final analysis – just couldn't take it once they got here, and were so desperate to go back home, they ended up going against God really. To take any life is so wrong – even if it's your own and you justify it that way. You'll just have to meet those challenges in another life anyway. There are no short-cuts, and the first thing you realise at any rate is that you're not dead. Then the guilt generally kicks-in as you witness the confusion and sadness of your loved-ones left behind. Some suicides are so distraught, that an amnesia type of effect is sometimes induced by those helping, until the personality can gradually accept what they have done. No one outside of yourself judges or condemns your actions, regardless. For those left behind who are wise enough to realise they can help, love and forgiveness must be sent from the heart.

The most uncreative thing you could do – Seth said about suicide, and that always worked for me, even in the darkest nights. But my life had been a paradise through and through compared to other parts of the world, where the lives of some people were barely comprehensible or endurable – this part of the world also, no doubt. I had to remind myself they had chosen that too, they were part of the same balancing act we were all involved in, but that was no excuse not to feel the utmost compassion for them.

The worst thing you can do with the knowledge that people choose their basic challenges before they get here, and then continue to create their own personal reality with their thoughts – is to use it as an excuse not to care, and help.

No, not everyone comes here, not even when the opportunities for advancement are so great. One life here is probably equivalent to ten or twenty or a hundred somewhere else, in terms of spiritual growth, but I don't blame anyone for passing this by. No, sorry, they probably said – I'll take my time somewhere else thank you, I'm in no hurry.

That being the case though, all of us should take a moment each day to congratulate ourselves on a very courageous decision.

So much for not thinking about things too much Neli.

Number eight was turning up everywhere now, and I knew it related to the octave feeling with the vibrations rising, and I couldn't stop thinking about faeries, castles, and Greensleeves. Greensleeves is the first song I fell in love with as a child, and if I ever had my doubts as to why, they were laid to rest when Gordon had told me I was a minstrel in another life. He had mimicked someone playing a lute, (I knew it wasn't a modern guitar somehow) saying – does this make sense to you? It sure did. I knew this song had followed me here, and it all made sense – I play the guitar here as well as the piano, and I'd thought about a minstrel connection myself years ago. I thought of my mediaeval boots again – one pair is knee-high.

I also couldn't stop thinking about Persephone, and Orpheus in the Underworld, and later I would find out she was the Winter Goddess (snow!) in one aspect, and her function was change and regeneration. She also represented spring and rebirth. Things didn't fit much better than this.

I was led to Hrastovlje Church, a church in Slovenia built in the 1400s (there's 1400 again), with an interior fresco of a Danse Macabre of all things, and I later found out Persephone's Christian counterpart was Mother Death.

Well, I'm dealing with my "dead" mother here, I laughed, and also death is still pretty close to me right now, I can tell that, so maybe I'm doing a bit of a dance myself. There's more to it than that though, isn't there? It's the end of something big and the birth of something even bigger.

Something else floored me, this church was also called – Church of the Holy Trinity. Holy Trinity – My church and school in England! And the word love is in Slovenia. Holy cow! Love backwards, is also the first four letters in evolution come to think of it.

This-just-will-not-stop.

I decided to go for a walk on Bayview Avenue – that would be a good idea.

On the way, I thought about healing again, and how heal was part of the word health, and how they both meant wholeness. Healing seemed to be part of the deal somehow – and I heard "healing shouldn't drain you," not from my mum, but from me, or someone. "Your energy is used only in the directing of the universal energy." I was wondering about that, because I still felt so drained physically. Well, now I had my answer, and I really must sort these voices out, or do I? Maybe some things will just come directly to me, without any arbiter? That's what this felt like.

Once on Bayview, the video store yielded a discount DVD called "America's Most Haunted Town," so I knew why I'd gone in there, and it turned out to be quite enlightening. Lots of Orbs in that film, and Gordon had said to me on the big day, "Have you seen any Orbs yet?" While I was still in the store, my mother placed "An Affair to Remember" in my mind, and I knew she would like to watch this old classic film with me, it was a favourite of hers. No problem mum, we can do that.

The bakery next door had a cone on the roof, and I had to go in there to see if I could stand under it. It turned out to be mostly behind the counter, so I bought a loaf of bread and leaned over as far as I could. They must have thought I was crazy – but I didn't care at all. I had to notice the signs and follow my impulses.

I knew this related to Jane Roberts again, and the pyramid she felt above her head when "Seth-Two" came through, like a funnel or flue concentrating her consciousness as it zoomed up that much further. This is wild.

I walked across the street to the stationery store and stared at the door pretending to look at the hours. I'd stood exactly here in one of my out-of-bodies when I'd looked at my reflection to see if I looked the same. I *had* looked the same, more or less, I wasn't transparent or anything, but I did have that greenish tinge.

Somehow standing in the same spot was exhilarating and amazing and I looked up at the name of the store – "Write Impressions." Great name for a stationery store, but it was the word "impressions" that grabbed me the most. Isn't that what psychics were always on about – impressions? Come to think of it, that's what I dealt with every day at work at Positive Print. In the printing business, you charged clients by the number of impressions their job contained. Everything was connected to everything, and these were just the incidents I noticed.

Riding my bike later, I saw a lilac-point Siamese come through the hedge and I whispered, Mao-Mao. He was the other cat my first wife Lindh brought into my life, alongside Mintski. I dismounted and went over to him as he just sat there and waited.

You just don't see Siamese cats on the loose that often, and Iffy on my street was odd enough, but here was another little guy. He let me stroke him as I enquired, Mao-Mao? I was getting another message here, and I didn't miss it.

I could have taken any number of different routes, or gone out at a different time, but here we were, and he was there just for me. He didn't "say" anything, but as I moved away he took a swipe at my hand as cats often do, and from the outside it might have looked like he was hitting me. I knew differently however, and I'd just gotten my first feline high-five, or four. As I rode away I looked back to see him disappear back into the hedge, another little brother helping me on my way, another little soul saying "we know about you."

Open channel D – mum are you getting this?

"I sure am."

Without balance, I wouldn't be able to ride this bike, and I felt I'd developed a certain psychic poise now to ride this wave in a similar way. It all seemed to be about delicacy and finesse with these energy vibrations, or as Gordon put it on one of his radio interviews when asked about communicating with the dead, "It's very subtle." Indeed.

୬ ୬ ୬ ୬ ୬ ୬

It's Monday morning again, one month to the day, and still I wondered if it was all some kind of dream...

"It's because it's working so well that you find it so hard to believe."

I can hear you as clearly as my own thoughts.

"It's been a month, and every day you've ended up believing it again."

She was laughing at me, and signed this last message *"the boss,"* just like she used to when leaving notes in the house for me to do certain things after school – every word was chosen to reassure me, to comfort me.

"Roll with it – was the mantra for that weekend I believe."

Yes it was mum. She was also overjoyed that I'd begun to eat and pull myself back from the brink.

"Five pounds more of you – and alive!"

What if I don't make it through this though? I'm so tired – I feel so weak and tired.

"I already said you could live with me."

I know, just keep telling me that okay? Just keep talking to me.

"'Till I'm blue in the face."

When I would get thoroughly scrambled, she would say:

"All right, as always – we go back to the beginning."

"Did something happen on June 2 with Gordon?"
Yes.
"What happened?"
You and Sri Bhundari spoke to me through Gordon.
"And now?"
You and he speak to me directly.
"Has the world totally changed?"
Oh yes.
"Are people completely different around you?"
Yes.
"Are you happier?"
I can't describe...
"Are you worried?"
I can't worry anymore.
"Are you safe?"
I'm safe in your arms.
"How's life?"
I'm surrounded by miracles.
"Are you really so surprised?"
No. The magic is real.

I was learning that the point was not to give me all the answers, and that growth was more dependent on finding my own most of the time. Even trying to remember something I may have forgotten, she made it clear the mental gymnastics *trying* to remember were as important as actually remembering. When I asked the really heavy questions about life, death, the universe, and everything – where was it all headed, and what would we become, she said:

"I'm not Seth."

I thought maybe I'd die laughing, and I didn't need help in that direction! Just stay positive, that's all I can do – all will be wondrous well – I told myself again.

"Being positive is the natural state of mind."

I can see that now. Worry was as bad an invention as coincidence. Worry creates the terrible tomorrow we all wish to avoid. We have had our power taken away.

This is the life of all my lives – this is the one – this is really happening isn't it?

"If it had not really happened, the world wouldn't be agreeing with you."

What's next?

"You being comfortable and becoming more comfortable is number one, work and everything else is number two."

Edna had taken over the front line from Sri Bhundari, she was under *his* tutelage, she was apprenticing as it were. This was something she'd wanted to do regardless in her new life, but now the subject was me, it just made even more sense.

I smiled when I thought of Sri Bhundari giving me the debriefing of my life so far, through Gordon. There was a moment when Gordon stopped and said, "You're mum wants to say – she agrees with everything he's saying!" Can you imagine?

ત ત ત ત ત ત

It's Thursday, Steaven died three years ago today, and it just didn't surprise me now that his father went into a coma on this day – he never came out of it, and two days later his body died. I saw them together now, and I knew Steaven's dad had given him a very special death-day present – himself. The word coincidence should forthwith be eradicated from the English language.

On the weekend I get to visit Treaca at her sister Angela's in St.Catherines – she has come all the way from Arizona and I haven't seen her for a long time.

Treaca is my number one teacher, she always has been – she placed "The Seth Material" in my hands when I was eighteen, three years after I'd "left" the church.

I didn't know what to believe for those three years, but I knew this dying business wasn't the end, and all those situations defined as "unexplained" were of the utmost interest to me.

My nature has always been to find out how things work, and I'd been taking things apart ever since I was a child. As an adult, "no user serviceable parts" meant – pass me the screwdriver please. This is the way I felt about death – what's going to happen? Isn't there some way to find out? Surely this is the top question on everyone's mind, isn't it? I found out it wasn't.

I'd quit school. In grade twelve a speech I delivered in English class about the "system" churning out automatons, didn't go down too well with my teacher, and I only lasted three weeks in grade thirteen.

Worth mentioning, is the day I went to the office to leave school forever and the secretary drawing a thick black line through my name, saying, "Just like you were never here." Why would you say that to someone? I was always a good student, but it didn't matter, my real education had begun, and Treaca opened the doors.

Along with Seth came Carlos Castaneda, Alan Watts, J. Krishnamurti, Ram Dass and Madame Blavatsky's Theosophy.

I started a dream journal and read Ann Faraday's "Dream Power."

Next came the Buddhists, Hinduism, Taoism, the Sufis and Confucius.

I became aware of Gnosticism, the Essenes and The Tibetan Book of the Dead, (with help from John Lennon and the song "Tomorrow Never Knows.")

I read Aldous Huxley's "The Doors of Perception," and Hermann Hesse's "Siddhartha." Timothy Leary just seemed to be everywhere. I read about Findhorn.

Philosophy opened up as an entire world to dive into, and I discovered Descartes, Albert Schweitzer and Gurdjieff, who used the word automatons too.

The Existentialists popped up with Kierkegaard, Albert Camus, Nietzsche and Sartre.

Psychologists and this new business of psychoanalysis came along, and I read Carl Jung (I didn't like Freud but dutifully read a bit), I loved what Fritz Perls was doing with his Gestalt Therapy, and Elizabeth Kubler-Ross released "On Death and Dying."

Then came feminism, and I read some Simone de Beauvoir, Germaine Greer and Betty Friedan.

I also read anything else I could get my hands on to do with religions, spirits, and belief systems, but Jane Roberts immediately became my yardstick, my measure, my filter, with which everything else was compared. She just didn't take anything for face value – she thought she was losing her mind – she thought she now had a split personality, and by the time she accepted what was happening to her as "real," I accepted it too... completely.

In fact at the very beginning, I said out loud – come on Jane, just look at this material you're getting, it's incredible, it's the best I've ever heard (not that I'd heard much channelling at this point, but I did know about Edgar Cayce), it just feels so true! I just had no problem believing an "energy personality essence, no longer focussed in physical reality," was relaying this fantastic information to her. Then again, it wasn't happening to *me*.

Now I was having a small taste of what she went through, I was a bit more understanding, she didn't have "The Seth Material" as a foundation to help her through it. Without that complex, detailed information, I don't know what I would have done. I had every book pre-ordered before she'd even finished writing them, and I've read them all backwards and forwards so many times I'm on my third and fourth copies of some of them. For more than thirty-five years I can't imagine my life without her writings.

Thank you Jane – in your rocking chair. I love you so.

I really wanted to meet her – Elmira, New York is not that far away from Toronto – but she'd suspended her classes by then. I *did* correspond with her, and I sent her a reel to reel tape of some songs I'd written inspired by her and Seth. I'm not big on possessions, but the replies I received from her in her own hand, have to be amongst my most prized ones of all.

I knew of the "dream" classes she held, and I thought, well, I *must* be a member of those classes, I'm practically obsessed with her. But over the years I kind-of thought, oh yeah, right Neli, just because you want something so badly doesn't make it so. Or does it?

It would take thirty-five years and Jane herself to straighten me out – the dead Jane that is. She died in 1984, twenty-one days after my mother's death – I lost two of the most important women in my life at almost the same time. I was thirty.

Back to the present, the heart-shaped birthmark on my wrist seemed to be darker, or is it my imagination? Imagination is the real power plant – I thought, as my hands made yet another pyramid.

I thought about Steaven again, and his answer when I asked him if he was scared a week before he died – "a bit" – he had offered. What a simple statement of inner strength.

My dad was quite scared as he was getting closer to *his* time – he'd loaded a lot of bombs and bullets onto planes during the Second World War as an armourer in the Royal Air Force, and it was in and on his mind at the end. I said something useless like – try not to think about it....

᭢ ᭢ ᭢ ᭢ ᭢ ᭢

It's Saturday, day thirty-six and guess what? I'm on the train to St. Catherines. I actually get to go somewhere! I looked out the window and hoped/asked for an animal to comfort me, (I was a little nervous – what if Treaca asked me to "do" something, and I couldn't?) A Falcon soared into view and guided my eye to a jet contrail that was in the shape of a nose! Your nose is in the sky now mum! Holy smoke!

I couldn't think of any reason for a jet to deviate from its flight-plan like that, just to continue on, in exactly the same direction a minute later. Couldn't think of one.

Once I arrived, it was as if we'd parted but a moment earlier, and the old banter and cutting each other off just to get a word in, carried on like we were thirty-five years ago.

I got my first chance to convey a message face to face, from one world to the next – "My mum wants me to tell you, you're beautiful." She embraced me and my mother and we climbed into the van as I dabbed my eyes and noticed my legs were shaking. Not out of the woods yet Nelson – try to eat something on this trip okay?

I'd taken my guitar and we sang some of our favourite old songs together – Leonard Cohen and Donovan out of my old notebooks that were still with me after all these years. A lot of the songs were written out in Treaca's own hand from more than three decades ago – look at that, we're getting old man! I don't want to be on this planet without you.

Her sister Angela was away with her husband Don, and their daughters Sarah and Kayla, but they had left their two doggies! I'm all right now – hi Amica! – hey there Ori! I could already feel myself calm down with one look at these lovely dogs. I had two days and one night there, and still we barely managed to say all the things that needed to be said.

One thing I needed to be sure of right off the bat, as I gave her the latest news of my development/situation, was her opinion of all this, that was crucial.

"This is big, isn't it?"
"This is *huge* Neli."

This is the girl who created "Neli" thirty-five years ago. All through high school we'd known each other, but it wasn't until school was over before we started going out together and became boyfriend and girlfriend for four years. We each moved on to successive people, but nothing ever changed between us. If you really love someone, you always will and that's all there is to that. We could bridge a gap of years like this:

"I talk to everything now Neli."
"Yeah... so do I."

We went to visit her mum and dad Teresa and George who lived just around the corner, and I hadn't seen them for thirty years. They were always so kind to me when I was "the boyfriend," and I could hardly wait to see them. Teresa was like a second mother to me, and George had found me a job at his company many years ago when I needed one. He'd done the same thing for Angela, and that was where she'd met Don. At one point, the three of us had been working at Ferranti-Packard together, but that was so many years ago now as to be almost another lifetime.

I knew I'd fall apart when I saw Teresa, and I did myself proud.

I don't know what she thought as I held on to her for dear life and bawled my eyes out, but if nothing else, she must have felt the love I have for her. I also knew she wasn't in such good shape at the moment and I might never get to see her in this life again – which is what happened.

I had a wonderful time and almost drowned in delicious tea to go with my selection of biscuits sitting on the plate beside me.

Some things never change, and I wanted that tea and biscuits to prove they hadn't, because really – I wanted it to be thirty years ago, I wanted us all to be younger, and I wanted Teresa to *not* look like she was close to bowing-out of this world.

We all had our pictures taken, and Teresa thought I had to catch a plane for England so I'd better not be late. It was all so good and so heart wrenching at the same time. So many things in life are like that, aren't they?

Treaca and I knew that Teresa thought she was seeing her dead father and other dead relatives around the house, *because she was* seeing her dead father and other dead relatives around the house. She was half-way into the next world at least, and linear time had broken down for her, as well as dimensional barriers.

This was also the start of a pattern for me, of making a connection with someone who was about to go, in order to make potential contact later a bit, what... fresher? – maybe easier and stronger anyway. It helps to have a recent memory of a person's voice too sometimes, I learned.

We covered so much that weekend my head was spinning. Treaca established that this awakening was classic in terms of the Goddess Kundalini, and she'd even heard of the technique spirits sometimes employ, using lines from movies. Things like that really helped me. At one point though, she came out with a word that just rang like a gong.

"You know Neli, the new-agey people have been going on for a while now about something they call the *Ascension*."
"The Ascension?"

Immediately I thought of Jesus and Christianity – "He ascended into heaven, and sitteth on the right hand of God the Father Almighty."

"It's the Ascension of the Earth herself, and us as well. It's about evolution."
Evolution! Where have I heard that before?
"Well that sounds interesting." Little did I know.
"You might want to look into it – it relates to the prophecies of the Mayans and 2012 and all that."
"I'll be sure to do that – okay."

There was something about that term – The Ascension. I felt like I'd known about it for a long time already. The future me knew about this in great detail, and I was getting that feeling I've had before, the feeling of a bleed-through of sorts, of one part of me already knowing, but in linear time this was the "first" moment.

We were at the bus stop now, the weekend was over. I'd decided to take the train there, and the bus home, just to maximise the travel experience as I rarely got to really go anywhere. Maybe that would change one of these days? I didn't know. A part of me has never liked being away from home very much, but I liked the idea anyway. For now, the cats were waiting for me (I like to believe), and I had to go back to work tomorrow.

Treaca and I held on to each other like we might never see each other in this reality again, which was potentially true of course – you never know when death will tap you on the left shoulder. We were a lot older now too. I could barely get the words out:

"I will always be there for you, in any place or time, in any dimension I will always be there, I will never let you down – I love you"
"I love you Neli – you're my favourite soul."

I'll be glad to be in the next world where there are no goodbyes.

I climbed aboard clutching the book she was lending me "The Reluctant Shaman," and the article from Tom Kenyon and The Hathors, with a meditation for the ride home – The Planetary Creatrix Meditation.

It was a very important weekend, she had said, there was something special going on. It turned out that July 7, 2007 – the seventh of the seventh of the seventh, which was yesterday – was an energy event, a harmonic shift, and a precursor to something amazing going on. That was why she'd given me the article and the meditation for the way home. She had also picked yesterday as our day to get together, *and* the day to see her mum and dad. As I began to look into things more and more, I soon realised this was no accident either. What a sneak!

She was working on more than one level, this one.

Her teachings and manoeuvrings were gentle but precise. The same way she'd casually said I should go and see Gordon and my world had changed forever.

She's the best, and I would trust her with all of my lives.

I got into my seat and the bus pulled away, making the face I loved move two-dimensionally sideways through the murk on the glass, as we tried to hold each other's eyes for as long as possible. How many times has this dance been danced on this earth?

I thought of my Auntie Vera waving her scarf, as it slowly dwindled to nothing as we sailed away from port in Liverpool on our way to Canada. That scarf was the last thing I saw of England, and now Tom Waits sang in my mind:

> Planes and trains and boats and buses
> Characteristically
> Evoke a common attitude
> Of blue

My lord, Neli – you sure can be maudlin can't you? Let's look at that article. You'll know her for eternity and you *know* that, first hand. How many people can be so sure?

Last Quarter

Namaste

People on the other side change the way they look, the way we decide what clothes we're going to wear for the day. When you can change your body and therefore your face, hairstyle and everything that goes along with it, you do so.

So far, she had looked like my mum, only younger, which is what most people do, although her clothing had tended to be more flowing.

Now she introduced me to her current or favourite look for the time being. Her hair is straight and black and just below her shoulders with a fringe – or bangs as they say in North America. Her face is different, but the funny thing is, she is still completely recognisable as herself. It's the "essence" of a person that you recognise, and not the outside appearance. She looks somewhat like a forty-ish Anjelica Huston when she doesn't want to look like my mother, which I gather is mostly for my sake anyway, and the connection to the word Angelic didn't go unnoticed either.

In this particular appearance, with her long simple gowns that I must say are very appropriate for the occasion, she calls herself Edwina.

Upon looking up the name, it seems to be the original name from which Edna was derived.

It was Edwina who spoke to me this morning:

"You are a white knight."

You are very friendly – I thought back to her as I rolled out of bed.

She was in a great mood this morning – I could feel it.

You would think people back "home" would always be in a good mood, considering the living conditions and the freedom, but this isn't always the case. People are people no matter where they are – and a lot of the time on the other side, they are so very concerned about us.

Back to earth, I thought about her high spirits last night too, when the TV came on by itself, and when random on the CD player just didn't seem to be exactly random anymore.

"Ours is not to reason why – ours is just to die and die."

She was laughing her head off, and it was infectious, so now *I* was in a good mood – thanks mum!

She wanted me to look at the TV captions before I went to work, so we played spin the remote and I had a look – "People have gotten together," was today's message, and somehow I knew this had something to do with the Ascension. I must find out a lot more about that.

It was a beautiful stormy morning, the middle of July, and there was a face in the clouds as I got my bike out of the garage. I looked up, and "guessed" twice the exact moment lightning would occur. This is more fun than I've ever had in my entire life.

On the way to work she made it clear she wanted to do more with photography, and I remembered again how much she'd enjoyed taking photos herself in physical life.

Well, that was just fine by me, I never went anywhere without my camera now, but I was still a tiny bit nervous about taking more pictures in the pitch black. At the same time I never felt more protected in my life, this was wonderful – everything was wonderful.

As the morning progressed and the sun came out, I noticed there was a certain edge to the way my mother sounded. It wasn't the way she sounded actually, it was more the way she felt somehow. There was something different about the contact in a way that was hard to put my finger on. It wasn't until I went outside at lunch time, that I realised how hot and humid it had now become since the sun had managed to blast through the clouds and dispel them. It was stifling.

That was one thing about working in the printing business, air conditioning was a necessary part of maintaining the correct moisture content of the paper to ensure optimum image quality and printability. That it made for a much more comfortable working environment was a welcome by-product.

Now I was outside, I could feel just how thick the air was, and I knew it was the reason for the odd feeling I had. It was the feeling of interference. I would have possibly thought the more moisture and electricity in the air might have made for better conductivity somehow, but this was clearly wrong. We were communicating trans-dimensionally after all, and it was obvious this atmospheric condition was presenting a slight thickness that I could psychically feel – like a slight static.

It wasn't a big deal, and I chatted with my mum about this and other things, all the while gauging the effect. Everything was working fine the way I was now used to, but it seemed to require just that little bit more energy to cut through the atmosphere. It didn't take long before I remembered Seth mentioning this to Jane Roberts, and subsequently cutting a session short because of the added strain on her, as he put it.

To be able to personally feel something from that world I'd read about for so long put me in an ecstatic mood, extra strain on me or not.

I can feel it Jane, I can feel it! – I announced to her as if she was listening, and I climbed the steps to go back to work.

The workday went on as usual, until Marie came in. This was the person I'd been waiting for, as Marie was old, both physically and spiritually, and I'd been wondering when she was going to show up. I knew she would.

She was French, a yoga instructor, but she taught the teachers, and I'd printed her book for her and learned she'd been on many TV and radio programmes – she was a pro. I felt she was another ally.

She handed me her folder and explained to me the procedure for her next printing job. I took a deep breath.

"Marie, what do you know about Kundalini awakenings?"
"Well, Kundalini is the energy – it comes up..."
"But what do you know about Kundalini *awakenings*?"
"Well if you're not prepared, it can be very frightening and..."

At this point, she looked at me as if she'd only just seen me, and her eyes narrowed slightly, "Why, do you know someone who..."

But now she knew something, she could tell, there was no fooling this one, and she looked at me closely.

"Some people are born with a mark." I could see her dropping "some people" in her mind.

"You were born with a mark – you are a seeker – you see beauty, no?"

"Yes." She was eyeing me very, very carefully now.

"Every day is up to you, whether you have a good day or a bad day, it's all up to you. Positive or negative, it's up to you."

"Marie, all negativism is... gone."

I knew the power of my thoughts more than ever now, and I knew none of us really, could afford to be negative. The universe is responsive no matter what, and I noticed it was easier than you would think to be positive. It was natural.

She went on, "You *know* something?"
"I know a lot of things."

A month ago I wouldn't have said that, as it would have seemed too arrogant and not like me, but now I felt confident and I meant it.

She began to smile with a gentle indulgence, but it ended on a more serious note, as she realised I wasn't being cocky or anything other than honest and accurate.

She gathered her things from the counter, and headed for the door. I didn't know this would be the last time I would ever see her at Positive Print – I'd been serving her for over ten years. As she reached the door she just stopped, and she knew – she knew everything – and if I had any doubts about that, they were dispelled as she turned around and looked at me again – hard.

She put her hands together in front of her chest and bowed her head – Namaste.

I did the same with no volition on my part. Not a word was spoken as our eyes met one last time in complete understanding before she spun around and headed out the door.

Oh my.

New Moon

The Calling

It was Saturday, six weeks in, and day forty-three. I would probably be counting the days forever since that incredible day of emergence. Thank you Gordon – you little dickens!

On "impulse" I decided to go out and buy a tent. In my mind I called it a meditation tent, although I still found it harder to come back to this reality, than to go somewhere else.

Off I went to Zellers and quickly found one I liked. The price was good too as they'd already started putting things on sale for the end of summer, so that was handy.

I noticed I was right next to the toy department, and it reminded me of all those years ago in England at the Co-Op, when you would get a magical ride in Father Christmas' sleigh, and then get to choose a toy based on your age. There were toys everywhere, just like this department I was in, and I decided to buy one – I never stopped loving toys. What should I get?

It was almost like my hand reached down and pulled out the jigsaw puzzle all by itself – I couldn't believe what I was holding.

The image was Native American. It consisted of a small figure with his back to you standing in front of a fire and the mountains with his arms raised up to the sky. The background was deep black space with stars and nebulae all blue and purple with beadwork down each side. In the centre was the large golden disc of the sun, and inside that, a gigantic figure of an ancient ancestor with long flowing gray hair looking down at the man. His hair became feathers as it reached down to the earth, (feathers!), and he was holding his hands as if to look at the palms. In between his hands was a great eagle chest high flying straight up. It was magnificent.

As amazing as this image was, the name of the puzzle was just as astounding. The series being "Sacred Spaces," and this particular image itself entitled "The Calling."

That was exactly what I felt had happened to me – I had been called. It just tied in so perfectly with the agreements I'd signed and the way

I'd been interrogated in a way, by my mum and Sri Bhundari through Gordon.

If I hadn't been in the middle of this large department store, I would've screamed with pure joy. As it was, I headed for the checkout counter with my tent and my puzzle, feeling about a foot off the floor, and saying thank you over and over like a mantra in my mind.

The next day I put my tent up in the backyard and it turned out to be a pyramid tent. How not surprising! I got it all arranged, and felt I'd now completely accepted what was happening to me. If I thought I would never have any doubts about anything again, I was wrong, but I knew I was still just at the beginning of this incredible experience. My life had just begun and Edna had something to say:

"Have fun with this beginning time - you will relive it with great affection."

Once again I knew by this that I wouldn't always feel this way, I knew I had to come down somehow, I knew I had to rejoin the land of the living. That's funny - I'd never felt so alive in my life, but I knew what she meant, and it seemed a little sad, but I knew I had to integrate what was going on *into* this life, and not just fly off into the more rarefied realms. I decided that "realm" meant "real dream."

I'll be with you soon anyway, right mum? I'm not getting any younger.

I'd been researching a lot now, so Edna told me to slow down a bit and let her and the other spirits do what they were here to do. She said the writing was okay, but just to cool it with the internet. I now had a journal I wrote in every day, and I was still writing on the new July wall calendar at work. June, I'd taken down and was safely at home.

The July calendar wasn't quite as hysterical looking, so I felt a bit safer with that, although I did now have a folder called Bardo buried in the computer at work, and if anyone found that, I didn't know what they might think. I also didn't really care, and part of me hoped someone actually would find it and start asking me questions, because in reality, I wanted to shout from the rooftops and tell the world what was happening to me. Not yet though, I had to see where this was going, and make sure I knew what I was talking about.

She also told me to keep Positive Print together because as much normalcy as possible was still a good idea. Well I had to agree with that one, although not much of anything seemed normal anymore since all this had begun. I was still being comforted and coddled and boosted as much as possible from my family on the other side.

"Just look at what you've done so far."

"Am I going to see you again? More than the black shape I saw before?

"You ain't seen nothin' yet."

"All this is still pretty hard to take in you know mum."

"You are the real deal."

ನ ನ ನ ನ ನ ನ

It's Tuesday and I was riding to work, when I decided to silently call my groundhog as I zoomed down the hill and went under the bridge.

There he is waiting on the concrete wall! What are the chances of that? What are the chances of any of this?

I pulled over to talk to him as he looked at me with that ancient animal face, before scurrying behind a bush and disappearing down his not-so-secret entrance to his underground abode. I must buy some more peanuts to leave here on my way home.

After work I went over to my tent and noticed there was a shadow in what I now called the sacred grove. The shadow looked exactly like a Celtic Cross and I wasn't surprised, just excited and grateful, and I made sure I jotted it down in my journal.

My head was still full of Druids and Faeries and Hindus and Native Americans and Merlin, but now I have a new word – Brahman. It's an all too familiar word but I didn't exactly have a definition off the top of my head. After looking into it I find the Brahmins (with the "i") are the Hindu priest class, and they are the scholars, educators and law makers. On a larger scale in the Vedanta philosophy, Brahman is your true self, God – the Infinite One – Brahma being the Hindu God of creation.

This could get confusing.

Then I found out Brahmin also means – twice born.

All right, well you just fit right in there don't you? Welcome to the club!

I go for a walk and the cicadas singing high in the trees on each side of the street seem to be balancing the two hemispheres of my brain.

I sense White Feather and Duncan – they just want to say hello and let me know they're still with me. Whenever – the feeling is, whenever you're ready, we'll be here. We are always here.

On the weekend my new old piano arrived. I hadn't had an acoustic piano for a long time and this one looked just like the old piano my grandfather had, the one I learned to play on originally and I couldn't have been happier. I am truly blessed.

Some more furniture of Mum B's arrived too, and took its station in the house, causing me to feel she's even closer, and it's a very good feeling.

No matter what happens now – no matter what happens for the rest of my life, I've seen some things not everyone gets to see. The magic is in every moment – it's in every breath.

First Quarter
The Ghost and the Rainbow

It's Monday morning at Positive Print and there goes the door chime again. It's a motion detector and it's been doing that for years now, just going off all by itself regardless of whether anyone's there or not. Other people have been saying oh, it must be a fly, or it's just overly sensitive, or it's defective, but for years and years now I've been saying – "It's the ghost."

The ramifications of those three words now hit me with an impact that made me psychologically shudder, as I now knew beyond the shadow of a doubt that what I'd been saying was a literal fact, and not just a fun metaphor. Not only that, it was my mother, it had always been my mother, ever since we'd gotten the stupid thing.

Oh this was just too perfect, this was too funny, and I was as sure of this as I was sure of anything at all. I didn't have to change a thing, I didn't have to say anything different, all I had to do was just carry on saying "It's the ghost" and there was yet another source of secret fun. This was like psychic espionage!

I wished I could tell them it really was a ghost – or a free spirit actually, as my mother certainly wasn't earthbound – but I thought it best just to keep it to myself. How long had this lady been trying to get my attention, and in how many different ways? I'd even said what it actually was, and I *still* didn't get it until now.

The fact she hadn't come out and said to me in the past fifty-two days – by the way, that door chime thing is *me* you know – was another example of what I've mentioned before. There really seems to be something gained from figuring things out for yourself. I was elated by this simple revelation.

After work I was going downtown to see my friend Jane (another Jane – that's three now, not including Jane Roberts). She was here to perform a couple of her songs at a songwriter's gathering. I hadn't seen her in thirty-odd years, and she'd been invited to come all the way from British Columbia to join these songwriters – I was quite excited.

It was about a twenty minute walk to the bus stop I wanted to get to, so off I went down the hill and under the bridge once again on this bright sunny day. About halfway there, something above me caught my eye so I looked up and saw the most beautiful rainbow directly above me. I was always looking up, so it was kind of strange I hadn't noticed the rainbow until this particular moment, but there it was in all its glory. The funny thing was – it wasn't raining. There were a few clouds all right, but they were *below* the rainbow! I decided this rainbow was just for me, my own personal rainbow, but just to be sure, I looked around to see if there was anyone else looking at it.

There weren't many people on the road, but the people I *did* see weren't looking up, and passengers in cars didn't seem to be noticing it and it was quite a startling rainbow, not one of those you can barely make out, but intense and vibrant.

Okay, I thought, I have my own rainbow.

My thoughts now veered off to Tibet, and I thought of various Buddhist masters, and incredible things that happened upon their deaths. I have a book called "Graceful Exits" and many such tales are recounted in this book. Sometimes flowers would fall from the sky, or their bodies would lay there for days and days without decaying, and sometimes – rainbows.

It was a very old symbol of spirituality, and I prayed I wasn't just an arrogant newcomer to presume this could possibly be meant for me. At the same time, I wasn't going to be blind enough to ignore that God was looking down upon me – and all of us – if we would but notice. I decided I had noticed, and – you guessed it – said thank you.

I had a great time at the club, listening to all these brave songwriters, and it was interesting to notice that I didn't care if other people heard *my* songs or not, really. There was talk about feedback – all perfectly natural – and letting the audience help you to decide if you really had written a good song or not, but it just didn't matter to me anymore what other people thought in that way.

I'd always been such a nervous ninny anyway, and that stopped me from performing in the past the way I would have liked to, but I came to see I was secure within myself, and if others thought a song of mine was really good – that would be a bonus, a very welcome bonus to be sure, but not necessary.

I realised I was independent of others' opinions in a way that wasn't arrogant, but simply assured. At last.

The next day at work I added to my screensaver: more animals, beautiful angels – one with the caption, "the messenger has arrived" – a clip from "Highlander" as he's in the throes of becoming the *only one*, and an image of a figure in the lotus position with all the colourful chakras.

you have no knowledge whatsoever of your potential

I heard this line from Highlander and knew it was from Sri Bhundari. He'd gotten the accent just right too. I thought – yeah, tell me about it – and laughed.

The voices I'd called the chorus were either him or from my higher self, who I called Neli-Two or Malcolm. Neli-Two was a bit of a joke because of Seth-Two (a "higher" version of Seth), and Malcolm was one of the names my mum may have called me but didn't. It just seemed appropriate somehow. In my reading I found out it had taken one lady six months to separate her guide's voice from her own thoughts, so I didn't think I was doing too badly.

I was on a roll. I found myself alone and I wasn't going to stop here.

Not having my own computer, I was actually years behind in what I would have looked up on the Internet. This started to work to my advantage now – of course it did! The web began to place things in my lap strategically.

I found images of space, planets and nebulae, and chose a select few – this is exciting! Two images of Persephone, two Buddhas, a feather, a faerie, The Yorkshire Rose to go with the Lancashire Rose, My Lady Greensleeves, and another gorgeous rendering of a seated figure again with the chakras, and him I grabbed to be my new background picture.

Then I began searching for Hindu Goddesses.

For years, every time I've seen an East Indian female I've said – there goes an Indian Goddess, so it wasn't so strange to start hunting them down. I found a dozen or so I had to have and snagged them, and then I saw a statue and everything stopped still.

I saw *her* and I choked – I *know* you Hindu Goddess!

Parvati couldn't wait to be free. I-know-you! I couldn't take my eyes off her. I found out who she was exactly, and gave myself to her. I was in love. Does that make sense?

If I needed to personify All-That-Is, if I needed a face instead of energy or the ultimate vibration of Love – she was it. An avatar (avatara) of sorts for me, as in bhakti-yoga, although I don't believe there is any real separation between us and God.

Still, I knew her, the mountain Goddess version of Shakti, representing erotic and sensual love - where the snow would be! Perfect.

I made sure I would be able to find this site again, and printed her out as well as adding her a few times to my collection. I would see her and the other images circulate as I went through my day. I retrieved her from the printer and stared... I have to get some air.

Outside, elated, I took a moment just to make sure my mother was with me, and I heard:

"I'm watching you like a hawk."

Sri Bhundari sent me an image of himself as well. I'd been seeing him in a suit lately, looking very dapper like a Sidney Poitier type, his face becoming clearer each time I saw him, but now he sent me an image of himself from a distance, rowing along in a small boat on a lake, just gliding along and whistling. Okay, everything's fine.

Back inside, I took a moment to add Parvati and a new phrase to my collage of pictures, quotes and photographs on the wall in front of my work table - "I only respond to kindness and respect" I wrote, and placed it next to "Open unto yourself."

That was the way I felt now, not higher than anyone, but not beneath anyone either and I would do my best to treat all the eternal beings in my life the same way.

I finished some copying and thought of my monk again, and how it must have taken him months or even years to complete a few pages, depending on the complexity. I would've liked that job - I *did* like that job - but my how things have changed. Now it was just get it done as fast as possible.

I rode home and three butterflies flew across my path closely - two Monarchs and a white one - about chest high. I was still thinking about how beautiful they were as I put my bike away and picked up a couple of feathers off the back lawn.

Moon Three

Granddad

I have to take photographs of the full moon tonight – I thought, as I looked at the pictures on the bedroom wall. I'd started a little collection there as well as at work. I looked at a photo of my dog Rex and heard him say – I'm waiting for you. Oh my.

I was two months into this now and my feet still hadn't hit the ground.

I didn't want them to, but I'd read enough by now to understand this was the way it worked for human beings. My mother had also recently made that comment about remembering the beginning time with affection, so I knew there was no way around it.

There was an explosion of complete knowing, and oneness, and then there was the integration of the experience, and a kind of slow climb back up to what you glimpsed.

You were forever changed, but there was always a yearning to be there again. To be held by the Goddess again. Tears spring at just the thought.

This is the gift we all have waiting for us one day.

I used to think instant enlightenment would happen on the day we died regardless, but I know now this isn't the case. There really are no shortcuts, and the work has to be done somewhere.

After the last two months, I knew it was impossible to remain in this mesmerised state, and be anywhere near functional. Then again, being functional in the old way didn't seem to matter that much anymore. But one still had to eat – especially me.

Helping other people understand and remember who they really are became the main reason to maintain some sort of coherence, and to stay in this world. If there could possibly have been a downside in any way, it would have to be the desire to go home.

Not yet.

It was Monday morning and as I got ready to go to work, I still couldn't believe two months had actually gone by. It was all a dream within a dream.

That first week I'd wondered what it might be like and how I would feel a few weeks or months ahead – assuming I lived that long – and even though it was so far in the future, I knew it would be here before I knew it, and here we were.

Time was still even crazier than it was before, in my old life, when everything was just going faster and faster. It was like pieces on a checker board, and it moved with a will of its own. It looped all over the place, and I had a hard time trying to straighten everything out and keep it linear in my mind. Almost everything seemed to be a déjà vu, either as it was actually happening, or after the fact. I was dreaming the days before they happened or I'd hit a dimension of experience where time just really didn't matter that much anymore – or both.

I had to begin e-mails to friends who knew what was going on with a little disclaimer – "I might have already told you this, but just in case I haven't...."

I also figured it was time to start telling my family and other friends what was going on with me because I was not the person I used to be, and never would be.

The Ascension had something to do with this time business I now knew, and I'd gathered enough information about Kundalini and shamanism for now, to start moving on to the bigger picture.

This awakening had been triggered by my own personal crisis, but I learned it was also connected to our planetary crisis, and the two were very much intertwined, but for now, I had to go to work.

I got my bike out of the garage and checked that my friends were with me. My mum, Sri Bhundari, Sherrie, Steaven and Mum B. were all there – I could feel them.

One thought away.

I didn't say – open channel D – anymore, and I actually kind of looked back on that nostalgically, it was fun. Edna knew I liked to hear the words though, feeling or not, so I heard:

"I'm right here love."

Sri Bhundari had gotten a kick out of his row boat image and knew how much it had made me laugh, so he carried on and went further in the same vein. Today, it was an image of him skiing, but at the same time scrubbing his naked back with a huge scrubbing brush as he was flying down the slope wearing only a loincloth. It was too ridiculous, and I laughed out loud as I put my bike helmet on. He knew I liked non sequiturs, and this one was visual.

He knows everything about me, I thought. They all do – good – I have no secrets, and I've given everyone full access anyway, right?

I felt nothing but trust, and an aching love that took my breath away. I wiped the tears and rode up the street to work in a kind of bliss. As I flew down the hill to the bridge, there was a brand new billboard beside the railway tracks, relating to energy conservation, and in gigantic letters backed with the blue summer sky, the message was – YOU HAVE THE POWER.

I zoomed under the bridge laughing and crying and managed to shout: Hey Mr. Groundhog – hope you're okay!

I'm okay, I thought, I'm blessed beyond the beyond, but I guess I'm going to arrive at work with red eyes once again.

It was an eventful day at work as the new production machine arrived from Xerox. Hours of installation time later, there it was in all its glory – the NUVERA.

Well, if I needed a sign as to whether it was time to tell my family – there it was. How could I not think of my Auntie Vera? I'd been thinking a lot about her lately, and I knew she'd be the first person I would tell outside of the house.

It also looked a lot like "new era" to me, and it didn't escape me that Vera means truth, and faith. It was time to have faith and tell the truth – verily.

Before I left for the day I took down the July wall calendar, and put up August, even though I was a day early. July wasn't quite as crazy-looking as June had been, but I figured it was a good idea to fold it up and put it in my knapsack. All right, we'll see what August will bring – one last thing before I go – I went to my secret Bardo folder, and created a new sub-folder called "Ascension."

Once home, I decided to look at a Seth book for the first time since all this had begun, and within moments I'd found a section in "Seth Speaks" that related so perfectly with what was going on, it was uncanny. I'd read this book so many times I'd lost count, but now of course, everything was different. It was obviously about Kundalini although he didn't use that word, and here are some of the sentences I read:

"The energy generated by some such experiences is enough to change a life in a matter of moments, and to affect the understanding and behaviour of others."

"The knowledge gained must then be integrated by the physical personality...."

"The incredible charge is always in the initial experience. Contained within it is the condensed energy from which all other developments come."

"Expansion of consciousness, therefore, requires honest self-appraisal, an awareness of one's own beliefs and prejudices. It brings a gift and a responsibility."

I sat there stunned. All together, I had over fifty Seth books in my book case, and I'd chosen that particular one and simply opened it. This is the way things are supposed to work, this is being in the flow, in the Tao. I said thank you, and copied the section out.

Why are we out of the loop? I wondered as I wrote. Why do we doubt more than believe? Is there a greater irony than connecting with the universe and then interpreting it as losing your mind? We've been programmed, we've been held down and we've been conditioned to not see the magic for fear of being ridiculed and laughed at. Sometimes we do it to ourselves just to fit in. Or so we don't get locked-up.

"It's self-imposed, and terribly imposing."

Thank you mum! You always make me laugh and lighten up my thoughts. It's too easy for me to get heavy, isn't it?

I took the July calendar out of my knapsack to tuck away neatly in my room with June, but time wasn't so neat and tidy for me anymore. It seemed as though those two months existed in a space of their own somehow, and not really slotted into regular time.

I was thinking this when I heard: "Hello P."

It was my granddad, he was here and he had waited exactly two months before he came to me. This made perfect sense, it was another reassurance, a nice round number just to make sure I was all right and could handle his visit. He knows the way I feel about him.

The first thing he did was show me his hands. He held them palm up, and then slowly turned them over so I could have a good look. No arthritis now. I'd never seen my granddad's hands without arthritis, but I did now, and it was almost too much to bear. I just collapsed against the wall, leaning there with my eyes closed and the tears of ecstasy running down my cheeks, and I just witnessed.

He played the piano for me. He played beautiful music as only he could, on a keyboard that seemed to be suspended in a void. I saw all I needed to see and heard all I needed to hear to know that he was just fine. He was happy. He had his hands back and was operating at his full capabilities and then some – if that was possible. He'd always been the best musician I'd ever known, the most sensitive of players. Many times here, in physical reality, I'd seen him reduce his audience to a puddle on the floor. The love I felt for him was like my soul aching, and I was blessed with twenty-five minutes of his presence, until I felt him deciding that it was enough – for now.

"Love everything P" – was his final comment, and my mind went back forty years or so to a day when we'd been talking about music, and piano playing. His secret could be summed up in what he told me then.

"All the time you're playing P... you're loving it. You're loving every note you're playing," and he mimicked playing a piano with his eyes closed. He of course knew I'd just gone back to that day, and I could see him nodding, telling me without words that now I had to extend that love – to everything.

Oh Granddad – I'm going to die!

I could feel myself coming back from somewhere, I must've been in a kind of trance, and the last thing I heard as the world solidified around me was my grandma's voice – "I'm next!" All right Grandma, it's a date.

It was dark now... time to go outside and take some photographs of the full moon. I stood on the deck and stared at the Moon, noticing the clouds coming and going and seeming to frame her glory. They were doing it on purpose – there was no doubt about that. And the intensity of the light! Has the Moon ever been this bright before? It was like blue neon and I swear I've never seen her this bright. I took my photographs, and my mind went to Steaven. We stood here together on this deck many a time, and he was here with me now.

"Peteski – can you lend me ten bucks?"

I spluttered laughter, it was so out of left field, and so perfect. With Steaven to my left and the Moon above me on the right, all I could do was close my eyes for a moment, and feel *life.*

Last Quarter

Vera and White Feather

It was Sunday morning, day sixty-five, and Vera was coming over this afternoon, it was time to tell her about her sister – and her nephew.

I'd already told Officer Jane what was going on by now, and the universe had backed me up in everything I said. For instance, when I brought up the insects, and told Jane that "flies like me now" – at that precise moment – one landed on my left arm, one on my right shoulder, and one on the top of my head. I couldn't have prayed for more support. That, plus my spiritual journey before all this, had made my declaration somewhat believable from the outside.

It was already impossible though, to explain all the things that were happening in the detail they required. Not to mention that some things were almost beyond language, and I was still in another world. I felt giddy and overwhelmed. I was hoping it wasn't too early and that I didn't come across as a crazy wild man to Vera. I was still pretty thin, but at least not as skeletal as I looked a couple of months ago.

By now I had a stack of printed material about Kundalini and shamanism, and I got those arranged and ready on the floor of my room. Plus, I had my two aces, the photograph of the astral nose, and the piece of music my mum had written. I hoped it was enough, and I noticed Edna had been quiet so far this morning.

"I was being quiet to save your strength."

She now offered, and then carried on.

"Let Vera come, let her see Jane, your room, the cello, the photograph. Let her hear the music."

The cello she referred to was the one made by my great grandfather who was a violin, cello maker. He was Vera and Edna's grandfather, and I had one of his instruments. Vera hadn't seen it for a while, and we had just talked about it on the telephone.

"Let things happen."

Are you sure about the photograph? – I thought.

"Let her see it – my nose knows she should see it."

She had me laughing again, and I felt better already.

"Don't forget the genuine love we all have for each other – you're in good hands."

We were in the bedroom now, and for added reassurance, she told me to grab the remote.

"Turn on the TV – right now! Put on channel 31 with the captions"

I did so, and as the TV popped on I saw – "God bless you son."

Vera came over for five hours, and four of those were spent in my room alone together. I could feel Edna's presence, and between the three of us we created a triangle of energy. Vera sat there and listened to everything I had to say, and during the really far-out parts, I would say, "Are you okay?" and she would quietly nod. God bless her.

I handed her pages and pages, which she dutifully flipped through, and then I handed her the photograph. I knew I was home free when she said, "You know Peter, you've always been like this."

I hadn't realised how much my reputation had preceded me. I also knew how well she knew her own sister, and so could relate to a lot of things my mum had been saying lately, and to just the way she had said them. I told her about Granddad.

"I talk to them too you know."

Oh praise the lord! It couldn't have gone any better.

I mentioned 11:11 and numerology, and she wasted no time reminding me of the significance of the number 12 in our family. "I'm surprised you're not thinking of number twelve more." This turned out to be quite profound as the number 12 is very significant on this planet. Twelve hours on the clock, twelve months to the year, twelve eras within the 26,000-year procession of the equinoxes, and twelve strands of DNA. I was learning more about DNA and cosmic cycles as my research into the Ascension continued. The Great Shift – was another name for the event about to happen, or already underway.

Finally, I told her about the music – Edna's piece – and I hit the play button on the keyboard and left the room. When I returned a few minutes later, she was staring out the window with tears streaming down her cheeks, and I knew I was in the clear.

"One more thing Vera, your sister wants me to give you something," and as she looked at me enquiringly, I walked over to her and gave her a "butterfly kiss" on the cheek. Nothing else needed to be said.

Vera left after we'd taken a few photographs, and I sat alone in my room reflecting on how well it had gone. I seemed to have said all the right things, considering the unfamiliar ground Vera was on with all this Kundalini business, and I hoped it had all been the right thing to do at the right time. I felt drained and happy and that I had another ally.

"You have done something wondrous."

Everything seems wondrous lately mum, but I'm not sure it's all me – I thought back to her as I went into the bedroom – I think I'd better get something to eat though.

"The TV – now!"

Oh, what this time? I feigned annoyance, but I loved this game. I clicked it on, just leaving it on the current channel, and looked at the screen – "Don't forget the pork-rinds." This was too much, this was... fun! I seemed to have just about eradicated "insane" from my exclamations. I remembered my guide in the coffee shop, when I didn't even know his name, saying "Eat the rind of the pork." That was only a couple of months ago.

I took a deep breath – am I really surviving this?

"You really are a duck-egg."

ཉ ཉ ཉ ཉ ཉ ཉ

It was Monday and back to work, and my otherworldly feeling was compounded by my lack of sleep. I'd only had three hours sleep last night and three the night before.

"You're going whole-hog."

I know, but I'd better start getting more sleep or I'm not going to last much longer. I can't burn-out now that I've gotten this far.

Not surprisingly, the feathers I always found and cherished were now suddenly white. I knew this was because of my new friend White Feather. He was really making his presence known, and *I* felt as light as a feather, buoyant and free. When I got home, Jane gave me a feather she'd found – it was white. Oh my.

I threw two slices of bread out for the birds, and they both landed inside a bowl of seed that was there as though they were placed there precisely, the way you would balance bread on the side of your soup bowl. Give me a break!

Later, I clicked on the TV, having no idea what was on, and was just in time to see a programme about a "Modern-Day Shaman." My jaw dropped. He seemed to be a cool guy, and was using drums and jazz piano in his work. I had to tell myself to close my mouth.

Vera called me on the phone with a few questions about Kundalini, and told me she was doing research on the Internet, and had asked an East Indian friend of hers at work a few discreet questions. It was all I could do not to dance a jig.

Now I felt I could extend a little more, and the next day at work I sent a short note to my Cousin Judith – Vera's daughter – telling her a few things that were going on. She mentioned that she and her daughter Jenn had been hearing music lately. Music from nowhere – celestial music – and they'd searched high and low for a source, but had been unable to find one. "Do you think it might be Auntie Edna?" Yes Judith, I do. I think Edna the musician has been busy lately. This was bliss, through and through.

By now I felt I had a fairly reliable foundation, or at the very least I wasn't dead, and I couldn't get "the meek shall inherit the earth" out of my mind. I was starting to understand what that meant. It meant the people who were quiet and listened to the wind and the murmurings of the earth. It meant the people who would move an ant out of the way of the cart wheel. It meant people who were connected to the stars and revered all life everywhere. That's what it meant. I was learning.

A couple of days later I woke up to:

*"We've got friends gathering – waiting in the wings,
people who can dance – people who can sing."*

That's nice mum, I like that, and good morning to you too.

It was a beautiful day and I rode to work feeling as though I was part of the sun.

When the door chime would go off at work now, I still said – it's the ghost – to anyone who was there, but inside I said – hi mum. My life by now was a fantastic adventure story and the only drawback was I couldn't share it with everyone.
After work I had some errands and of course found a white feather before I started on my way home. Once there, I listened to the radio as I went about my business and endeavoured to keep my journal straight. I realised the synchronicities were virtually impossible to keep track of now, and gave up trying to log all of them in my book. They were however, constant and amazing, and I trust you can take my word for that.
It was now time for the famous bath once again, and I turned off the radio only to hear it turn itself back on as I was halfway to the bathroom. I was getting it all. It was like all the best parts in my favourite books and movies, all rolled up into one glorious story that was now my life. Thank you. There was no saying thank you too many times.

Once in the bath, as though he'd been waiting, White Feather came to me in earnest. We sat by his fire by the bend in the river, close to where Lorraine, or Walking Wolf Woman, meets her companion – Grey Wolf. Maybe we would all meet soon, and dance together. Right now this was all I could take, as the tears of bliss and wonder slowly made a river down my body, and home into the bath.
We smoked together and performed a ritual that was just ours, and was basically whatever we felt like doing. We danced, we chanted, and we laughed to the sky and held on to each other tight. At least that's how it looks in words.

We were in a place of no words and no time and no space and no separation and no problem my friend of course there's room for you around the fire. Come and join us. It was a taste of the world as it can now be here, if only we want it passionately enough. We must create this world of peace and wonder for ourselves. Right here – right now.

White Feather now gave me his first teaching. I'd been a little bit concerned that I couldn't seem to really meditate anymore after the initial firming meditations, even with my tent in the sacred grove. I'd gone from this and sometimes also sitting down for a few minutes before work, to simply finding it what? Unnecessary? It was strange – it seemed like being in *this* world was the challenge these days.

His solution was simple and perfect – "Take your meditation with you."

Of course, like with the music, like with riding my bike. What do you think being half-way in the other world *is* anyway Neli? I felt fine now. That took care of that.

Four days later I found an article entitled "The Wise Do Not Waste Time On Meditation." The idea was to *be* meditation, as a quality of awareness at all times, and it backed-up what White Feather was getting at.

This was the way things were working for me now. I would find things out for myself, or with the help of my spirit friends, and *then* the universe would verify. It was a perfect system for me. There was no way I could read something, and then think I was trying to force the situation to be that way. I realised it first, and *then* the articles or books would come. My confidence grew by leaps and bounds at this realisation.

The next day after work, I met my friend Johanna who was visiting from New York. As we were talking about synchronicities, she glanced over at a parked motorcycle, and contained in the name of the bike – Bullet 350 – was the name of her apartment building – Bullet Space. Everything was backing me up! The universe was underscoring everything. All we had to do was notice.

On my last day at work for the week, I found a beautiful image of a faerie-ring, with the faeries dancing a circle in the forest under a full moon. I added it to my screensaver and looked down at Roxy who was snoozing by my work station.

"Roxy bucks me right up!"

I know mum, she's a beautiful dog isn't she? She always cheers me right up too. I would have quit this job a couple of times already if it wasn't for her. She's the best part of working here. The universe must really love me to have blessed me with her company. I'm going to miss her.

I couldn't think about that right now. Positive Print wasn't doing very well as it was, but I sensed I was outgrowing it somehow, and when that day came, I hoped Roxy would be nowhere in sight. Edna had been following my train of thought.

"I know love – I know...."

new moon
Grandma and Jane Roberts

It was Sunday, day seventy-two and as I got out of bed I heard:

"You are so bright."

I knew Edna was referring to how I looked on the other side. According to many sources, and now my own mother, when a person becomes fully realised, or enlightened, that person shines like a beacon through the dimensions. I still felt a little shy almost, to define myself in those terms, (who me?), but I couldn't deny what had happened to me, and what *was* happening. I couldn't pretend it wasn't a big deal. That wouldn't be right. It seemed to be the biggest deal going, according to all the spiritual literature I was recently devouring.

"This is bigger than you – this is bigger than me – and you really agreed."

Okay, that put things in perspective a little bit, and I certainly did agree didn't I? I had visions of those documents floating in the air.

"You've already turned this life around, and made it extremely successful."

I needed to hear that – thanks for saying that. You don't have to tell me there's a lot further to go though. I know that. I still have to fit into the outside world somewhat better than I have.

I had the urge to play the TV game, so I clicked it on at that moment and had a look – "White Knight" was what I saw. How perfect considering my mother had just called me that last month, and I thought to myself – Holy smoke! I'm still okay – I'm still on track.

The universe wasn't just leaning in my direction – as Seth always said she did for everyone – but she was still throwing herself at my feet, and I prayed I was worthy of the attention and support.

It seemed to come down to helping others, sharing all this with others, and I felt this was the best way to serve humanity, the earth and the universe at large. After all, I'd said for the good of all – right? If I was proud of anything, it was of making that stipulation and declaration. I knew my heart was in the right place, whether I rose to the occasion, or failed miserably. I would put myself on the line for this, I would step to the edge, and hopefully holding each other's hands we could all step off and fly.

Wow, big dreams you've got there Nelson, are you sure you can do it?

I don't know, but something tells me I have an integral part to play, and hello to my own thoughts here... I don't get to hear you as much as I used to. I can really tell the difference now – how interesting!

There was something about this "integral part" business that was a paradox. I was happy about that because I'd discovered something interesting a long time ago. When I was in the realm of the paradox, I knew I was really on to something because so many spiritual matters seem to involve paradoxes, and so here was another one – a big one.

I was learning more and more all the time about the Ascension, and I felt I had a vital role – the key role it seemed – in what was going on. The thing was, I also felt that *everyone's* part was just as crucial. Now normally, with regular three dimensional thinking, this just wouldn't work, it wouldn't be a viable model. However, with the knowledge I'd managed to gather around me so far in this life, it all somehow made perfect sense!

It was as though none of what was happening would work without me, I was the secret ingredient, I was the most important thing. (I cringe saying that.) But somehow, absolutely everyone else was the secret key as well! How can be? But it is! What fun!

I had to do what only *I* could do, and each other person had to do what only *they* could do.

It's hard to string this thought out when in actuality it just came as a complete knowing. We are all part of this evolution, which seemed to be what the Ascension was all about, and we are all following this human destiny, but not a single voice is any less important than anyone else's. Somehow, we are all – "The Central Character." Everyone's personal part was going to change the entire universe. We each somehow have the final say. It was as though we each have our own personal universe!

So this "creating your own reality" was not only precise *and* all encompassing, it was so encompassing as to affect the entire universe. It changes Everything Everywhere.

As I thought about us all being one, or my feeling on day five of *everything is me*, it started to make sense. As difficult as it is to put into words, we would all end up in a universe of our own making. My lord, how powerful *are* we?

With that, I thought of something else Seth had said that I'd never forgotten, "The soul or entity is itself the most highly motivated, most highly energised, and most potent consciousness-unit known in any universe." That was quite a statement, and I believed every single word of it.

This was the best I could do with these ideas for the moment.

All these things were going through my head, and then friend Jane came for her piano lesson. That seemed to be part of everything too, as we started working on "Imagine" by John Lennon, and I couldn't think of a more appropriate song for this moment in our true history. With a genius lyric inspired by Yoko Ono's poetry, it seemed the song was a perfect blend of the masculine and feminine, but overall a song of the Goddess. A call to arms for love and peace, only these were the arms of an embrace.

I watched myself guide her through the song, and noticed I was really beginning to *appreciate myself* in a way I never had before.

There were a lot of things to think about.

The next day at work, I looked up on the wall and saw "I only respond to kindness and respect," and I felt like I'd become more in the last couple of months than I could have ever imagined possible.

Christ is still on our side you know

This came from everywhere again, or from my higher self, or Sri Bhundari, and I thought – oh boy here we go. I can feel the Christ energy somehow, and Jesus as the singular prophet of that energy. Am I going to be dealing with deities now? I'd better see what that lady wants at the counter.

I carried on with my day, and I could sense Sherrie and Steaven with me. It only made sense they would hang around with someone who could hear them and who loved them. Not that they didn't spend a lot of time with many other people whom they loved and who loved them, but from their point of view, for there to be someone who could hear them and see them must be a novelty at the very least. Not to mention they were now fully functional, multi-dimensional beings, and could be in many different places at the same "time." Just like us, only here we're simply not aware of it most of the time. Time and space overlap, all the dimensions are right here. It's as though we're stuck on a single station, but we're learning to change the channel, to focus on other frequencies, and we *will* learn, and we shall *see.*

The dream world is another dimension we tune into spontaneously every night, and is every bit as "real" as this place, and is in fact closer to our natural state. Dreams are the great connector. Whatever we may have agreed to, whatever we may have forgotten, without the replenishment of the dream world, we would not have been able to survive this dense reality.

I thought about all of this as I watched my hands do the work, and then Steaven decided to send images to me about his particular life on the other side.

He is taking "courses" on painting and photography, two of his great interests when he was here, in this world, so that made perfect sense. Only there was a twist where he is now.

In his painting class, as an exercise in seeing what other people see, each student literally views his own work through the eyes of the other students in the class. They take turns merging with each other. In this world we know everyone sees something different when they look at a painting, and in that world, you literally get to see what that difference is. How perfect! What a great idea! I was astounded.

With the photography, he was involved in photographs that "aged," or had a time element to them. For instance, he showed me a photograph of an apple tree and it was a beautiful photograph of the tree on its own in a gorgeous landscape. He showed me two versions of what he was doing with this photograph.

In the first, the photograph was static and simply looked the way it did, however the next time you looked at it, there would be an apple halfway from the branches to the ground, as though caught in mid-fall. The third time you looked, the apple would be on the ground, and maybe the sun would be in a different position. I love it!

In the second version of the same photograph, it wouldn't be static at all. The branches would be swaying in the wind, and the sun would be slowly rising and then setting, either in a real-time twenty-four hour cycle, or at a different speed, depending on your preference. You would look again, and it would be night time and windy, with the outline of the dancing tree gracefully etched by the blue light of the full moon. It was breathtaking.

I thanked him for this priceless view of his new life, and once again it made me wonder what I was doing here, with the machines churning away, and all the stress and strain of a current physical life. I only had to think about the beauty once again, the earth and all of her creatures and how close we were to something big. I couldn't leave now. I couldn't bailout. I knew I'd chosen this moment to be here, on the cusp of something never before seen on this planet, something so wondrous there were visitors from everywhere in the universe just waiting to see what would happen. This was the place to be, this was the show of shows, and I was here in a body that still wasn't too old and with my own part to play. I added the Goddess Durga to my screensaver, and my Ascension folder grew.

ॐ ॐ ॐ ॐ ॐ ॐ

It was August 15 and twenty-three years ago today my mother died. I knew this day had been coming and I wondered what she would say. I wondered what might happen. She'd been quiet at work as she was more concerned about me than anything else, and she knew I'd been holding off thinking about it too much as I went through my day.

Later at home, I stood on the deck and watched the birds and squirrels go about their sacred business. I thought about how much Edna had loved watching them herself, especially the birds, and how I'd been too young and busy with my teenage years and early adulthood to pay too much attention as she'd been saying – "Oh look at that one! I must fill the feeder." Then she would have been grabbing her bird book, and looking up whichever one she didn't recognise, before going out to top up the feeder and bird bath.

After she died, and I'd started to appreciate that sparrows were just as phenomenal as eagles or anything else, I'd often say things to the air like – "I love the little birds too now mum" – hoping she could hear me. Then I'd be crushing up the peanuts so the sparrows could pick them up as well as the larger birds. I regretted I couldn't have shared more in her passion for them at the time. I was thinking all this now, and as I sensed her with me, I said out loud – It's not too late!

We were enjoying the little feather-heads together now – right now! She was with me, she was standing right next to me on the deck. Good god, she really is right here! There was no doubt whatsoever – I could see her in my mind, and in my heart. It wasn't like an apparition in physical reality, it was better than that. Eyes open or closed it didn't matter, she was right here, right now, and I could *see* her perfectly. You don't need eyes to see.

I closed my eyes on the tears, and I felt the wind on my face drying them for me. My mother was the wind. She was the sun sliding over me. She was the birds singing. She was the spirit of everything as well as herself, and she embraced me and held me with everything at her disposal – with the living nature.

Twenty-three years ago today my mother did not die. Nobody dies.

༄ ༄ ༄ ༄ ༄ ༄

All day at work today was the number eight again. Eight seemed to be everywhere, and I was back to thinking about octaves and frequencies.

There really is something going on here – I thought, as the numbers swirled around me and through me. I was so glad to know what I knew about music, as it seemed to have everything to do with what was going on. The universe was a symphony of sorts, with vibrating divine harmonies, and I thought about celestial music, and all the many references to it in so much literature. There didn't seem to be any separating of numbers and music.

I looked a few things up, and there were so many references, from Pythagoras, to Robert Fludd's "Divine Monochord" to superstring theory. Once again, I found these ideas corresponded to my initial *feelings* about the universe, and I didn't look into them deeply. The term "celestial music" was all I'd ever really heard – from the religious or spiritual end of things – and I'd always thought there must be such a thing.

Modern keyboard synthesizers, with their ability to create unique sounds, also seemed to make a lot of the new age or meditation music possible, in a way that a lot of standard acoustic instruments didn't. There are many exceptions here though, such as drums and ethnic music, and instruments such as the Sitar and Tanpura. It seems like the droning sound which these instruments and the modern synthesizer are capable of, may come close to the sounds in the heavenly realm.

Was there any end of things to think about?

I decided to grab my camera and go outside for break, it was a beautiful mid-August summer day and I needed to breathe it in. Outside I noticed the old electrical outlet attached to the wall about chest high, and last year wasps had been attempting to build a nest inside it, much to the distress of couriers and delivery people as it was right by the shipping doors.

During the winter months I'd examined and touched the tough honeycomb they'd left behind, and was amazed at the engineering. Now I noticed the wasps were back in full force, working diligently to create a nest in a place that was basically not viable. They didn't seem to care, and here I was with a camera that had a macro capability. I'd been looking forward to using it as you could get some amazing close-ups, and zoom things up much bigger than life-size. Here was my chance!

May I take some pictures of you? – I asked the wasps, and implemented the settings on my camera. It took about a dozen shots, most of which involved the lens being about an inch away from them, and they didn't seem to mind at all. I could hardly wait to get back inside and look at the photographs once everyone else had gone home for the day.

Alone now, I connected the camera to the computer and one shot in particular was so stunning I immediately printed it in full color on heavy card-stock, and added it to my collage on the wall in front of my desk.

In the image the wasp seems to be looking right at you, and is about ten times life-size. I couldn't stop looking at it, and this photograph would remain there regardless of whatever else came and went. The beauty of this creature was breathtaking, and I stared hard, wondering once again how anyone in their right mind could possibly think that any of this, this world, this earth, this life, could be accidental. I looked at the other animals in my collection as well, and the sense of supremely inspired divine artistic design was beyond a shadow of any kind of doubt. You just had to look – just stop, and look, and feel. It was obvious.

I added this photograph to my screensaver, briefly wondered what people might be thinking when they saw all this adding up, and then locked up for the night.

The next day was Friday, and after work I sat down and unloaded the day's printed material from my knapsack. I was so lucky to work in a place where I could do this, and I thanked my boss in absentia for his assistance in helping me to understand my new life. If only he knew. In another job and another place where maybe I wasn't basically running the day by day show, everything would have been so different. This was perfect and I didn't take it for granted, but at the same time I thought – of course it's perfect, of course.

I had the evening to myself, and my grandma obviously knew that, because now it was her turn to say hello. It had been sixteen days since my granddad's visit.

She appeared with Lady, her and my granddad's black and white Border Collie, the dog I'd known and grown up with first, before getting my own dog Rex. I was standing in the bedroom, and then there she was. I closed my eyes to eliminate the distraction, and we were together, locked in an embrace that was long overdue. How many ways can I describe this obliterating love? It was a divine delirium, and as we spun around we started to dance.

There was music playing, "Place To Be" by Nick Drake, who I'd been listening to lately, and I guess she must have liked it, because I hadn't put it on. We twirled and flounced, and I couldn't remember ever having danced with my grandma before. Maybe we'd been saving it for this moment? It was sublime.

Then she took my hand, and we were back in her house in England, and she was showing me all the rooms and the garden, all the places I remembered so well but hadn't seen for so long. I didn't know if she was showing me her current home which looked the same, or whether she was reminding me that nothing is ever lost. Love is never lost, that's for sure – I was a wreck and I just could not stop crying and who cared? Not me. I was with my grandma again after over thirty years and time had a sense of the eternal. I barely knew where I was.

Very gently she eventually said, "That'll do," which tended to just make things worse, as that was what she would always say when Sandra and I were being naughty. She led me back to myself somehow, and looked at me one more time – "That's enough for now...."

As the words and her face faded away, I sat down on the bed and tried to compose myself. I laughed in a jagged sort of way and thought – should I compose myself in C major, or maybe in B flat? My grandma was an accomplished pianist herself, and I was sure she'd placed that little joke in my mind.

It was time for a cup of tea, that's what I need right now, a nice cup of tea. I noticed my knees were shaky on the way down the stairs and it didn't surprise me, nothing surprised me anymore, but I really must look after my body – this is intense.

I got my tea, went back upstairs and a phrase came to me – existence is interpretation. This seemed to be an original thought of my own, and I quickly jotted it down in my journal. I had a lot of things to write in there today, and I hoped I could remember them all. Things were coming in waves, and this last moon phase had been extreme to say the least, but the day wasn't over yet.

Jane Roberts was here in her skirt and turtleneck sweater, and now I started to feel a little concerned. It was Jane herself who had thought it was just oh so convenient that psychics always seemed to meet with famous personalities. Along with – oh yes I've contacted one of my other lives, and I'm royalty in Egypt. I found myself very tentatively saying – Jane? Is that really you? I thought I might have really lost it at this point. I'd wanted to meet her so much, and was I just constructing fantasies now?

Jane Roberts? But wait a minute, we *did* write to each other, and she *did* read my lyrics when her reel to reel wasn't working and she couldn't listen to the songs, and...

She was laughing her head off. She was rolling around on a couch and I could feel a rambunctious sense of humour overtaking me. She'd been listening to it all, and simply couldn't contain herself anymore, and it was infectious. I laughed out loud too, and marvelled at the universe and how it's never too late for all of our dreams to come true.

She sent me reassurances of a kind that made it completely plausible she would be here. She presented herself as a skinny mop-top with a wicked sense of humour, and she obviously knew I'd corresponded with her husband Robert Butts too, after she had left us. Bless her heart, she made it so understandable how she would be here at this moment that I simply let go, and basked in her personality. She knew exactly how I felt about her. She knows I love her.

It was a full twenty-five minutes of support and encouragement, and I thought – all these people are right here! And they know the moment you think about them. Like Aunt Ciss had said, they may not always answer, but they know the second they pop up into your mind.

I could tell our time was up for now, and as Jane receded there were two thoughts from her. One was her saying she would come again, (can this be happening?), and the other was something I was supposed to acknowledge or figure out. It was a little mystery or something to clear up.

By now I was getting used to this pattern from my new friends – never just coming right out and giving me all the answers. They would prod and stimulate and coax and steer, but let you find your own way and do it yourself. This was the only way to truly learn. You can only learn to play the piano, by playing the piano.

It was midnight, I was exhausted, and I wondered what would come next.

"If you knew what came next, you'd just be there – knowing."

Oh hi mum, yes I know what you mean – learning is everything – and in this reality it's really all about remembering isn't it? Remembering who we really are.

"Yes, and I'm not a-kidding of you!"

You used to say that all the time mum! Just the way you said it now. We did it didn't we? We pulled it off, and you're not going anywhere are you?

"We are unassailable."

All right then, I like the sound of that.

I got ready for bed, and thought of snow. As much as summer would forever be a special time to me now, much more than it used to be, I could hardly wait for the snow.

I climbed into bed and assumed the position, with visions of trees blanketed in white and the faerie-dust coming down. I saw myself twirling in the magic.

ᘛ ᘛ ᘛ ᘛ ᘛ ᘛ

The next day was Saturday, and Jane and I went to Blackthorn Avenue where I first lived in Canada. I had an overwhelming urge to go there. The house had been torn down, but there was a new one in its place with much the same configuration. There was still an upper deck above the garage where Aunt Ciss used to live, same front porch steps where I fell and my lungs collapsed, and the trees were older. We walked to my first school, General Mercer, where I'd gone for grades five and six, and the walk seemed much shorter than it used to. Everything seemed narrower and smaller, but inside of me it created an expanse. I needed to be here, I needed to create this circle in time – it had been forty years – and we took some photographs as I breathed it all in. Life was the adventure I'd always hoped it would be. I would have to come here again, maybe with my sister Sandra.

After returning home I needed to do a few errands, so I got my bike and set off for Thorncliffe plaza with the wind and a smile on my face. Was there any way I could impart this knowing to everyone so they would just know? I already knew the answer to that, but it was a nice dream anyway. Just for everyone to know they are eternal beings, beyond any doubt, would change this world drastically. How do you do that? Many very sane, intelligent, and respectable people would think I was completely delusional at this point if I told them what was happening to me, and what I thought.

I imagined myself being dragged away screaming – but you really are God! You are! We all are!

I thought of – "Forgive them, for they know not what they do" – and I felt that particular unease from even beginning to put myself in any kind of category with Jesus. But that was what this was all about now wasn't it? It was time for everyone to awaken to their own sainthood or godhood and become citizens of the spiritual universe. Jesus was a way-shower wasn't he? All the prophets were. Didn't he say you can do all of this yourself, and more? "...the works that I do shall he do also; and greater works than these shall he do...."

In my mind this means Jesus knew we are all one, he was just a lot further along on the road. He was way ahead, but knew everyone would get there eventually. It was inevitable. All roads lead to this place – this simple truth. You have to feel it for yourself though, otherwise you still won't see a miracle happening right in front of your face. On top of that, we've been conditioned to believe we exist only by chance. What a shame – all this to control the slumberers. I would never have believed things were so twisted out of shape. I do now.

This was going to step on a lot of people's toes. The word blasphemy was created to keep us from the truth, but the truth has a way of always seeping to the surface, and it was bubbling up now on twenty-first century earth.

I arrived at the shopping plaza and decided to park my bike in a place I don't normally leave it. I dismounted and walked the last few feet to see a praying mantis on the brick wall right where I'd decided to lock-up the bike. I put the lock around the wheel in a cursory sort of way – figuring if someone really wanted to steal this bike, they needed it more than me – and I looked at this amazing creature from about two feet away.

He was unmoving and awesome, about four-feet up on the wall and had managed to turn himself the dun colour of the bricks he was meditating on. I looked around and although it was a busy Saturday, no one seemed to be aware of him at all, even though he was about four or five inches long. This guy was here just for me!

I actually didn't know if he was male or female, but considering the size, and females always being larger, he was probably a she, but I just thought of him as, well... him. For fun I said – guard my bike for me will you? And I went inside to do my errands. All in all I was forty minutes total, but I went back to my bike twice to arrange things in my knapsack, and to see if "he" was still there. Each of the two times, he was still in exactly the same frozen position. He could have been a statue.

My third and final time returning, I got everything set in my knapsack and on my back, and I unlocked the bike.

Well little one, thank you for looking after my bike, you're really beautiful, that's for sure, thank you for being here.

He hadn't moved in all this time, but the very last time I looked at him, just before I pulled away, one front leg slowly raised up and moved sideways in what I can only describe as a wave goodbye. Stunned, but not anymore, I also waved goodbye to him as I wiped my eyes so I could see where I was going, and set off for home.

ふ ふ ふ ふ ふ ふ

It was Sunday and I thought I'd turn on the TV to see what was in store with the weather forecast. I'm always hoping for a nice thunderstorm.

The first sight as the TV popped on was a huge Celtic Cross. Oddly enough it wasn't a spiritual programme, but a room makeover on a decorating show. They were applying this wall-sized cross as wallpaper to one of the walls in the room. I watched as the room transformed. I thought it was a brilliant idea and something I would love to do myself... especially with that cross.

There just didn't seem to be anything happening around me that wasn't a message of some sort. I was in a universe of my own making – a "you-niverse" – I thought, and chuckled again at all the secrets hidden within words.

I went downstairs to make some tea, thinking – *We* are the biggest secrets of all though.

First Quarter

We Rise Now

It was day eighty, another Monday, and I couldn't believe so much time had gone by already, although I was prepared for it, what with the way time had been quickening so much in general over the years. Here I was at work again on a Monday morning and I noticed I had two e-mails waiting for me.

One was from Gordon – "It *was* an awakening," and I thought, good job for that, or I've been on the wrong track for almost three months now! Of course Gordon couldn't possibly have known everything that had been happening to me so far, but I'd given him some idea – enough for him to come to that conclusion and agree with me. He was particularly taken with the channelled music, and encouraged me to keep up the good work. Thank you Gordon.

The second was from a client containing an order, and I thought, oh yes, that's what this computer is supposed to be for isn't it? All right, well I'd better get that done then. As I was downloading the attachment with the specifications for the job, I happened to notice the spam folder and thought I'd better check it as sometimes messages went there by mistake, and that could be a problem if from a customer.

I opened up the folder, and there was one message in there – one blank message.
However, there *was* a sender, and there *was* a subject for that blank missive.

The sender was simply – "Edna."
The subject was simply – "I miss you."

At this point I'd seen a lot of stuff, but with this I just had to sit down... or collapse down I should say. The sender's address was listed as @positiveprint, with nonsense letters in front of it. It made no logic at all, and certainly wasn't from anyone here. It was from the ether. That must be what e-mail stands for! – I laughed.

I had to send a quick note back to Gordon about this one. This was just too good! It seemed to be a natural extension of the TV captions, but this was the internet, and a different type of energy for my mother to be working with. This had come to my own personal e-mail at work – my own address! We all had our own individual addresses here. It was hard not to do cartwheels in the office.

At break time I went outside and took more photographs of my wasps, then before leaving for the day I received a note from Walking Wolf Woman reminding me the full moon coming up was a red moon, due to the total lunar eclipse, and she told me to "look out." This sounded very exciting.

I took more wasp photographs the next day, and by Wednesday I decided it was time to try the moviemaking feature on my camera, and with that I managed to capture these beautiful creatures in action as they were busy at their work. They very gracefully put up with my presence. The macro feature worked on the movie setting also, so it was amazing to see, and I couldn't stop watching the little movies I'd made.

The next day I saw my groundhog again after asking and looking for him for the last couple of weeks. Hi Mr. Groundhog! He scurried away and ran down his hole before I had a chance to grab my camera and take a picture of him, but that didn't matter, I was so happy to see him.

On Friday my thoughts revolved around the number eight and octaves still, and my tabla drums. There was something about those drums and the way they felt so familiar. It was a wonderful feeling.

Now Sri Bhundari chimed in:

your drums are magic encapsulated

Yes they are. I know exactly what you mean.

Once everyone had left for the day, I decided to sit down and make a list of the people who had spoken to me so far. It was getting to the point where it would soon be easy to lose track.

There was Edna, Sri Bhundari, Sherrie, Steaven, Mum B, Aunt Ciss, Granddad, Grandma, Jane Roberts, and another relative Alice, who had died recently. She had recently just popped in quickly to let me know she was there. So all together that was ten. I didn't think that was bad considering it had only been eighty-four days now, but I really had nothing to go on. There didn't seem to be any way to gauge things really, but in my own heart I felt this was quite an accomplishment. Good for me!

I rode home with another week under my belt, and a sense of actually thinking I would survive all of this now. Although not every part of my life was smooth sailing, and I still had my problems like everyone else, tomorrow would be twelve weeks and I was still here.

On Saturday I thought about actually becoming a working psychic, and I thought about all those people with their "test questions," just trying to catch you as a fraud, or maybe secretly hoping you weren't. What if someone was waiting for me to say something no one else could possibly know, and I couldn't do it? What if they asked me outright? How could you explain to people that it wasn't just like talking on the telephone and that you're dealing with multiple dimensions and timelines, and infinite realities. They wouldn't care about the working intricacies of things, they would just want the correct answer.

you want test questions more than anyone else actually

Sri Bhundari had a point there. How much was it really about me, and wanting to prove it all to myself? I came to the conclusion that if I didn't have confidence in myself, no one else ever would. It came back down to faith again, but I guess a track record of sorts wouldn't hurt, once I got going.

abilities and confidence rise hand in hand

This guy was good! I could think about that sentence for a long time. Do the abilities create the confidence, or does the confidence open the door to the abilities?

Oh that's deep Nelson, but then everything's deep lately isn't it?

I'd left the wading pool behind, and now I was in the deep end for sure. I was growing up all over again – spiritually this time – and there were bound to be growing pains. No matter what would happen though, I felt I was where I was supposed to be in a way that had nothing to do with space and time. I felt the Goddess had shown me the way to my own heart.

I looked at the statue of Parvati on the bedroom wall, with the swan gliding by behind her, and my heart clutched – she was the one. I laughed at how I'd called her Pavarti a few times at the beginning, not being used to her name and mixing it up with Havarti cheese! I got the distinct impression I could hear her laughing at that, and I said – sorry about that Parvati – and laughed myself.

I sensed a joyful understanding from her and I wondered if it was just my imagination, or if maybe talking to God, or All That Is, would come next. The funny thing about all of this inner communication was that it seemed to happen in the same realm as the imagination, so it was easy to think you were "making it all up." Fortunately I'd learned enough by now to ignore this feeling if it did crop up, and to believe in myself and trust what was going on – or try to. It was a fine discrimination you had to learn. I also understood that on another level we are making *everything* up, and nothing was really objective at all.

I needed to do something ordinary, so I decided to shave, but that didn't really take me too far away from all the esoteric business, because now I was checking the condition of my thyroid gland. It seemed to be almost back to normal after a couple of weeks of being quite swollen.

Kundalini did a lot of work through the endocrine system so I hadn't been overly concerned, and had actually been happy to see the swelling as it was a classic symptom of the body changes. I'd found and read just the right material to reassure me about developments such as these. I'd had a slight problem with a section of my gums too, and that was now almost over as well. I envisioned nothing but good cleansing situations going on, and I felt negative energies were being purged.

This was altogether too incredible.

Edna was now just adding things to conversations I was having, either with other people or with myself, and it was anything but annoying – it was amazing. It seemed even funnier when the one thing my mum feared the most, after I'd left home, was of being – an interfering mother. She had always been adamant about not playing that role. We both had a good laugh at this, as now here she was in another world and as close as a thought. I assured her this was not interference, and that I'd waited lifetimes for something like this. I could tell she really needed to hear that, and we both knew I still had privacy every time I really felt like being alone. This was an unspoken agreement.

I'd be concerned about going somewhere with a lot of people, for instance, and if she didn't pull out the standard – more the merrier – I told you about, I'd hear:

"It'll be a bit of fun – It'll do you good – Let your hair down."

Or I'd be trying to describe a situation where I felt I was being manipulated:

"You're being pushed and pulled from pillar to post."

These were phrases right out of my past in England, and every time she placed one in my mind I felt stronger and more certain about things. This was really happening and there was no turning back now.

During the day on Sunday I took some photographs in the garden, and was fortunate enough to take some beautiful shots of a bumblebee going about her business. This macro feature was amazing, and once again I felt the bee was fully aware of what I was doing and happy to let me get as close as I needed. The insect world knew all about me, of this I was sure.

That night the Moon was almost full, but I couldn't wait so I took some photos anyway, and in one of them the Moon was an eye and the clouds were eyebrows, a nose and a mouth. The nose was quite prominent and I could feel my mum laughing as she made a comment about the Moon's "hooter."

I went inside and suddenly felt a little off-kilter and overwhelmed by everything. There was almost too much happening, and this time I heard a voice telling me I was on track and everything was going splendidly, and I knew it was Sri Bhundari and my mother together. The voices were getting a bit easier to sort out now. It had come through as one voice, but I knew it was the two of them.

Telepathy is voices in your head, and we're not taught how to organise them and separate them from our own thoughts. It all comes back to my mum's lesson number one – the difference between thinking and listening – then comes the categorising and learning to feel who it is. We're used to seeing a face when we're talking to someone most of the time too, and even here in physical reality when we can't see someone, such as when we answer the phone, we can be unsure of who we're talking to for a moment.

I turned on the TV to see Mother Teresa's face and a programme about a new book coming out in just over a week. The book "Come Be My Light" is primarily letters written by Mother Teresa over a period of sixty-six years, and they reveal someone who felt she had lost her faith for the last half or so of her life.

I couldn't believe my eyes.

Doubt again – first the Buddhists and their writings on the matter, and now Mother Teresa. As much as it upset me to hear about this, it really put a lot of things in perspective and actually made my own occasional uncertainty seem perfectly understandable, or so small as to not even be in the same realm. This lady had been operating on another level entirely.

We play the game, but Mother Teresa was hands-on, neck deep in dirt and blood and never went home. She humbles us all.

It was distressing to think of her as unsure and shaky with her belief in God – but understandable. It must've been the suffering – I thought. She was in the thick of it. No matter how much you hear about the love and the light, you take a look around sometimes and you think – something must have gone wrong. Something must have really gone wrong. Never mind about karma and balance, just look at this – if you can.

Oh my goodness. Oh me oh my. I can understand her feelings. We must be the universal example of how far the wrong way a race of beings can go.

And so that is why...

Yes, that is why... we are going to be the shining universal example of how you can go so deep into the abyss but somehow wash off the dirt and let the blinding light come shining through from inside. Light that doesn't blind though. Light that does the opposite, and lets you finally see.

I have to believe this. I have to believe we can change everything. I have to believe the past will be changed by the Now. At what cost though?

Dear God please show me it was all worth it.

Please Parvati, let me know we would never have become the greatness we will become, without all this terror and pain. I have to believe you know what you're doing.

I know we chose to come here, I know it's not compulsory. What were we thinking? It has to all eventually be worth it, and I have to believe it is. And I do.

We rise now.

I lifted my head and changed the channel and the universe rescued me once again.

There was Lawrence Welk. Lawrence Welk! I was laughing now. It was one of the shows I always watched with Aunt Ciss when we first came to Canada and we didn't yet have a TV. She always let me watch TV with her as long as I didn't mind watching her preferred programmes: Andy Williams, Ed Sullivan, and this one, to name a few. She always watched the music programmes and that was fine by me.

"Proclivities."

Right mum, they were one of her proclivities – good word, thanks.

I decided to watch it and immediately sensed Aunt Ciss there with me. I could see her front room down on Blackthorn Avenue, and we were both sitting in the same positions as we used to. It was an image we were both seeing, and her presence filled my heart as we sat back and watched the bubbles rise up behind the orchestra. This was perfect. We did this together every Sunday for the next three months until the cable was replaced with satellite and I couldn't get the station anymore. By then I'd discovered it on You Tube, and I would find myself going there whenever I felt like we needed a hit, and she would always show up. It was heaven.

Moon Four

Bodhisattva

It's Tuesday, day eighty-eight and today is the day of the red moon.
Some say this eclipse is an omen that bodes well for the future, and some say just the opposite and that it's a sign of dire times ahead. In my own way I have to say things look good as I saw my groundhog on the way to work yesterday, and today I saw him once again on the way there as well as on the way home. For me, his appearance three times like that was a good sign indeed. Maybe he doesn't want to miss that Moon!

I didn't want to miss it either and I went out that night with my trusty camera. Although I wasn't in the right place on the planet to see the effect properly – and I couldn't stay up all night to keep looking just in case – it was spectacular nevertheless.

At one point I had a strange idea about taking photographs with a slow shutter speed, and randomly waving the camera around at the Moon. I found out that in this way I could effectively "write" with the full moon and get some interesting wavy lines and squiggles.

I decided to call it "Moon Writing."

My camera is basically automatic with various presets, but I tried some manual settings too before finally deciding on one particular preset that worked the best for my purposes. The display on the camera said – twilight, shoot low light scene without flash – and there was a tiny graphic to represent this setting. The graphic was a crescent moon! How perfect is that? I went through every one of the eight presets, and it turned out to be the one with the Moon.

I thought to myself – well, I guess it won't be easy to forget that one.

The universe was taking every opportunity to show me the magic no matter what I was doing. I felt that feeling again rushing through me, the feeling of capturing the bigger picture. That's funny! The feeling of peering through the veil and finding out a secret. Elation was becoming a companion I'd forgotten about since childhood.

I took eleven photographs this way and ten of them seemed no more than scribbles or doodles, but one of them stood out. It looked like a child to me. There was just something about it that had an effect on me, so I called it "Child" and filed it away after sending it to a couple of friends, just for fun. They liked it.

I decided to keep this moon writing business in mind for the next full moon, and I had a thought about it possibly being a type of divination. Who knew what you might find and see? I'd never heard of this before, and it struck me again that whatever was going on with me, certainly was incredibly creative. People might think the whole idea laughable, but to me it was a discovery. We use the tools we have in any given era, and right now we have these cameras, and we don't even have to waste film.

I had to chuckle to myself though, at the thought of someone seeing me jiggling the camera around while pointing at the heavens – the whole thing with photography was to keep the camera still, usually. That would look pretty funny.

ಪಿ ಪಿ ಪಿ ಪಿ ಪಿ ಪಿ

Vera had left me a biscuit tin full of family photographs to go through, and I slowly tried to get them organised with the idea of scanning them. I was obsessed with blood now, and I needed to get to know these people once again, especially if they were going to come a-calling. The bloodline was something I couldn't stop thinking about now, and DNA. It was fascinating to go through these old photos, and of course when it came to the ones of my mother, I couldn't stop looking at them. There was also one of the family visiting Arundel Castle in West Sussex in 1955, and how I wished I could have been there with them, but I would've only been one year old.

I was also starting to get a real feel about the Ascension, and my folder continued to grow. There was so much information about it, and I found that some of it rang true while other material just didn't jive with me – or my mum.

"That's a load of nonsense."

Yes, I'd have to agree with you there mum.

It was picking and choosing and embracing and dismissing.

One thing I *had* found out was that 2012 wasn't the end of the world as such, but it sure was the end of an era. A lot of cycles were coming into play now, and I could feel it in my bones. I also knew we definitely couldn't go any further in this way as a species.

We are profoundly insane, and the earth herself isn't going to wait around anymore for us to become sound of mind. Soon there'd be no clean water or fresh air but we *would* have the latest electronic toys and the latest wars. We could make a call on our cell phones with our last breath – if there was anyone to pick-up.

This is it folks.

It amazed me how the phrase "save the planet" had been rendered impotent, as if it didn't *really* mean exactly what it said. Now it was used to sell bathroom tissue. The extent of our fall from grace was stunning, but we were so busy with the "important" things, we really just didn't have the time for all this doomsday stuff. We'd be okay.

No we wouldn't, unless consciousness changed – now.

And lo and behold, it appeared to be happening. There was evidence of a shift going on. The internet had changed everything, and had somehow bypassed the controlled media. People were getting unofficial information and were acquiring a taste for it. The truth was becoming addictive. People were becoming able to discriminate by using their hearts to decide what information felt right, and what didn't.

My feelings for the human race had continued to grow, and I cried and held myself when I saw people working tirelessly to untangle a whale from a fishing net, or something similar that showed what we were *really* like. Those people were the true human beings and it seemed to be happening more and more that the light was shining out. Underneath it all, we were good souls, we were worth saving, we bought each other ice cream and we knew how to kiss.

For ninety days now I'd cried every day and it didn't seem to be slowing down. There were so many things to cry about, but I was crying for joy at least half the time and I felt proud to be a creature who could *feel* so much.

I am proud to be a human being. I used to feel ashamed, but something is happening and I can see we have been misled. Now every person must lead themselves and let their true nature shine through. It's going to be miraculous.

༄ ༄ ༄ ༄ ༄ ༄

Sometimes Edna liked me to just talk out loud, instead of silently or her merging with me and gathering the information for herself.

"Tell me without me permeating you."

So we would just converse like any two people, but to an observer it would seem like I was talking to myself. We tried everything, and I could always switch in midstream and carry on mentally, or not say anything one way or the other and know she would be on top of things anyway. I gave her full access, right?

One night, the purple pen-light I use for recording dreams in the dark simply turned itself on in my pen holder. There's a cap covering the on and off button on this pen and it was still in place, so there was no way it could have been depressed. I knew it was my mother, and I knew this was the reason she'd chosen it, and of course it was the pen I sometimes used for dreams so it all made wonderful sense.

On that Sunday, Jane and I were at Colin's new apartment and I was putting up some venetian blinds for him:

"I like this kind of work, especially if I'm not doing it!"

Thanks a lot mum, you're a big help.

I still couldn't say anything to Colin about this remark, or about Mum B's visits, and I wished with all my heart that one day I could, and that he would believe me. Who knows, I thought – one day I might really write a book and then I could just give it to him. I hoped he wouldn't mind being in it, but I could hardly say anything first, without being in the same position I was in now.

It was all so much more complicated than I thought it would be initially, I had to be so careful with people. I was dealing with very personal stuff, and I had to remind myself that not everyone liked to think about the afterlife at all, even if they did believe in it. It was like winning the most supreme lottery in the universe and hardly being able to share it with anyone. Then if I did, would they even believe me? I had no ticket to show them. It was the oddest type of frustration, but I accepted it as well as I could – it was all part of the deal.

Back at home, I was eager to try another book after the success with "Seth Speaks," so I went to the bookcase and found myself taking out "The God of Jane," one of Jane Roberts' own works, as opposed to a book strictly written by Seth through her. Once again, I just opened the book and was presented with a section stating that the centre of the universe was at every point, and the individual person *is* the centre of the universe from that viewpoint. I thought of my day five, and – "the centre of the circle is everywhere." It was astounding.

I could have carried on reading all night, always a problem when I opened one of Jane's books, but I forced myself to close it after noticing her term "heroic" just before I did. Jane Roberts had a lot of things say about the heroic dimension and of our reality springing from it, as I mentioned before, and our "heroic nature" was a term she used to describe *being* – fully being.

I put my left hand on the cover of the book and took a moment to take my pen and trace my hand onto it.

All the great teachings ended up saying exactly the same things in different ways.

I loved the way Jane had done things though, because she'd taken you along for the ride, instead of merely presenting the final revelations. Without thinking about it, I somehow decided that if I ever did write a book concerning my own experiences, I would like to document the journey itself too. This I decided would be the most valuable way to present the story – from a human perspective, with all the inner turmoil that went along with it. Maybe someone could learn from my experience that they weren't going crazy, and certain situations might be expected along the way. At the very least, maybe I could pass on a phrase that seemed to pop into my mind frequently – It's a rocky road to Babylon.

I then opened Steaven's "The Teaching of Buddha" and immediately found a section on faith. It was perfect. I laughed and thought to myself – okay, I'll meet you down at the corner of faith and doubt. On a more sober note, I thought about how sad it was for us to be so unsure of our own supreme divinity. I read on:

"One who understands Buddha is a Buddha himself; one who has faith in Buddha is a Buddha himself."

ॐ ॐ ॐ ॐ ॐ ॐ

Hi Mr. Groundhog! I shouted as I zoomed past on my way to work the next day, and I hoped I didn't have too much work waiting for me as I wanted to look a few things up. It was perfect I still didn't have my own computer, because it forced me to be fully focused in the experiences themselves, and not to have my head buried deep in research. This was no accident – there are no accidents – but still, I was anxious to check a couple of things, now that I seemed to be "allowed" to. Research now came in phases, and then I would know I had to stop for a while. Breathe in – breathe out.

Alone finally, I went into personal mode, and I punched-in Buddha. It was Buddhism day today as I couldn't stop thinking about Steaven's book from last night.

Okay, let's see...

I read about Siddhartha Gautama and I remembered the movie that came out in 1972 – Siddhartha – based on the Hermann Hesse book. Treaca and I had gone to see this film, and I went back to that time and place and remembered the scenes by the river.

This was what interested me now, the period of discovery when the young boy had just begun to think that something was wrong with the world. Again, I had that odd hesitant feeling in my stomach for even daring to put myself in the same category, but I could relate very easily because right now, right here in the early twenty-first century, I knew something was very wrong with the world. I could almost hear Siddhartha saying to me – it's all right, feel what you feel, I'm no greater than you, we are one.

Almost? Was I actually hearing that? Oh my lord, am I truly hearing the Buddha? Dry your eyes Neli, you can't see the screen.

I was lead to Buddhahood and to a definition of what it strictly means to be a Buddha. It was simple – it was one who has become enlightened.

How many times had I walked on my way to high-school, chanting Om and wondering if I even dared to hope that one day I might reach such a state in this lifetime? Did I even really know what it meant? I read on...

In the Theravada tradition, the oldest Buddhist school, they emphasised attaining this state all on your own, without a particular teacher, during a time of darkness or ignorance in the world and passing the knowledge on to others.

Well times were dark all right, but I had my teachers. Not in the sense of one Guru, or signing-up or joining a club, but I had the animal kingdom, I had Jane Roberts in her apartment in Elmira, New York scribbling away and smoking her head off, and I had Treaca. She'd put my little boat in the river and given it an ever-so-gentle push to get it going. Then there were all the people I loved who loved me back, and said little sentences that changed everything. I saw now that everyone had taught me, I could name all their names but it didn't matter, it was all of them. Everyone who had nodded their head to me as we passed on the street too, everyone who said hello, and everyone who had said get lost.

As far as passing the knowledge on, I had an absolutely overwhelming desire for everyone to experience this knowing. It was an innate feeling or drive inside of me now. It was a basic need – like washing your hands. Teaching was breathing and could be just as invisible. All you had to do was be.

Classrooms were fine and I love classrooms, but I felt the real teaching was walking down the street and emanating love and light. This could be done anywhere and everywhere and I thought of the reactions I'd gotten those first few days of being at work after all this had begun. I also knew that practical physical action was also required in this world and I wouldn't get off quite that easy.

Now I was looking at Bodhisattva. I must have punched something in or clicked somewhere because now I was reading a description of this word. The main element here is the overwhelming desire to take everyone along with you. To unceasingly attempt to help others awaken to the greater reality all around us.

It was describing the new me.

Again I had the security of feeling things and coming to my own conclusions first, and *then* finding corroboration from information that just fell in my lap. The beauty of this method couldn't be surpassed, and I felt the arms of the Goddess pulling me tightly to her chest.

I was still here, a physical being on this planet, but I'd also gone home earlier than most because this was surely heaven.

Next I somehow came to Jivanmukti in Hinduism and it revealed a self-realised person who remained in the physical body: Realisation being the knowledge of our eternal nature, our oneness with All That Is, and the full awareness that the world is not real of its own accord, but a mirror of our thoughts. There is no outside – Jane Roberts said.

It was all beginning to make a whole lot of sense in a whole lot of ways. I clasped my hands together and pulled my elbows to my waist in gratitude of all the ancient seekers who worked all of this out and wrote it down for people like me. People like me? Yes, people like me and like you. Priests or middle-men are not needed to touch God.

Later on I was led to Nirvikalpa Samadhi as the perfect description of my day five, a state from which people sometimes never return. When one does return, and somehow manages to continue to function in the physical world, it is referred to as Sahaja Samadhi. I'd found terms and descriptions that made sense to me – a great deal of sense.

I was lucky I was the last one here at work as I got up and walked around in circles dripping tears and chanting thank you, and hoping a customer wouldn't walk in at that moment. Feelings were crashing inside of me like waves from the holy ocean – I couldn't feel any higher and still be on the planet. Maybe this was what heroin felt like?

I had that idea again about all the drugs and artificial highs being a cry for this. A cry for something we'd lost so long ago but knew we could find yet again somehow if we could just hold on and believe against the monstrous odds against us in this world designed to keep the sleeping forever asleep. Heroin. Looking for the hero-in me.

Hold on dear sisters and brothers hold on! I wept for all of us here as I'd done before, but now it was different, there was something in the air. If this could happen to me... well, wipe those tears away and give me your hand. We will do this together.

I gathered my things and put my new notes into my knapsack. I thought of my mother and her cousin Alice, and I heard Alice's quiet voice as I saw her smiling face – tell Tom I'm here and I'm okay and I love him... if you can. This was the number one message from the dead without fail, but I noticed she'd added – if you can. She was aware of the delicacy of this proposition, and I thought – good, this full access thing is working, she knows what's going on.

Riding home, that silver rose was in my mind, and thinking of the Tudor rose being a symbol for the balancing of the feminine and masculine to me, I saw easily that the silver rose was the next step to the integration of everything. I saw the necklace around my mother's neck at that party so long ago. We never stopped dancing.

Last Quarter

The Blue Jay

I found myself at the video store again and I found "The Messenger" and "Excalibur" on sale as old movies they wanted to dispose of. The messenger was the story of Joan of Arc, and was enlightening and brutal. I took from it the message of courage when it comes to believing in the "voices," and there were terrible scenes that gave me insight into the times of my man John. Although not in the film, I was reminded of what is reputed to be her final words – hold the cross high so I may see it through the flames.

The 1400s were not a very friendly time to be alive.

Excalibur put me back into the world of – the Merlin – which is a title given to a High Priest of the Druid faith. I read more about the Merlin, an ascended master, and how he was connected with the Essenes who Seth had talked about. We were in the fifth century and on the island of Avalon at the mystery school where the Merlin is said to have prepared Druid initiates for Ascension! Oh my, this was getting good. My head was swirling with Stonehenge and Avebury and Glastonbury Tor. When I thought of England, I thought of lying face down on the ground with my arms out holding the earth.

I hadn't been able to get the song "Turn Me Loose" out of my mind for the past three days, so of course at work it came on the radio. I wanna fly! He sang. There was a reason for everything and I could easily see how my mind was working and why things were coming to me the way they were.

As beautiful as the world is, once you know where to look, there was still a part of me that would always want to be back in that place of light and knowing. The word light, taking on the extra meaning of *lightness*. Everything was so heavy compared to what I'd felt and become on my precious day five.

I remembered my father whenever things would get tough, and he would say, "We're English!" I decided to acquire strength from that sentiment now, as well as anything else I could get my hands on, but with a small adjustment... We're Human! It was time to think galactic or universal, and although we as a race are no better than any other, we are no worse either. I felt we were finally coming in to our own as equals.

My father's situation was still a mystery to me on the one hand, and something I didn't want pursue right now, on the other. I thought of his one main thought on the afterlife, and his resounding statement, "If there's no beer, I'm not going!" I'd heard this altogether too many times, and the ramifications of such a focus were fairly clear from a spiritual point of view.

They say you don't take anything with you when you die, but I'd learned something different. You take your knowledge with you... and you take your addictions. This can sometimes have untoward implications on the other side.

I couldn't go there right now and I figured it might be quite a while before I could. He was quiet anyway, I couldn't hear him, and maybe that was just as well at the moment, but he was always at the back of my mind.

I love you Dad! I sent out into the universe. If you need me I'm here, and the slate is clean.

Still at work I went over to the computer and found another message in the spam folder. This one had a message that said – true about jewels. I took this as an affirmation about the power of crystals and the mineral kingdom in general. However it was the sender again that staggered me. Along with that same nonsensical Positive Print address as before, the sender this time was – "Edwina Nelson." Oh my.

I don't know how long I just sat and stared at the screen as my mind went off to my mother's current home, which seemed somewhat transparent to me, or could be if she wanted it to. One time she'd tried to let me experience it more as it really was, and I felt like the walls and floors were moving and I found it hard to get my bearings. I think she solidifies it somewhat for me. I saw her work station, and the large monitor that gives her a moment by moment view of my life when she isn't actually "here," or fully focused in my reality – fun but unnecessary props I'm sure were there mostly for my benefit. She had all the bases covered.

I could hardly believe the things I thought about on a general basis now. It was all too incredible for words. I saw my dog Rex padding about in her house and he turned to me and said – see you soon! Somehow he'd split the words up, so it was more like "I see you" followed by "soon."

I was dying with love and longing as I robotically added the ether-mail to my Bardo folder, and got ready to go home.

🕉 🕉 🕉 🕉 🕉 🕉

Vera came over on the weekend with more family photographs and we had another lovely visit. She's the closest person I have to my mother obviously, but that's not why I love her, it's the person she is apart from anything else. She's my friend as well as in my blood.

Vera's seventy-third birthday was coming up, and my mother was amused at this as Vera *used* to be the younger sister by thirteen years.

"Tell Vera she's the older sister now!"

It was pretty funny, and the three of us ended up having a good laugh.

Vera and I talked, and she listened again as I droned on and on about the latest things that had happened to me. She thought I was still far too thin, and even though I'd gained a little weight at the start (the five pounds my mum had mentioned), I'd started to slip a bit. So we talked about that, and I'd gone on to bring up more esoteric subjects like levitation for instance.

*"If you get any lighter – you **will** levitate!"*

There was no end to my mum's humour.

The next day was Sunday and a strange looking Blue Jay landed on the deck. It didn't take long to see he was being shunned and was dying. He just didn't look right, but he was still beautiful as he seemed to be drifting off into sleep. I took a couple of photographs, not knowing if I'd be able to look at them later, and I gently put him in a rabbit hutch to maybe look after him and fix him up.

Once safely inside, I was stroking his wings when with one mighty squawk he extended himself to full attention and flapped his wings, and died.

It was like flipping a switch – the transition was that fast – and as terrible as it was when he died, I couldn't help but think that at the last moment, he'd died so full of life! Does that make sense? There was so much to learn from this. I knew it was a huge lesson and I would think about it forever. One thing I did know, once again, this bird was a supreme teacher and I'd been blessed and honoured to be a part of his crossing. I knew this was part of the training I'd agreed to, and I would try to learn all the lessons here.

Of course I couldn't escape the recriminations on myself – maybe I should have left him where he was, maybe I killed him off by touching him, maybe maybe....

I had grown enough spiritually to know my intent had been pure, and that was all that mattered. The Great Spirit knew I was trying to help, everything knew, and as I wrapped him in a purple silk shroud, I prayed and made up a little song as I buried him in the back yard with many other sacred little bodies. I had to cry of course, and I felt good that I did.

Death is all around us – I thought – all around.

ॐ ॐ ॐ ॐ ॐ ॐ

A hundred days had gone by now, it was day one hundred and one, and I was slowly coming back down to the ground in a way. I didn't want to come back, but I knew there was no other way of living here and not returning somehow. The other alternative would have been to carry forward full steam ahead, and to have left this realm altogether with a big smile on my face. I'd decided not to do that, as you full well know if you've been following along here. I had to try and help people know what was going on, and 2012 was coming. So was the snow, it was September 10 now and we were coming into autumn. If that wasn't enough, with all the beauty of the trees getting ready for bed, well just hold on a bit longer, because the snow would be blowing soon. I could die in the snow. I was thinking of all these things as I got my bike and set off for Monday morning at work.

There was the sign, still up there – YOU HAVE THE POWER. What we needed was a media blitz like that to remind everyone on the planet that they do indeed have the power. If only, I dreamed, as I swooped under the bridge and shouted my hello to Mr. Groundhog and his family.

It was a regular kind of work day, but nothing in my life was really standard anymore, and even though I could feel the return of gravity on occasion, I knew I was truly reborn and I had a look in my eyes.

I grabbed two more castles for my screensaver, and gathered some information on Kundalini for my cousin Judith. I really didn't want to forget or ignore the people who were genuinely open to what was going on, so I sent it off and hoped it made sense to her. There's no real way of knowing what it feels like without experiencing it, but it was the best I could do at the moment.

I realised I could talk about skydiving all day to someone, but they would only get an idea that was far removed from the reality of actually jumping out of a plane. If I could just help someone to see what was possible though, maybe I could help them jump right off this plane of existence.

It was going to happen. It would have to happen to all of us eventually.

What I had going for me, was that everyone actually knows all of this inside themselves. It was a matter of helping people to be quiet and remember who they really are.

This was the mission now, and a huge part of it was knowing when to shut up. Learning/remembering came in stages and steps, and I had a tendency to be like an avalanche and overwhelm people, but I would hopefully learn better. Until I did, I trusted people would realise it was simply out of excitement and enthusiasm... I was fired-up.

Getting on my bike to go home, I paused a moment and just listened to the life buzzing and squawking and shuffling everywhere. I felt that energy again, that primal feminine energy. Shakti. Kundalini. It doesn't matter what you call it really, it's the source of everything and I felt it as sexual energy once more. This made so much sense to me – it's the power of creation. This energy is the same as when two people create a child on this earth, and when a star is born in the far reaches of the cosmos. I pulled away from the building and laughed out loud as a thought entered my head – the universe is one big orgy!

I saw myself riding along as if from a great distance, and I knew I was part of the dance too – a guy laughing and crying on a red bike going under the bridge and heading for home. He belonged in this universe, and has a part to play.

White Feather was waiting for me to get home. I gingerly asked him about his name as it seemed so commonplace in a way, and he agreed as I could hear and feel him laughing:

if I had a nickel for every White Feather I've met...
it's my name for me, it suits me

All right, fair enough, and you got to actually choose your name didn't you.

Come to think of it, if I had a nickel for every Peter I've met....

He was so in touch with nature and animals, and that was a huge connection I now understood. He was the animal person, the nature teacher – and that took you a while to figure out didn't it Neli? I mean his name alone might have given you a bit of a clue there. You sure are a bit slow on the uptake sometimes, but you *have* been going through a lot, I'll give you that, better late than never.

I sat down by the fire and we chanted together – hewe-shewe-hewe-shewe...

He and she and we, it's all the same. There's only us together, and in the larger picture, there's only one. I Am That I Am.

sing Walk for me

You want me to sing my song, Walk?

sing it

This was a song of mine from 1988 and one of my best in so many ways.

I was honoured and awestruck, and I started singing as I stood up next to the fire in that place by the river with White Feather – "listen to the wind, call your name" – and he joined in. He-joined-in.

He knows the words of course he knows the words he's one of your guides isn't he and he asked you to sing it he must like it he's probably heard you sing it a million times before right what's so weird about that listen to the way he wants you to hold on to the word walk longer than you usually do oh my lord I can't believe this is just another day in paradise that's funny I think I should just accept what's happening and sing just sing your little heart out Neli ...

And we walk
Under and over
Spiralling higher
Reaching out for what we lost

I recalled writing those lines nineteen years ago and thinking about DNA when I wrote – spiralling higher. This was all meant to be, everything was the way it should be, and I was fortunate to have written certain things down so long ago to generate these revelations now.

The weather seemed to join in as we finished the song, and I could feel his love and his humour washing through me. I heard his accent clearly as he gave me a word for a good dream "Ecawa" and one for a bad dream "Bejawa." He was laughing and I knew these were humourous words of a sort, and I could *feel* their meaning. The part of me that might at one time have wanted to start doing research and trying to verify these words, was long gone. This was real and these words were his words if no one else's, and now they were in me. Believe or doubt, take your pick. I had chosen a long time ago.

New Moon

Parvati

The next day I went to work as usual. I never took time off in general, and I was amazed I was still living up to that, even though life was so different now and my hands were still forming mudras with a mind of their own. I was getting used to the wonder somehow. Once again that seemed a little sad, but I knew there were so many more things in store for me the way things were going.

I really was accepting talking to so-called dead people with much more assuredness than I had on day forty-four when I'd written – complete acceptance. That made me laugh when I thought about it, as I'd still experienced more doubts about the whole thing after that, but now with over a hundred days under my belt, I felt there really was no more uncertainty in me. I really was getting used to living with miracles on a daily basis.

That evening, Jane Roberts came to me once again. We had another long talk about the situation, and laughed that she was now on the other side talking to me. It was hilarious really. Now I was the one who was in a trance of sorts, and we had a most joyous meeting until things came to a close with her asking, "How many days now?"

For some reason I looked at the clock first before checking my journal, it was 1:02 in the morning. I then looked at my journal to verify the day that had just officially ended as day one hundred and two!

Somehow I knew she'd wanted me to look at the clock so we could share this synchronicity together, and that was why she asked me what day it was. I was truly living in another world now, there was no doubt about that, and as she laughed with me and started to fade away she offered, "Oh, by the way... you do, and always did attend my dream class."

That was it! That was the little mystery she'd left me feeling the first time she visited. So it was true - after all these years I finally knew, right from Jane's mouth... or mind. I always was a member of Jane Roberts' dream class.

I got undressed, climbed into bed and suggested to myself that I would head straight there to say hello to my classmates, and to thank my teacher Jane for coming to me and not forgetting those of us still in this world.

༅ ༅ ༅ ༅ ༅ ༅

The next couple of days were about thinking things through, as indeed everything was really. Integration was the word of the year.

At work a Kundalini article appeared in the spam folder, and it was the one I'd been looking for earlier in the day, "What is Kundalini?" Something was telling me to read it again, and I stopped what I was doing to do just that, as by now I knew it was best to follow the signs as fast as possible. You could tell this was the best way to go, but in daily life it wasn't particularly feasible, so I was blessed by the universe every time I managed to just flow. I thought of all of us being free enough in whatever way, to be able to find this place, this way of living, and our actual natural state. It seemed perfectly obvious that this level of magic was available for anyone who believed it possible.

Believe first – proof after.

This is a quick and efficient way the universe has of making you have faith, instantly and on the spot. Without belief, there will be no evidence to find. The evidence doesn't exist until you believe it's there. It's funny that. So it turns out that the only answer to "show me" is – show yourself.

If I could, I would have everyone on this planet awaken now to their true nature in one way or another, and it seems this dream itself has awoken on our earth. I was gathering more and more on the Ascension, and I was beginning to see the dream of a mass evolution in consciousness as something that *was* happening in the only way it could – as something growing.

That's if I could believe all these people. It's not like I went out there and did some kind of survey myself, but I felt good in my choices. It was easy to feel through and determine what was coming from a much deeper place, and what fit in with me and this endless moment. When the information all starts to say the same thing, whatever spiritual angle you come from, then you know you're on to something – and all the information was saying the same thing. The Bible was suddenly making sense if you just listened to what Jesus was saying, and forgot the rest.

Love is it.

Love for all and everything throughout the universe – or it's not the kind of love we're talking about here.

Sometimes I felt my mother couldn't fully grasp what had happened either, and a sense of being awestruck would come across from her, and I would say – I know. I felt this now as I got ready to leave work, and then I said hi to Steaven and Sherrie who I hadn't said hello to for a couple of days. This was a new development and I hoped I wasn't ignoring them, but I was reassured with waves of understanding that they remembered all about time in physical reality. It must be weird to hear us and contend with all this stuff, and still deal with being there – they sent me.

After work, I got my bike and looked at the empty wasp's nest; it was the middle of September and they'd gone now. Maybe that was just the way it worked, or maybe they'd figured out the nest was really not viable. I wished them well with all my heart and rode off for the home part of the day.

As I went up the stairs and crossed the hall to the bedroom, I noticed something out of place. There were comic books in a holder down along the skirting board, and they were always neatly lined up and standing along the wall, so the one on its back on top of the holders and staring at me from a rakish angle, really stuck out. I had a closer look. This was from my friend Paul who had passed along some of his comic books at one time or another, and on the cover it was the – Fantastic 1st Issue!

Ghost Rider. That's right, Paul always *did* like this ghost rider character, and look at that! There he is with his flaming skull-head on his motorcycle and it's the first issue and everything!

It wasn't until a moment later, when I lowered my eyes and saw what was written in large bold letters at the bottom of the cover, that it hit me how important this message was, so I stared and read it over and over as I wondered how it had come out of the holder to end up here. Would a hidden camera have caught it slowly drawing itself out of the group and floating up to land softly on the top?

I looked at the words – A Spirit Reborn! – was written there, with the exclamation mark.

This was getting good now, this was getting really good, and I think I'll put this backpack away... I seem to be just standing here in the hall wearing it. Oh my. I couldn't have put it better myself – a spirit reborn – no question about it. I have two birthdays now and thank you for the verification.

I awoke on Saturday thinking about numbers, tuning forks, crop circles, the symbol on my leg and birthmarks.

"Let's put a spurt on!"

I know it's Vera's birthday mum, don't worry I'll give her a call.

Yes I'll have to call Vera, but you're dead and all I have to do is think one thought about you. I pondered this type of communication, and the subtleties involving uncounted numbers of things, including the atmosphere, even though the dimensions are part of each other. It was fascinating, and I was considering that there really was no distance in those terms, it had nothing to do with distance at all, it was about wavelengths.

"It's not the length – it's the width, or better – the breadth."

I could really see what she meant. It was more the depth of things, the emotional dimension of things. It was when things connected together sideways by combining their shapes – their waveforms. It's the universe's way of sorting things.

I thought of millions of people talking to their friends on the other side as a matter of course, then I thought of *everyone* on the planet being fully aware of this and living it.

This is one of the places we're going – death will never be the same.

The weekend was a dream about roses and music and a particular life on planet earth when the walls came down and light found the corners and Monday came without any warning whatsoever but it was wonderful and I was having the time of my existence.

Whatever led to this was worth it, and I could feel the focus behind this new life winding through times and places. This was meant to be and the plans went deep.

At work the Hebrides Overture by Mendelssohn came on the radio, and I stopped and listened as I remembered the history of this piece of music in my family. It had always been one of our absolute favourites, and I recalled many an occasion listening to it and conducting along in a kind of ecstasy. It was one of the first pieces of music I'd ever become aware of as a child, and I knew my mother was here and listening too.

Now it served as a connector between realities, and as the two of us followed along with the music, we merged together as the strings swooped and surged to paint a picture of Fingals's cave in Scotland. We were doing the exact same thing in two different realities and it didn't seem strange at all. No systems are closed, we aren't separated and we're never alone... we've just forgotten so very much.

Luckily I was alone at work again so I just let the tears flow. It really was a crying day today, and I laughed when I thought that because a day hadn't gone by since day one when I hadn't cried, and today was day one hundred and eight. The music stopped, and I'd just pulled myself together when I heard a female voice with a thick Irish accent...

my name is Gwen - it didn't stop at ten

This was said because - as I'm sure you remember - I'd just counted the number of spirits who had contacted me so far, and had arrived at the number ten.

the whole world is one family

I could *feel* this person, and I could see her inside of me. She had long red hair and was twirling in an ankle-length dress with both arms straight out. She was dancing on a hillside to some music of her own. They were Irish hills.

I know you and I love you

I know you and I love you too! Thanks a lot Gwen! I'd just stopped crying...

so it's Peter Nelson now is it?

This simple statement said a lot of things, not the least of which was - I've known you before this name. She was so present, so *alive*. It's true, dead people put us to shame with how vibrant they are.

You're pretty feisty.

I prefer inelegant

As I laughed with her, I saw her skip away like some kind of Irish Heidi, but with a look over her shoulder that said – I'll be back. She felt like part of me, and as I had that thought I knew she was. She was an incarnation of mine, or I was an incarnation of hers, and she was aware of other versions of me, or should I say other versions of herself?

I had to try and keep things simple. We were part of each other and from her perspective I think she knew more about these things than I did. All I really knew was that I was ecstatically happy she'd come to me, and I hugged myself believing it was her. In a way, it was, and I felt that ultra-joy through and through my being.

Man, the things that happen around here when everyone's gone home! I was still laughing as my mother popped in.

"What do you think?"

I think she's wonderful, and I think I'm reeling.

"Now that you have Gwen in your repertoire, I guess you're going to have to redo your list. She's a lively girl."

Yes I suppose I will, and the way things are going I think I'm going to be updating it continually. I hope so, please God don't let this ever end....

A customer came in which was just as well. I needed some grounding back into this reality and once again the universe provided exactly what I needed. By the time he left it was time to go home, and I stared at my collage as I packed-up my things. I couldn't take my eyes off Parvati.

༄ ༄ ༄ ༄ ༄ ༄

It was bath time again and everyone was asleep except for me and the cats. I got undressed with my eyes gazing unwaveringly at the photograph of the statue of Parvati on the bedroom wall. She was beautiful and amazing and divine and I slipped into a dream where I was wearing a robe in another place and time when the Mother had held us all in her arms.

I bid you

Did I hear that? Bid me what? Does she speak to me?

I don't think so Neli, I don't think this Goddess who you have decided represents All That Is or God to you, is really talking to you right now, do you? And what kind of greeting is – I bid you – anyway? What does that mean? Maybe it was that Sheltie from years ago who snapped at you when you and Treaca were trimming his claws? Maybe it was him saying – I bit you.

At the same time as I was being flippant, there was something bothering me, because if this really was Parvati, then my lack of belief would be somewhat disrespectful wouldn't it? I wandered over to the bath and slowly got in to let the sacred water ground me, and I felt a little strange, a little uneasy with my own behaviour. I'm just some kid from England who's read a few books. I don't know what I'm doing – do I?

As though waiting for me to be sitting in the bath, the message came through loud and clear this time, with no question as to the source or the power behind it. I went stock-still as every cell of my body and every nuance of my spirit stood at full attention to hear what was spoken...

take this fraction of my Love
if I were to release the smallest imaginable portion of my Love, it would be thus
this is one fragment from the most minute particle
take it

I obviously knew something was coming, but there was no time to think, there was only time to acknowledge, and feel, as my body was thrown backwards into the water. I heard a loud splash as I saw my legs fly up into the air with the force I was experiencing, and I watched as the water ran up my legs before I saw them return to the water in a kind of slow motion. I had one micro-moment of astonishment as the observer, and then I was adrift and lost in a sea of almost unbearable Love.

This was more than bliss – this was undiluted ecstasy. With bliss I think you can still walk around and function somewhat, with this, there was none of that. This was paralysing, and I knew I was flat in the bath and could breathe and wouldn't drown, but that was really all I knew. My eyes were closed and the water had the job of telling me I was still actually in my physical body. A meaningless amount of non-existent time went by before I was able to slowly open my eyes, and then draw myself up to a sitting position. If I was in shock I felt remarkably calm. It felt more like I was coming out of a trance.

I was alone now. Parvati had delivered a knock-out blow and left me to ponder the ramifications. If I'd have been unsure about being capable of communicating with the Creator before, I sure wasn't now. I was reeling and I added a bit of hot water to the bath, the sound of the water running was ancient and soothing. How long had I been lying there? I tried to absorb what had just happened to me as I ran the scene over and over again in my mind. Association took me back to the time with John when he'd pushed me in the bath, and the difference suddenly became clear.

With John, I could physically feel the push on my back as he forced me to the side of the bath on day five, with this, there was no sensation of being pushed or pulled at all.

I thought it over yet again and it was true. I hadn't been pushed or pulled – I had been *moved*. Every cell of my body had been physically shifted at the same time, so there was no localised sensation of touch. The dissimilarity between the two was blatant and awe-inspiring. I came to the conclusion that only God could do that.

I finished carefully washing this sacred body that had just been touched by the Creator, feeling more blessed than I'd ever thought possible, and as I stepped out of the bath and began to dry off, I looked down to see my private hair and another revelation hit me with force.

My lord I couldn't believe it. It was all so obvious!

I'd always liked to keep things trimmed and tidy in this area, but in 2005 I'd done something a little more drastic. I reversed the usual look by creating an upward triangle or a pyramid. I'd always liked this look, but on that day I had an overwhelming desire to just go ahead and do it for myself, and I called it – the arrow. This wasn't that long ago, and since that time the inverted V has been conspicuously showing up here and there.

Now the connection between this and Kundalini became abundantly clear, the energy beginning at the base of the spine and surging up like a freight-train as had happened to me. I stared at my arrow and saw how it was right there, at the base of my spine but just on the other side – like a road sign giving directions – start here and move up! How incredible is all of this? I even had a sign of what was to become on my own body!

Elegant – I couldn't get away from that word as a perfect description of the way the universe worked, and as I thought that, I heard my mother.

"Eat something."

I hear you mum.

"Well if you hear – then obey!"

Laughing now, and knowing she was oh so right – I put on a night-shirt and decided to obey.

꙰ ꙰ ꙰ ꙰ ꙰ ꙰

The next day at work I was outside having a break and missing my wasps. I made myself feel better by thinking about all the beautiful snow that would be coming along soon, as autumn was almost here, we were days away from the equinox.

White Feather, obviously in a jovial mood, decided to break into my reverie at this point.

your love of snow is universal

As I was basking in this statement and enjoying that the universe knew me so well, he finished the sentence with gales of laughter.

we all think you're an idiot!

I wonder if anyone saw me double-over with laughter myself for no apparent reason.

First Quarter
Jesus and Siddhartha

I decided to very gingerly mention talking to Jane Roberts to a few people and I squeezed my eyes shut just waiting for each response. This would probably raise a few sceptical eyebrows I was sure, even for the people who were with me this far. I was wrong. I could hardly believe it, but the typical reaction was – oh that doesn't surprise me, not with you and Jane Roberts all these years.

I love my friends! Thank you one and all. I was a bit concerned you know.

Bolstered by this, I decided to tell Treaca about Parvati on the phone at work. I was very excited and got her name wrong again, but Treaca quickly corrected me on it, knowing how to pronounce it properly because she was particularly enamoured by this Hindu Goddess and I didn't even know! She'd never mentioned this to me before, and I could hardly believe what I was hearing. Out of all the ones I could have chosen, or been chosen by, it was this one who Treaca knew all about. The synchronicities were constant and they were getting more and more profound and powerful. I was getting used to this level, but I told myself never to take the wonder of it for granted, even though it was actually normal to have life unfold around you this way.

By the time I'd finished the story with Parvati and the bath, Treaca was already saying, "You've got to write a book Neli – I need to read this part in a book with all the details."

Well, there's someone else coming to the same conclusion as me – I thought. There's no other way to explain what's really going on without an actual book is there?

"I think I'm going to have to," I found myself answering, and now I believed I really would. It was too early yet, and too many things were happening, but there would come a day and who knows? Maybe it would be helpful and entertaining as well as beneficial for me to relive it and put it all together. It could help solidify things in a powerful way – and I could see a book in my mind.

Later that day in the drifting place that seemed to be my usual state of mind now, I sensed John, my not-so-pleasant 1400s incarnation join me, and he had a few interesting things to say. The feeling was a little different this time and he came across as friendlier and a bit easier to digest.

He told me he had secretly thought women to be equal to men or even superior, and this was his very dark secret of the time.

This was amazing! Life was stories.

He found his power, or his chance to wield his power, on the battlefield, and he was really impressing upon me the power of the eyes. He felt he could be naked in front of his worst enemy and not be vulnerable, because of his eyes. He genuinely wanted to share this information and I could feel him emphasising it with a kind of forcefulness.

Satisfied, he left like a mist, and I was left feeling there was a heart in there somewhere and for the first time a wave of compassion went out from me to John.

There was hope and healing in the universe, and I saw now that I loved the part of me called John – because not to would be truly insane. He was/is an aspect of me for a start, and everyone's journey had to be respected anyway. I saw how simple it all was when the answer was always the same. Love truly is the answer to every question – I thought, as I sent some out to him and noticed my cheeks getting warm.

On the way home, I stopped for a second, got off my bike and rummaged through my knapsack for the peanuts I knew I had in there. It was Mr. Groundhog's lucky day and I peppered the area around his entrance with the dusty peanuts-in-the-shell. I rode on and was struck anew by the beauty and mystery of everything around me. It didn't matter what I looked at, it was as alive as the smell of September sailing on the air.

"Beauty is rearing its ugly head."

Don't make me laugh while I'm trying to ride my bike, okay mum!

After the house grew quiet I composed my new list, adding Gwen, and when I got to Aunt Ciss, I made a mental note to remember Lawrence Welk this weekend. Then I thought of birthdays and death-days and wrote down all the ones in September before I had to stop staring at the numbers for a moment, and turn my attention to the radio. They were playing "Loch

Lomond" and I quietly marvelled as I remembered singing this very beautiful old Scottish song earlier today at work. The synchronicities or connections were flowing along like a comforting river, and were always there to dip into, and refresh – you just had to notice.

I couldn't believe my blessings the next day at the office, when Mendelssohn came on the radio again with the Hebrides Overture. I laughed thinking maybe they just forgot to put the disc away and left it on the desk at the radio station, but I knew really it was being in the magic, and this was another gift from the universe.

I wasn't alone this time, my colleagues were still here at work, so I had to keep it together on the emotional front as I drifted along with the music. What better time for Edna to drop a clanger into my consciousness in the form of a vision and a statement:

"I've seen Mendelssohn conduct this himself."

And with this I saw Mendelssohn at the helm of his masterpiece, head back and conducting with passion, looking to be in his early twenties. This was a concert in the spirit world and he was taking on the appearance of himself at the time the composition was written. I felt a joyous excitement because I was so happy for my mother to have been in attendance on such an occasion, but then, the ticket would have been just to think about it and be there. Others of my family were at this event too, as I got a glimpse of Aunt Ciss dressed to the nines with one of her hats on, and meanwhile I was standing here in the store with my eyes closed, following the majestic music and the vision of the performance for as long as I could....

Nudged back to this reality by the business at hand, I thought to my mother – well you got me good that time, don't rub it in okay? How incredible, and thanks for letting me be there with you! As I dealt with the next job I realised I probably was at the concert all along, and I actually just caught up with me being there. We are multi-dimensional beings, and sometimes that's easy to forget when your awareness isn't big enough to contain it.

The next day was Friday, my granddad's birthday, so I thought of him and Rex and Sri Bhundari in an easy combination – my granddad always having a dog, and Sri Bhundari being a grandfather figure no matter how you looked at it.

"From a little old piano teacher" – that was how my granddad signed his gifts and letters to me when I was small. My mind drifted to a calendar he gave me before we came to Canada, with a close-up of a beautiful Alsatian's face for the whole year. German Shepherds were my favourite dog for a long time after that, and I wondered how much it had to do with this calendar. Happy Birthday Granddad! – I know I'll see you soon.

Later on, I was so consumed with thinking about the dream world and how we shape events there like sculptors, that I didn't notice the time until it was already past five. Yahoo! - the weekend was here again, and as I rode home from work Duncan was on my mind, and I wondered how long it would be until the Druid would talk to me. All in its own good time – I thought, and I was grateful that he'd come along to say hello in the first place. I sent a thank you out to him, and tried to keep my eyes on where I was going.

Sixteen weeks today and Saturday, so after the piano lesson I went for a walk and attempted to reflect on the last one hundred and thirteen days. It was almost impossible. So much had happened by now I couldn't keep it all together, and the notes were turning out to be for me as much as anyone else. I decided to just walk along and be one with the day, and I was fortunate enough to see fine people out on the street with their fine dogs. I came to the conclusion that dogs are pure happiness and joy cast out into the world, and I thanked the universe for dogs.

I thought of sending happiness out into the world myself, so I came up with the idea of laughter bubbles. I could send them floating out into the world, and wherever they ended up they would pop and shower the lucky bystanders with mirth. It didn't seem like a bad idea and subsequently, I launched laughter bubbles far and wide. On one level it would seem childish or naive in a world such as this, but this was first-rate psychic work really, and I had no doubt as to the benefits.

White Feather had been listening in and following along, so now he decided to add something to the flow of my thoughts.

> *when you laugh*
> *you are happy*
> *when you are happy*
> *you love*

I quickly jotted this down.

by the way, Parvati likes it that you had such a hard time getting her name right

So you guys laugh at me when I'm not looking?

I was laughing myself as I arrived back home and went upstairs to drop off my knapsack and sit down for a minute.

White Feather was still here with a clear, strong connection so I closed my eyes and joined him by the river. He had a large fire going this time, and it seemed to be twilight as the sun was leaving a red parting glance on the mountains for a moment. He bowed to me from the other side of the blaze, and perfectly pantomimed accidentally setting his hair on fire and dancing around slapping himself on the head in an effort to extinguish the flames. It was hilarious.

you can call me fire-hair!

This was in response to calling myself snow-hair from a photograph taken last winter. Walking Wolf Woman subsequently offered the variation, snow-hare.

attend

The phone was ringing so attend to it I did. This was White Feather's standard comment whenever we were interrupted. I noticed he never said – ignore. The idea wasn't to turn your back on the physical world, but to be well balanced and to embrace this life fully while here.

White Feather was still standing on the other side of the flames when I returned, and his face was serious now as he stepped into the fire, reached out and pulled me toward him into an embrace with the mystical flames dancing around and through us.

we burn together...

As we rose up towards the sky and then space, I felt pleased that fire was part of me and I could hear White Feather's words as if emerging from somewhere.

...teachers talk to teachers...

We were zooming through space now, but I managed to focus on his voice now I knew it was there.

if you have people's interest
you can teach them anything
if you don't have their interest
you can't teach them a thing

For some reason I found this inordinately funny although completely true, and I was still laughing to myself as the room came back into focus and I thought – I tend to blend. Yes, this would be my third T-shirt after "One thought away' and "Don't resist the urge to merge."

Always back to the water I went, and the nightly bath had become without fail, the number one grounding ritual. I swirled the bubbles around and saw snow as I tried to grasp the scope of what had happened to me so far. Whatever else was going on, it was obvious that friends and family were always friends and family, whether on this side of the veil or the other, or both. I was reminded of the first day or so when I was told – "roles change – loyalties don't." This was very reassuring.

Now my feelings distilled to land on my grandma and I heard her say, "Everyone knows everyone really," as I was engulfed again in that tangible blast of love. She then focused on specific family members and gave me a kind of fast recap of names and places and dates, ("you like numbers") and all I could do was bathe in the information and her presence.

I came back to myself sitting on my heels in the bath and feeling the water around my thighs like loving arms. I added some hot water and took a few deep breaths before another presence adhered to my mind and filled centre stage where my grandma had just been. It was Sri Bhundari, and I was figuring this holy man out somewhat, he came with his own signature that felt strong and by now familiar.

I want you to expand your sense of pride
be proud of everything
you had a hand in creating it

That was his message for today, and then he was gone.

Climbing into bed I thought of a few more facts and figures. It was one hundred days since day thirteen and the Autumn Equinox was in a few hours. My grandma and granddad's wedding anniversary was tomorrow, and there was a full moon on Wednesday four days from now.

I do like numbers Grandma! – I thought to her, as I said a prayer for the world and let myself fade from one dream to another.

ॐ ॐ ॐ ॐ ॐ ॐ

It's Sunday and I must get something to eat before I do anything else.

"If you'd eat something, I'd be eternally grateful!"

That's pretty funny stuff mum. Thanks for starting my day off with a laugh.

After dutifully eating, I looked at an old photograph on the wall of me and my sister Sandra, and I survived the ecstasy/love feeling once again as it surged up and took me over leaving me drained and full at the same time. Now I knew this feeling wasn't restricted to dead people or cosmic-level realisations – if I'd been wondering about that at all. Love simply transcends all dimensions and states and times and places and, well... everything.

Sometimes I just had to try to stop and catch my breath, but there was no stopping the whirlwind of my thoughts and emotions, revelations and sensations.

St. Francis popped into my mind as someone the animals knew well, and I remembered images of him surrounded by birds and other creatures. He could communicate with the animals and felt at one with them and with the rest of creation which he called a work of art. This was someone I could seriously relate to, and I thanked him for being him, as I thought of a world where animals didn't shrink and run from people as a matter of course. One day – I prayed – one day.

I felt something at the back of my throat and spontaneously opened my mouth as though to dislodge it, but I knew this feeling and I knew there was nothing stuck in my throat. Someone wanted to say something, and they wanted to say it through me and not just in my mind. I hadn't wanted to go very far in this direction quite yet, so the other two times this had happened, I'd not let it go any further. I saw this as a precursor to deep trance channelling, and I figured it was maybe a little early for that at this stage.

This time I wanted to try it, but if I went too deep I might not be aware of what I was saying and that would be useless with me being solitary here, so I thought maybe I could just dip my toes in without any danger of going too far. I didn't want to get stuck or something either.

I closed my eyes, took a deep breath and immediately had a vision of a 1920s Chicago gangster-type, talking around a cigar. He reminded me of Edward G. Robinson and I decided to let my mouth and throat go...

you're on a roll kid

Okay, I could hear what I/he was saying, and even though I had this gangster thing going on, he seemed like a pretty nice guy, and that sounded like a compliment to me. How many incredible things can I absorb and integrate? This was like a psychic landslide for the last three months and can you believe it? My own voice is talking with that gangster accent!

there's no stopping you

That was all there was to it, and as he receded leaving a residual feeling of being pleased with himself, I received the name Denny. Sometime later when I thought all this over, I acquired the last name too – Grazer. His name is/was Denny Grazer.

I was thrilled with what had happened, another potential had come forward, and it felt like all these natural, related abilities were coming on-line and making themselves known. This was an interesting Sunday so far.

After the house had gone quiet for the night, I sat and drifted. I considered the irony of people searching, questing for God, when God was right in the mirror and everywhere you looked. That was some powerful amnesia we came into this life with.

The Egyptians floated into my head and I recalled sensing/feeling a squared-off ceremonial beard on my chin during the first week of all this. I'd forgotten all about it, and I wondered how many other things had occurred that I would never consciously remember. These feelings seemed to indicate a possible Egyptian life or two – not necessarily as anyone special, I might have been a youngster making a fake beard out of clay or something – and I just had to shake my head at everything and laugh, especially in light of the recent Egyptian royalty joke. It was all about how much you could accept of your own true infinite nature. The more my mind was opening and the more I could allow – the more the universe was willing to reveal.

With my eyes closed now, I saw Parvati sitting under a tree by a stream, so I silently joined her and put my head on her shoulder. I called this our picnic place and we had just started to be here in this way when I needed to be filled and connected.

I now entered a dream within a dream and saw Jesus deep in the forest. This was the Jesus I knew as a child without the horror of the crucifix or any biblical drama, and it was all mixed together with Christmas and snow and animals and joyful magic. Wearing a long sumptuous robe he was surrounded by animals with birds circling above his head like a living halo. It was a secret gathering in the woods when the animals held council, and tonight they had a very special guest.

As a child I'd had a hard time sorting a few things out. Was Jesus God? How could he be – he's the *son* of God, right? And what about this Holy Ghost? Was that Jesus after he'd resurrected, or is it the Great Spirit behind everything?

It was kind of confusing, but things were simpler now after over half a century on this earth and I'd come across Kundalini and Holy Spirit or Ghost, as interchangeable terms. And in the end, with Jesus – of course he's God too, just like everyone else. Every part of God contains the whole – while at the same time, the whole is more than the sum of its parts. We see the term – Holographic Universe – now, which means the same thing.

One more time those paradoxes made me feel like I was on the right track, and it never hurt to sometimes get back to the basics. God steps the energy down, and ascended masters and deities are simply beings who are vibrating at a high refined level and have a propensity to teach.

Jesus is a master teacher and came here as a prophet, as the embodiment of the Christ energy, and as I looked I remembered how I felt from childhood when he was all I knew and I realised how much I loved him, the Father Christmas with Love and knowledge of eternal life in his sack. He opened his arms toward me and I could barely look as love and goodness flowed into me....

From this vision I returned to Parvati's shoulder for a moment, only to be transported to a barren, sandy landscape with a tired, young adept stumbling along a narrow pathway. I watched in wonder as I felt like I knew this person, or was this the archetype of all monks?

The scene shifted now to another time and place and I found myself in a cave, knowing I was in a rocky, mountainous setting. I saw a very old monk sitting and meditating, who was clearly the Buddha, and there was a moment of bliss and recognition as I realised that the struggling adept was the Buddha too.

Once again the scene changed like turning a page and this time I was sitting beside a peaceful, beautiful stream with Siddhartha. This was the time I was so interested in, just at the beginning of his journey, but after his self-realisation. He was young, much younger than me, but my current situation was akin to his at that particular time, if I dared....

I was sitting with the brand-new Buddha and we chatted about ageless things. I tried my best to notice everything around me so as to fully appreciate this gift, this dimension of experience I was in.

I heard Siddhartha's voice, "If you're practising anything..." but it was all a dream within a dream within a dream, and his voice came and went like the warm breeze.

As we talked under the white sun of the day, I noticed it was too intensely bright to do more than occasionally glance up at his face, and now I wondered if the light was coming from his eyes. I wondered if I was actually ready to look into those eyes, and so out of a natural reverence – imposed upon myself, I knew – I kept my head down with just a glimpse now and then. I could still barely think about myself and prophets like this in the same breath, never mind sitting quietly with him and adding our own words to the song of the day.

There were things said to me here in this place I knew I wouldn't be able to recount, but at the same time I knew my true-self would never forget – it was more like an *imprinting*.

Still not looking directly into his eyes, the reality faded, and as it did, I suddenly knew what I would see anyway – the cosmos. I had no doubt they contained the depths of space, and could also radiate the living light at the same time.

I came back through his last words and his fading presence until I was back with my head on the Goddess' shoulder.

When you have a physical body, whatever dimension you find the body in is home base whether you like it or not, so I reluctantly opened my eyes and reunited with the physical room. Yes, quite a Sunday indeed.

This gift was about depth of perception, all these levels or dimensions being inside of each other and dancing together. Focus was the key to the tuning in of the various frequencies that were all there at the same time, and the more you could contain or hold, the more you became aware of.

I was tired. I thought of teachers being energetic instigators. I thought of roaming through the subtler levels by association. I thought of Edna being contained within Edwina, but still free to grow independently. I thought of paradoxes. And I thought I'd better go to bed and try to be in decent shape for the beginning of the work week tomorrow.

I assumed the position and thought – goodnight universe! – knowing I was part of everything.

༃ ༃ ༃ ༃ ༃ ༃

Monday's were good days for reflection now and even more so this particular day as it was Edna's birthday.

"Did you get me a present?"

I could hear her laughing, and I thought – isn't what's happened here present enough?

"It sure is."

I gave her a happy birthday spirit hug and noticed she was wearing the silver rose.

At work, a courier came into the store and was about to kill an insect who had come in with him, riding on his electronic signing device. He didn't have a chance before I swooped in like the insect angel and took the little creature safely outside.

"Are you a Buddhist or something?"

I had to laugh, "Or something..." I managed to say before he flew out the door to his next stop – couriers are always in a hurry. If that was all Buddhists were known for on this earth, it would be enough. Compassion for every living thing. How's that for a reputation?

Later on a regular customer came in, and somehow the topic of Buddhism came up again. We'd never talked of these matters before, but the world was a different place now and he offered the observation, "It's not a religion you know."

I looked at him, "Define religion," and I almost wished I hadn't. He spluttered and hemmed and hawed until I had to jump in and rescue the poor guy, and I realised people sometimes just repeat things they've heard without really knowing what they're talking about. I was learning so much, and I knew people were being sent through the door for my education, one way or another. The world had become thicker, richer, and I'd started to really see the inner workings which gave me a feeling of childish glee and brought tears of joy to my eyes.

People were starting to see something in me too, and I suddenly remembered day sixty-seven when I went to the video store to buy a copy of "The Secret." On the way out, the girl who sold it to me enquired, "So what is this all about anyway? I haven't seen it yet." I started, "Well, it's about the law of attraction actually..." and then something happened. I just started to talk as though I had a polished script in front of me, and I had to consciously stop myself from going on and on about the supreme power of thought. I came back to myself to see her wide-eyed, and as I left she called out, "Thanks for the enlightenment!" and seemed very genuine about that. Oh my.

I came back to myself and somehow the work-day was over. Getting my bike for the ride home something caught my eye, and I looked up to see a beautiful white and grey feather slowly floating down right to me. I probably could have reached up and plucked it out of the air, but I didn't want to damage it, so I waited until it had settled by my feet before reaching down and picking it up, saying thank you and reverently tucking it in my chest pocket for the ride home.

ॐ ॐ ॐ ॐ ॐ ॐ

The next day was ten years to the day since my father died, and somehow I'd never really thought too much about this being the day after my mother's birthday. There was meaning here – there was meaning in everything if you just knew how to decipher it. Some people with a penchant for tidiness choose to die on the same day they were born for instance, neatly culminating their lives to the day. I thought about things like this whenever I had the chance during the course of the day.

At five o'clock I was still adding photographs of lightning striking water to my screensaver but I was tired now, and figured I could carry on later. I thought I'd better get going and head for home.

"Come on Toscanini!"

I forgot about that one mum! That's something else you always used to say, and yes, I know – you still do.

I rode home and went into the bedroom noticing a jar on the storage unit with a name on the lid –"Tosca." The jar originally held marinated artichoke hearts, and this was the brand name. I couldn't help but laugh at the connection between this and Toscanini, it was all just a matter of course now, not to mention the hearts, and living through the heart.

Sitting on the bed I thought about Walking Wolf Woman and somehow knew we were blood brothers in another life. Don't question it Nelson, just jot it down in your journal, it feels right and you know it is. This is how information comes through unofficial channels, meaning not through the outer senses. Sometimes it just drops into your lap without any warning, and you'd better get used to it.

Something else then came out of nowhere, and at first I thought it was a poem or a saying, until I saw Merlin in my other sight, and I realised it was a spell – a banishing spell.

  out of loop
  out of time
  out of sync
  out of rhyme

My very own spell! Just in case I might need to banish something or someone, and "peace be with you" wasn't quite doing the trick. How kind of you to give me this verbal charm – thank you! The vision faded and I quickly wrote it down, still feeling a little guilty for breaking the "spell" and going for my journal, but I was writing things down without looking half the time, and sometimes with my eyes closed. I just had to have some kind of record of what was going on, now I was coherent enough to know what pen and paper were. I put the pen down and my hand took on another mudra.

I don't know how long I sat in the bath and stared at the water as though seeing it for the first time. Water is a miracle all by itself and I looked at it in wonder as I washed.

Slowly climbing into bed, I looked at the doorway were I'd seen my mother before, and again a shadow formed before my eyes and I knew it was her. "There you are!" I said out loud and watched the shape slowly fade away.

"Goodnight mum," I mumbled as my eyes shut of their own accord, and I faded away myself.

Moon Five

Moon Angels

Four months today, and despite all the wonder in my life now, I still had all the same problems as everyone else, but at least I knew it all meant something. My mother quickly chimed in:

*"Yes, the **gravity** of your situation there on earth."*

Already I'd started to laugh...

*"I'm just **lightning** things up."*

And you have mum, thank you.

I decided to think about more uplifting things, so I thought about nature being the main doorway to enlightenment in so many ways, and I thought about that celestial music being the sound of love.
Now that I'd completely accepted what was happening to me – despite the occasional doubt and complete disbelief of course – I knew I had to build my confidence now, and I had to take it to a supreme level as well as I was able. The mystery of the universe might always be somewhat unfathomable, but I had to try to be meticulous and impeccable if I possibly could. I'd been given an overwhelming gift from the universe, from Parvati, and to accept it was one thing, but I had to feel I was worthy of it.

"You deserve everything that's happening to you."

Thank you mum, I'm glad you think so.

I was thinking I'd better get my camera and go outside to take some photographs of that beautiful full moon, when I was completely distracted by Aunt Ciss who wanted me to write something down. Whenever I'd thought about Aunt Ciss over the years, I could see her standing beside the piano so long ago, and singing "Have Some Madeira M'Dear," with her sister – my grandmother – on piano. It was a silly, somewhat ribald song in the style of the old English Music Hall tunes, and she did a truly wonderful version of it. I'd seen her perform this many times.

Now she was motivated to write one of her own, apparently inspired by the Toscanini name that had been in the air lately. I quickly got my notebook and proceeded to take dictation from my dead Great Aunt Cissie who was laughing and in a "daft" mood:

> look at Toscanini
> in his old bikini
> making quite a scene he
> was showing-off as needs be
>
> crying oh won't somebody see me?
> this is how I want to be, see?
> I'm an enchanted mystical genie
> won't someone come and free me?
>
> poor old Toscanini
> how he's holding up's beyond me
> they took away his TV
> and his baby blue bikini
>
> now he conducts his music fiercely
> all his attention where it need be
> but I miss my old bikini
> says dear old Toscanini

I was laughing along with the inevitable tears, and I could hardly believe what I/she had written. This was so much like her! This *was* her! She had sent this message because she knew I always thought about the Medeira song.

She really had this personality, and if I doubted, all I had to do was think back to another one of her favourite naughty Lancashirisms, it was quite rude and still in use in Lancashire I found out via the internet.

With the gift of this lyric as a kind of reassurance, my self-professed mentor took her leave as I told her how much I loved her and how I wished I could hold her in my arms for just one moment. "Soon enough," I heard – and then she was gone. I stared at the photograph of her on my wall for a long time.

ᚾ ᚾ ᚾ ᚾ ᚾ ᚾ

The magic of water was still on my mind the next time I was having the sacred bath, and I imagined writing my name upon it. Part of me would always go with the water physically once I emptied the bath, but now I added the energetic essence of my name to go with it psychically because of my intent. There was intent again – the secret of so much.

I wanted to add love and hope to this water, and I saw it being distributed and becoming a part of all the water in the world, the same water that's always been here, the same water that flows through all of the creatures and plants that are, or were, or ever will be... and through Gaia herself.

I was getting carried away with this idea, and the blessed water was getting cold now. Enough Nelson – let the water go and dry yourself off.

I was reminded of my laughter bubbles, and both these ideas were fun and interesting techniques, but I thought no props were really necessary to send love and hope out into the world and the universe. Yes, the universe and beyond. This reality was not a closed system – none of them were – and thoughts themselves transcended all realities. If only we knew just how powerful we really are – was what I was left with as I went to bed.

On Friday I decided I must take those photos of the Moon tonight before it was too late, the waning had already begun. I rode to work with the Moon in my heart, and noticed it was getting a bit chilly now, but I would ride my bike as long as I could.

Once I'd parked and gone inside, I was hanging up my jacket as I heard an Irish voice:

it's only cold outside when you're inside – my old da' used to say that

Gwen! I was so excited she was here, and I knew what she meant. Once you were out there and dressed for it, you were fine. It was difficult not to laugh out loud, but I had to be normal, say good morning to people and get to work.

This really was like having a secret identity, but this one I sincerely wished I could share. The irony caused me to snort a short breath – oh man, was I really going to be able to assimilate all of this and still walk these streets with a modicum of grace and balance?

I was beginning to understand that I would absolutely never be able to share this with certain people, and that was simply the way things were at this time in this world – for now. Everyone would discover their own truth in their own way, and if not before, that discovery would begin on the day they died. The hope was to see some of these universal truths now though, and I had no desire to say "I told you so," in the afterlife. I would rather people have their own experiences now, in this life, and start to feel their power and eternal natures before that day, if possible – and be somewhat prepared.

Gwen wasn't going anywhere for a while today.

do you find me delightful?

I sure do Gwen! I was laughing despite the work in front of me – I love this girl's attitude!

I know you pretty well darlin'

I bet you do.

maybe better than you know yourself – we'll find out

Well that sounds interesting! I'm just so elated to be talking to you.

I'm excited too, and I'm very excited for you

I noticed it was break time so I went outside and lit a cigarette, noticing that Gwen frowned with a kind of disapproval.

You know that doesn't really help anything – that's all I'm going to say...

I was beginning to feel a little chastised, until I heard her laugh and saw her sitting on a large rock smoking a pipe! You're a little Imp, Gwen! Today she looked like an Irish Faerie.

I look like a faerie because you really want to see one – besides, I like the look

This girl was hilarious, and we both laughed like a couple of kids.

Back inside, I was frantically scribbling this exchange down and the universe was helping by holding off the phone calls. I could keep my notes next to the machine and it just looked like one more sheet of paper. How perfect!

write down Gwen says – amazing things happen to nice fellas

Can I put Gwen smokes a pipe?

*I smoke a pipe **occasionally!***

I knew she was retreating now, and I noticed I was getting used to these feelings, as sure enough, she started to skip away. I felt giddy.

I like beer with the pipe!

She faded from my inner vision as I heard one last comment.

don't forget to write down the beer thing!...

And with that she was gone. I had no doubt I would be visited by her again, and I realised she was probably only one thought away too. It was a good, solid feeling.

ଙ ଙ ଙ ଙ ଙ ଙ

I was home now and darkness had descended as I checked my camera before going outside to capture the Moon. The overture to "Swan Lake" was on the radio, and I remembered asking my granddad the name of this piece when I didn't know what it was or who the composer might be. I went outside with the swans dancing in my head.

Putting the camera on its "moon" setting, I took several photographs waving it around, eager to try out my moon writing to see what would develop, if anything.

Going back inside and hooking the camera up to the TV, I started to have a look at what I'd captured and wasn't surprised to find the squiggles I'd seen before, until four of them jumped out at me as something to behold.

One of them was a double circle with a cross inside and I stared at it in amazement. What on earth? I was just waving the thing around, but of course I must have made the necessary motions to produce this effect. Still... it was astounding how it had turned out considering my random actions with the camera. I was sufficiently impressed but I hadn't seen anything yet, there were three other photographs that were obviously a series. They looked like Angels! Right away I said "Moon Angels" under my breath – I couldn't believe what I was seeing.

The striking thing was that the three images were of the same thing from three different angles. Angel angles! I had a good laugh at that. What were the chances I would somehow get the same image three times from three different angles? Checking the embedded photograph file numbers, I noticed they were not taken sequentially either, which made it even more astounding considering the means of their production.

It was late now, but fortunately there was no work the next day, so I finally put the camera away and had fun thinking maybe a moon angel would make an interesting book cover.

୧ ୧ ୧ ୧ ୧ ୧

Over the course of the weekend, I turned on the TV at one point to be presented at that second with a golden Indian Goddess dancing, her arms multiplying and then re-unifying as she continued her sacred dance. This just won't stop – I thought again for the hundredth time.

"You do like to keep the pot on the boil don't you?"

Oh hi there mum! Yes I guess I do at that, especially when it comes to you. You won't just figure I'm okay now and disappear one day will you?

"Not on your Nellie."

Before turning the TV off, I flipped to another channel just to see what would happen... the caption read "baby it's you" from the Beatle song of the same name which was playing as part of the show's soundtrack. Saying thank you, for yet one more assurance, I clicked the TV off.

Later it was the radio's turn as I put it on to hear the refrain of a popular song playing, which began with "you've got to find your balance..."

I couldn't have agreed more – balance was something I really had to try and maintain amidst a seemingly unending series of profound events. The song also mentioned grace, which isn't so common in a pop song and was perfect for me at this moment.

So how are you doing Nelson are you feeling balanced at all do you still think you might not make it through all of this are you okay I mean really okay do you know what you're doing do you know what you will do just relax okay that's the key that's the ticket okay relax relax breathe and breathe you can do this you can be this you've waited forever for this come on you've made it this far you've got what it takes you do you do you do...

you're tenacious

Aunt Ciss! Thank you for saying that. You're right, I am... I can be... I will be... I won't let go of this gift... I won't waste it on doubt when I know what I know what I know. You just keep popping in with your mentoring okay?

Yes, I know a few things... I know – you couldn't die if you tried... I know that. Maybe that should be my fourth T-shirt.

I wandered over to the bedroom window and had a look at the beautiful Japanese Lilac tree on the front lawn. It was the end of September now and the tree was still very lush although next month the leaves would be falling and not long after that the snow would be falling too. Oh my – I could hardly wait for that.

I stood and looked at the tree for a moment, and then felt an actual jolt as I saw a face staring back at me. One of the leaves dancing in the breeze had a distinct face, an obvious face, and there was a presence to go along with it. A nature spirit! A Deva!

I found my camera and quickly took some shots of him. What if he should fall off the tree and I couldn't find him? Better be quick! Him?

Knowing I was just personifying him for my own sake I christened him Mr. Green and took photos through the window as well as opening a side screen and leaning out as far as I could. There he was... right there in the photos clear as day! Thank you for showing yourself Mr. Green!

What is just my imagination or did I hear – "My pleasure."

You're right Aunt Ciss, I am determined to walk this path no matter what. I wouldn't have missed this for the world, and I don't care if people want to lock me up and throw away the key. I'm in this for the duration.

I remembered a phrase from my recent readings about Kundalini, it's the first mantra of the Rig Veda:

"I invoke the fire and place it in the forefront."

How ancient was this? Yet alive right now today in me and I'm sure many others. This was timeless knowledge and basically meant that once the sacred fire of Kundalini was ignited, it must take precedence over all else. There were no half-way measures here – you committed yourself or you didn't. The regular world wasn't to be ignored though, or belittled, but to be enriched and permeated with this gift of grace.

I sat on my heels and placed my palms on the floor in front of my knees – bowing forward to place my forehead on the back of my hands. I stayed that way for a minute or two as a dedication of sorts to this path and this wonder.

I couldn't remember deciding to do this – I just did it – that's the way things were happening now, and as I got back to my feet I thought – you can't always time the ritual Nelson.

༄ ༄ ༄ ༄ ༄ ༄

I rode to work the next day – Hi Mr. Groundhog! Suddenly it was October. So many things had happened since June, I could hardly keep it all together, but this was just as well. This moment was all there really was – this ever-expanding moment.

Flying on my bike now. Walking into work now. Answering the phone now. Time was actually just one now after another – no matter where you were, or what was happening, it was always now.

I'd learned to accept (basically) what was happening, but I just couldn't credit it, as we used to say in England. Edna used to say that sometimes too, but I was fairly sure it was my own thought this time. The merging still made it a little difficult to identify individual thoughts sometimes, but there was nothing uncomfortable about this now, or unusual, it was just the way things were.

I had a stack of work in front of me, but it didn't seem to be a problem, the world was exciting again and I wondered what would happen next.

"Do everything with joy or don't do it at all."

I understood what Edna was getting at. It was how you approached things, life was all about perception. That stack of work was neutral and not a good or a bad thing in itself. To someone wanting to go home on a Friday afternoon it could be a source of distress, and to someone who had been out of work for a while it would be a source of pure joy to dig into it. Marie the yoga master's words came back to me – "It's up to you." I was sure I would hear those words in her French accent for the rest of my life and beyond. I decided to get going with a smile on my face.

there's been enough supplication on the planet – it's time to stand up and meet the Gods...

This popped into my mind as I was working away and I wasn't sure where it came from. There were still the occasional things that came from nowhere, and sometimes I didn't bother trying to identify the source, and sometimes I did. This felt like it may have come from me, the more I thought about it, and eventually I decided it was from my inner (or higher) self. I was still referring to this part of me as Malcolm.

When I thought of people meeting the Gods now, I imagined someone looking in a mirror and truly *seeing*. There you are!

The word blasphemy came to mind. I was lucky to be living in the twenty-first century, but I sensed in other lives I wasn't quite so fortunate. People were killed for this kind of thinking, and isn't it interesting that people were persecuted for knowing and trying to share the truth? More and more it became evident that the church's number one agenda had been and still was keeping people in the dark about their *own* divinity. Many things were becoming clear.

I understood that all the answers were within each of us if you just looked deeply enough, but sometimes you could learn a lot by asking the right teachers the right questions.

it's asking the person who wants to answer that question too

Okay, that was funny! I sensed Siddhartha had thrown that in there, and once again there was that common thread of humour. These master teachers were hilarious, and I thought of all those images of the Buddha laughing, and it was a true indication of their natures.

Riding home I thought of healing and my mum's thirty-second cure:

*"You can **send** the thirty-second cure."*

Yes I guess I can mum – I'll keep that in mind.

This made me think of long-distance healing in general, and of course I thought of Jane Roberts and "Helper," an energy force she could send to people in need. This kind of healing was completely viable, even though it sounded absurd without an understanding of energy and intent.

This made me consider how far removed most people were from their own awesome power, and another movie line sprang to mind. This time it was from The Matrix, and it came from nowhere (or everywhere), and I realised just how profound it really was – "Billions of people just living out their lives... oblivious."

Last Quarter

In for a penny

Why won't someone ask me something?

I was waiting for someone to say – well, what's it really like to talk to dead people anyway? But this didn't seem to be forthcoming. Even the people who were behind me and believed me, or at least said they did, seemed to be very quiet about the whole thing and I was finally beginning to understand that as difficult as it was for *me* to fully accept – for others it was all theoretical or something... and I couldn't blame them.

I didn't need to go into trance, I didn't need to perform a ritual or at least take five really deep breaths, I didn't need to do anything it seemed, and it was almost impossible to fully accept the scope of what I was telling people. Thankfully Gordon and Lorraine had been doing amazing things for years, and more and more people all over the world were channelling and coming up with information from "somewhere" I was discovering, but in my small world I was now a bit of an anomaly, and – you'd better get used to it Neli.

It seemed my only hope now was to actually write a book, and *that* way there would be a chance of at least some slight idea of how things really were now inside of me. At the same time I knew it would only be a shadow of the real deal, the way it was when I'd read all *my* books and fully accepted most of what I'd read, but still was thrown into a world and universe I was barely prepared for. All I could do was press on and love my world and my fellow travellers no matter where they were on the path. All roads lead to the same destination in the end.

I rode to work thinking about feathers and arrows pointing skyward, which reminded me of pyramids which reminded me of Egypt....

There were so many things to think about. I ended up just feeling the wind on my face, and marvelling at how this life had taken a sharp turn into the unknown, and I knew I wouldn't change a thing. Actually, that reminded me of one pointed question I *had* been asked – "Do you wish you could be 'normal' again?" No, I don't. With that I was at work, and I quickly went inside.

Once the machines were running, I sensed who I thought to be Sri Bhundari with me – it was a warm and reassuring presence – but for some reason I doubted myself yet again...

Sri Bhundari, is that you?

who else?

I just thought someone might be pretending or something. (Why did I say that?)

why would anyone pretend to be me?
for that matter why would anyone pretend to be Parvati or Siddhartha or Jesus, or anyone else you've talked to lately?

To exert some control or influence over me maybe? (I'd heard about this.)

and have they?

No.

and have they offered positive advice and radiant visions of bliss and love?

Yes they have.

you can't fake that
and why would anyone pretend to do that for you anyway – as someone they are not?

(He had me on the ropes – what was I talking about? This is what you get for reading that stuff about devious entities Neli.)

do they want your fealty or worship?
do you kneel and bow?

Bow a little, sometimes. (He really had me now.)

but more as an equal – a friend

Oh boy. Of a sort, but yes, I guess. (He'd made the word "equal" come alive in a way italics could have only dreamed of.)

you don't guess
*what would **you** do?*
*how would **you** do it?*
we come back to this over and over
these are also people, just like you and me
would a gentle friend be a logical place to start?

Yes it would.

when you need a ball of light, you'll get a ball of light – but what if it's pretending?

Yes, okay, that's pretty funny.

you know what you know, and you can't borrow faith

Yes, I understand. (You can't borrow faith – definitely T-shirt number five.)

*by the way little one, if **you** want to pretend something*

Yes.

pretend there is no doubt and all is wondrous well!
now I am using your phrase – it's a good one

He was gone, and I wrote down what had transpired as well as I could. I read it over and thought – it's amazing these people are putting up with my nonsense.

On the way home I thought about my father, and I knew it would be my job to find him and to make sure he moved on. I'd always known this right from the beginning, and it fit into the entire scenario of my new world somehow. I would go into the underworld, or the lower astral realms if you prefer, and I would somehow get his attention and I would send him into the light one way or another. I knew he wasn't suffering, but I was sure he was confused and he needed me to break through into his thoughts. His guides had tried but he couldn't hear them, so they were just keeping him company and keeping an eye on him.

After the talk with Sri Bhundari this afternoon, I easily recognised him again (and didn't doubt) as he dropped a phrase into my mind, referring to my father:

a tricky extraction

This was said not to deter me in any way, on the contrary, it was meant as reinforcement to my own conclusions about the situation, and as such, it did the job.

I knew this would be some time off in the future. I wasn't ready yet, but one day I would be and I had no doubt I'd be able to pull this off, especially with all my friends on the other side. It would be two years later and beyond the eleven moons of this book before the time came, but I would never leave you hanging like this, and I can report that when we found my father and released him from that place, it was a glorious moment.

ॐ ॐ ॐ ॐ ॐ ॐ

The next day at work I was thinking about St. Francis again and I punched his name into the computer to find out a few more details about his life. When it came up that this very day, October 4 was the feast day of St. Francis, I pressed my hands together in joy and thanked the universe for yet another indication that I was on the right track, and everything was just fine.

If I needed more assistance in this department, it came after work in a small post office where they also sold children's books, should you be short on ideas for a gift to send someone. I looked at one on the display table as I lined up for my stamps and was flabbergasted to see my name – almost. The book for toddlers featured four blocks attached to the cover with a letter on each side. They could be moved around to form basic four-letter words, and the word staring at me was PETR.

That was about as close as you could get with only four letters available, and I said thank you under my breath as I passed by and reached the wicket.

This was all-encompassing now, the messages were everywhere, and all I had to do was keep my eyes and heart open.

In for a penny – in for a pound.

Hi mum! Yes I guess I'm in for a pound at this point, or maybe even a guinea! (A guinea being twenty-one shillings to a pound's twenty.) I remember you saying that a lot when I was little too.

I rode home and fed Henry with six other cats hoping to get some of Henry's dinner. Sometimes it was a little too much trying to keep the other ones at bay long enough for Henry to eat his canned food – it was the only type of food he would eat.

keep your shirt on!

This came out of my mouth, with that Irish accent, and it was Gwen of course. How interesting that it wasn't just in my head this time, but had come flying out of my mouth seemingly of its own accord. This was all she had to say this time.

I went upstairs and sat on the bed, thinking about my family and the people who had come before me. I decided to send a note to Vera from work tomorrow asking for her help in trying to put the family together, if nothing else, I knew she was enjoying my sudden obsession with the bloodlines, and I knew families reincarnated in groups and there was so much to discover and learn. It was the women who fascinated me the most, but better check into those men too, right? I'd better try and keep a nice balance here.

My mind drifted away again to insects and I thought about the wasps and the flies. I was so ecstatically joyous to have connected to the animal kingdom and the insect world had come-on so strong. I despaired that I hadn't been taught to respect these amazing creatures right from the start.

At that moment I felt something on my wrist, and I looked down to see a tiny fly sitting there! Oh my goodness, this universe was something else altogether! It was as though this little guy was consoling me, forgiving me. I now felt honoured and blessed when an insect landed on me, or walked on me, and people would probably think me bonkers at this point, I mused. "He thinks he can talk to bugs, and he thinks flies really like him! - ha ha ha here you go Mr. Nelson, put this nice white dinner jacket on will you?"

Well, if this was madness, I'd take it any day over the insanity I saw all around me in the everyday world - any day. I'd just better be careful who I say what to - that's all.

Colin and Joy came to mind. The months were flying by, and I wondered when or indeed if I would ever be able to tell them about their mother talking to me from the great beyond. I just wanted them to know she was alive and well and watching over them. If they wanted proof, well maybe I could give them some, but if not my message still might ring a bell of sorts. Mum B knew I was thinking about her and so she placed a nice precise thought in my mind:

They do think about me, maybe they sense me sometimes...

Okay Mum B, well that's a start anyway, I just don't know anymore. I'll do my best - I promised you I would - and I'll never give up trying.

᚛ ᚛ ᚛ ᚛ ᚛ ᚛

The next day at work was Friday and I came up with the idea of "Survey #1." It consisted of nine questions about life and death, but the first question was all that really mattered. "Do you think death is annihilation?" After that I wrote, "If yes, please stop here." I had fun with this and subsequently gave it to a few people who came into the store, and they seemed to have no issue with answering it.

When I gave it to Colin I was overjoyed to find out he did *not* think death was annihilation! Now we were getting somewhere! Buoyed by this, I e-mailed it to his sister, emphasising the just-for-fun aspect, and it was a total disaster. It just rubbed her the wrong way in every way imaginable and the response was crushing. The only thing to come out of it was that she thought death was "the end," but maybe there was some residual energy. This didn't bode well for telling her about her mother, not to mention that she seemed to think I was a total idiot.

I'm sorry Mum B! I seem to have completely alienated your daughter, so I guess Colin's the only hope now.

I felt a wave of complete understanding and support from her – no words were necessary – but I still felt I'd made a huge mistake somehow. Something good has to come out of this somehow though, right? With any luck, maybe Joy would just forget all about it in a year or so... or maybe she wouldn't.

Once again I came back to my intent. My intent had been pure and I was only trying to lead up to telling her about her mum and how happy she was where she is now, so even though it had backfired, I'd done my best and in the end, only wanted to eventually comfort her. My mum and yours have tea!

So, I found even something done with the intention of helping someone can blow-up in your face – how interesting. Finesse came to mind again. I must have finesse with what I'm doing here.

After work I went to visit a friend by taking a cab and the driver began to talk about Hindus and "a white man who was really an Indian" and various prophets like Mohammed and Moses without any steering in that direction on my part. This was incredible! I chimed in with what I'd learned recently about Guru Nanek and Sikhism and I was almost sorry when we reached our destination.

Once home, my mother had a lot of comments to make about my situation and it was so evident how well she knew me and how she truly had watched my life in action and knew "everything that's going on."

"I know you like the back of my hand."

She also revealed to me for the first time how upset she'd been with my father when I'd begged him to let me move back home for a while, and he'd refused. She had considered him to be her representative after she'd gone, and was very disappointed in his behaviour at this juncture. I assured her it must have been for the best in the end, and I didn't hold this or anything else against him when all was said and done.

How sad it all was a month later when he now asked me to move in with him as the only way to avoid being relocated into a senior's home. I had to decline, as by then I'd already made arrangements to move myself and I'd made commitments. Instant karma seemed to be at work here, but it didn't make the situation any less unfortunate.

She made it clear she'd been very unhappy about all of this though, and I thought – wow, there's always someone watching isn't there? How frustrating it must have been for her not to be able to intervene.

It was Saturday and pouring rain outside so I went into my tent and just listened to the rain performing its drumming song. How magical is this? I could have stayed there forever but finally emerged and decided to go to the Goodwill store to see what I could find. I just had the impulse to go there and knew I should follow these nudges if at all possible.

It didn't take long to discover what I'd gone there for – "The King And I." There was the record in pristine condition for one dollar, and at home I actually had my turntable set up and ready to play these old vinyl LPs.

Shall we dance mother? I put the record on and as heart-wrenching as it was to listen to, it was glorious and I remembered all the comments she used to make at various stages of the recording. We sang and danced – her in one reality and me in mine – and the music brought both worlds together magnificently. I was in heaven too. Life had gone somewhere too exquisite to put into words and the magic swirled around the room.

The next day on Sunday I turned on the TV to immediately see the famous painting of My Lady Greensleeves appear before my eyes. I wasn't sure what could actually surprise me anymore, and I said thank you once again and over and over for all of these blessings.

Edna had been quiet so far today, so I cast my mind out to see if she was there.

*Of course I'm here. We figure you don't want to be nattered to **all** the time.*

Oh but I do mum, I do. Don't you ever worry about that.

"Write this down right now:
<u>*The conversation will not be broken.*</u>
Underline it.
Okay? That goes for all of us."

I could see she'd signed it "the boss" again, and I laughed out loud from joy and relief.

Sorry mum, it's just that sometimes I still think I'm losing it.

*"You're gaining it.
And I will never ever leave you again."*

I went out into the backyard. There was a high wind gusting about and I wanted to feel it and be a part of it. I looked down and saw a white feather sticking straight up from the ground, somehow managing to remain in place without being blown away. I gently pulled it from the earth and held on to it as I heard the wind and the spirits laughing and dancing together.

New Moon
Big-wigs and Mr. Green

I found my granddad's shirt-sleeve garter this morning after misplacing it a few weeks ago. It had always been a treasure to me, so finding it in a pocket today was like mana from heaven.

"You mean Mama from heaven!"

You really are hilarious mum, I thought I was the king of puns. Maybe I get it from you!

The week was over, it was Friday night and now Parvati decided to appear and say a few things. I'd been thinking about her and wondering if possibly there was something she wanted me to do.

my command is command yourself

I was thinking about you and wondering when I would hear from you again.

you don't have to hold me or try to keep me – I am always here

I still sometimes wonder what is happening to me. I can barely contain it. What am I becoming?

you are becoming beautiful – fear not – the stars were born somewhere

You are infinite possibilities aren't you?

I dream

Parvati was gone now, and as my mother came back I realised she'd receded far off into the distance when Parvati was here.

"I stay in the background for the big-wigs."

I spluttered with laughter. Just the idea of calling Parvati a big-wig was hilarious, and again I could hear my mother saying that term when she was alive. It was definitely her all right. Once we were both in the same dimension we'd have a lot of fun reliving these experiences – I could hardly wait, but yes, I know mum, I have some things to do first. No matter what bliss I knew was in store for me, I knew it was of the utmost importance to see this life through and I was determined to do so.

It was mid-way through October now and the leaves were changing and getting ready to fall. Mr. Green was still clearly visible, looking in the window and swaying in the wind. I was beginning to feel quite upset at the prospect of him shrivelling up and falling to the ground – as silly as I knew that was. Four and a half months had gone by and I was still crying every day – this was the reason for today's tears.

don't be upset, this is just a representation of me

This time I heard him clear as day, and my joy at this just seemed to make me cry that much harder. I was still a mess, but I found the tears to be cleansing and I was glad to be able to feel so much. Without feelings there's nothing.

Will I see you next year? I had a profound feeling I would somehow.

I'll be here – you will just have to find me

I'll find you Mr. Green, have no doubt about that. I'll look for you and I'll find you!

I know you will

I drew a sketch of him to go with the photographs I'd taken, and then I had to step away from the window and pull myself together. Oh my lord, I'm talking to a tree, to the spirit of a tree. My mind went back to Findhorn and the nature spirits I'd read about all those years ago. Now I was talking to a Deva myself and all my dreams were coming true as fast as I could handle it – or faster. I really was a wreck, but it felt like home somehow. I knew I was finally becoming the me I was always meant to be.

I woke up on Saturday thinking about Zoroaster and Zarathustra for some reason, and as soon as I could look up some information, I quickly found out these were two names for the same person. Here was someone else who believed in one God, or All That Is, and I took the information in and was pleased to learn about him. I wondered how much work I was doing in the dream world to wake up with names like this forefront in my mind.

So much was happening and I went back to the beginning when I thought I was smart enough to fool myself about all of this. It seemed like so long ago now and that didn't work anymore.

"I kept thinking – why would he think he was pretending? Until the obvious – disbelief mixed with ultimate hope."

I know mum – can you believe what I went through just trying to except what I always believed in?

what a to-do!

It was my grandma and she chimed in with a phrase I'd heard her say a thousand times before. It set us off and the three of us laughed at the poor guy who was still physical here on earth trying to figure it all out.

Then I thought of Sri Bhundari and Edna and myself, as another group of three – I'd always liked the number three. I imagined us as the mighty threesome.

three people holding hands are the maximum, before you are not holding someone's hand – this is the original power of three

It was Sri Bhundari who added this, then it was Edna's turn again:

"Remember Jane Roberts – she is your true mentor.
Even if it's all nonsense, it's the most creative time ever.
Didn't she say something like this?"

I heard her laughing after the nonsense part, and I had to agree with what she was saying. We had written music together, I was on my third notebook, and I was fairly sure the book would come to pass – and Jane Roberts *had* thought similar things when she didn't know what was really happening to her. There was nothing to worry about – even if I could worry the way I used to.

That night I wrote all this down in my journal and was amazed again how I couldn't spell basic words. Have I mentioned this? I couldn't spell and it was hilarious. I'd gone so far into the right-brain since all this had begun, I just couldn't do some basic left-brain functions, and I noticed it was still happening. It was actually exciting when I had to give up on some words after crossing them out and trying again several times.

What a laugh, I thought – this is what happens when you go dimensional.

"Are you happy?"

Yes mum – more than ever.

"See."

I did see. I'd asked for this, I'd searched for this, and there really was no going back now. How many times had I said this? Many, but with each day it became more my reality. So let's get on with it – I told myself, but first I had to go to bed and dream.

That seemed funny as I put the journal away next to my dream note-book, and realised again there was no difference between the two.

ॐ ॐ ॐ ॐ ॐ ॐ

I awoke on Sunday thinking of Parvati, so I looked at the photo of her statue for a long time. There seemed to be no reason to rush about anything, and I just stood there in at least two different worlds.

"She is paradise Peter."

I know mum, but I'd better come out of it and do a few things... it's Sunday and I have another day off.

I went out and arrived at the bus stop the moment the bus appeared, and during the course of the day several things happened: once again change fell out of my wallet in the exact amount I needed, I found a feather and a lovely black beaded bracelet, I looked up and out of the bus window the second we passed the "Goddess Hair Salon," and I saw an advertisement for a TV show called Heroes that was about evolution and people with "special" abilities.

Everything was still backing me up, and I sailed through the day in a blissful dream, getting home eventually to record Lawrence Welk for Aunt Ciss and I to watch later.

I glanced at the clock as I finally went to bed to see 1, 2, 3 on the display. This had recently taken over from 11:11, and I would now see sequential numbers like this everywhere. I couldn't help but think 1 – 2 – 3 – Go! It was like I'd finally entered the real life and I was on my way.

The next morning at work, 11:11 did show up again however, and I mentioned it to Ed the Xerox technician who was on the scene repairing a machine.

"Did you make a wish?" he asked, and I laughed as I thought that all my wishes had recently come true and I wouldn't know what to ask for next. It turned out Ed and his family had been seeing this for quite a while themselves, and in *his* house you had to make a wish. How interesting! And now I knew why I'd mentioned it in the first place.

Yes, clocks are doing some pretty interesting things lately – I offered to Ed, and I didn't know how true that would be in a very short time. I had a moment and wondered why I'd said clocks instead of time.

First Quarter

Time Flies

I awoke Friday morning to go to work and looked on my night-table to see what time it was and... my clock was gone. It was just... gone. This didn't make any sense at all. I remembered setting it last night all as usual and then I'd simply gone to sleep.

I checked one of the other clocks in the room (there were three) to make sure I wasn't late, and then I went down the hall towards my music room, basically looking for my clock. In the hall outside the room and on top of an upturned trunk – there sat my clock, with the cord dangling down in exactly the same configuration it would be had it not been moved at all. My friends on the other side were being quiet about this little trick, but I just knew it was them – humour is something else that just cuts through somehow. I was astounded.

If I'd have moved the clock myself (why?), I would have wrapped the cord around it, and I wouldn't have just left it sitting there in the hall. I've never sleep-walked, and even if I did, why would I do this?

All the time I was having these typical intellectual responses, I knew the clock had actually dematerialised from its place in the bedroom, to appear here with the cord and everything exactly the same. I picked it up and stared at it, turning it over and over as if it would suddenly start talking to me, and then I took it back where it belonged.

Being a digital clock, it obviously didn't show a time until I plugged it in and reset it, and I wondered what time would have been frozen on it had it been an analog device. I was left with that tantalising mystery as I got myself ready for work. I had a few ideas about that one all right.

I also remembered what I'd said to Ed just two days ago about "clocks" doing interesting things lately. There was precognition in that statement, and now I understood why it had seemed weird to say clocks instead of time. It had been to get my attention and set it in my mind somehow. What a way to start the day!

I sat down and had a cigarette before setting off for work, to take in and savour the clock story, and a perfect smoke-ring left the end of my cigarette like Gandalf or something. I could feel the magic everywhere as I stepped out into the day, and said hello to the birds and squirrels as I got my bike.

I looked at these little creatures and thought of what is probably my favourite hymn – All Things Bright And Beautiful. And the next line – all creatures great and small. I always really loved that hymn, and as I looked at the life in front of me chirping and scurrying, I saw that "life" is one category, with each identity being inviolate. Does that make sense? Not only is it one category, but it's everything – there is no "dead" stuff. There really isn't.

My lord Neli, all this before you've even gone to work? Grab that bike and get going! Come on, that's it, not long now before it'll be too cold to ride but today's okay – off you go – better get some air in those tires on the way home though.

I was at the mall after work and the traffic was so heavy, the cars were backed up coming in and going out of the parking lot. An East Indian salesman was standing outside of his store having a cigarette, taking it all in when our eyes met. He shook his head as if to say – just look at this will you.

It's a lesson in patience – I replied to his unspoken question, and he got the strangest look on his face.

Yes, and that would be a good lesson for us all to learn wouldn't it? – he added, as we smiled at each other and I walked on.

Just little things like that were happening now, and I hoped I'd helped him somehow, maybe just changing his perspective a little bit. I hoped so, and I realised my presence on this earth actually meant something. Teaching and learning seemed to be the same thing somehow.

Before bed that night, Gwen came to visit me again and as she was speaking to me I saw another one of those black shapes in the room. This was the largest one so far and I assumed it must be her. Again, there was nothing negative or threatening about it, and as she left it disappeared with her so I concluded that I must've been correct about its origin. I peered into the dark for a long time before finally closing my eyes and wondering what tomorrow would bring.

༄ ༄ ༄ ༄ ༄ ༄

My confidence was growing. It'd been almost five months now and how much reassurance did I need? I also realised I couldn't use Edna as a secondary type of conscience, and whatever conclusions I needed to come to, I had to come to by myself.

The time had gone faster than any I'd experienced yet on this earth, and in a way it made things a bit more difficult because it seemed like all of this had just begun yesterday.

I sensed Parvati's presence, and I could see her sitting in our spot under the tree by the stream:

it makes it harder for you to assimilate, because the months are gone like the wind and time is a dream

I wanted to pry open my vision and crawl inside, to actually be with her with all of my being, and I thought again of how perfect she was for me as an embodiment of the creator.

for you, with God... you prefer talking to a woman

I thought of the first time she'd come to me, and my splashdown in the bath.

I had to get your attention, and... I can deliver

She faded away with a smile, and I gasped a little at her leaving and at her having come to me in the first place, but I knew she was always here and I would never be alone.

During the course of the week I noticed that when I asked a question to a spirit on the other side and they didn't know the answer, or want to tell me, they would say:

I'm not occupied with it

I thought this was absolutely hilarious and I really had a good laugh with it. I had to remember that one the next time I didn't know something!

Sherrie dropped by and laughingly told me – I'm the happiest I've ever been in my life! With a certain emphasis on the word life which made it even funnier. She mentioned the "vividity" of everything on the other side, and I looked forward to the time when I would see her again and maybe she would show me a thing or two.

moon six

sea of feathers

I was trying to keep it all together as well as I could and not forget about anyone even though my own life was so awe-inspiring and intense. So on Sunday I remembered to turn on Lawrence Welk, and I was joined by Edna, Aunt Ciss and my grandma and granddad. Sitting there with four spirits I couldn't physically see was quite an experience, but somehow I managed to actually see some of the show through the blur of tears.

I could see them clearly in my inner-sight though, and they appeared to me on a long couch looking ready to share a programme and each other's company. I wouldn't have been surprised to see my mum asking if anyone wanted a mint – she never went anywhere without some mints.

The next day at work I actually felt a little low, and I could hardly believe it possible. Had it come to this already? I had to think about this for a minute. After all the wonders that had happened and were still happening, how could I dare to feel any less than elated?

I told myself I was doing very well actually, and that this was the power of a dense reality such as this. The way this world was set up at the moment just wasn't conducive to being happy most of the time, not with the fear and everything, and again I cheered all of us for having the courage to live physical lives here during these very trying times.

A young guy who worked for a company that had recently rented part of our space was a new face on the scene, and I noticed whenever I said – Hi, how's it going?, he would always answer by pointing forward and saying, "Straight ahead." That was all he ever said to me, and I couldn't help but think this was excellent advice in general and I took the idea to heart.

Almost five months had gone by, and I was going to be rather relieved once I'd made it past the six month window. My mother had said less than two years to live or more like six months if I didn't turn things around on one level or another, and I was wondering if I really had.

At least on the internal spiritual level things had definitely turned around and I wondered if that was going to be enough to abort the six months to two year timeframe for simply dying and leaving all this behind.

I was sure this was the summation life now regardless, and in a way it would be all right if things did turn out that way, especially now I had a lot of those answers I'd been looking for – first hand, but I decided after all these physical years getting this far, I wasn't going to just give up so easily, so I nipped out for ten minutes to get those chips and that milkshake while saying thank you to potatoes and cows for saving my life.

Sometimes I just didn't know how my poor body was carrying on day after day, especially dealing with these new extraordinary developments that were all I could have ever hoped for on the one hand, but left my body racked and drained a lot of the time, on the other.

The place was only three minutes away and I walked through a tunnel of trees that some thoughtful person had planted on the property next door. I walked through them with my arms straight out and I didn't care if anyone saw me and wondered if I was a little peculiar or looking for attention. I felt the energy flowing between me and the trees.

It was lunch time for the world and I looked at some folks sitting on the large boulders outside of the place, chatting and having their lunches – it was warm and sunny for October. As I got closer I could begin to see their faces clearly and my vision swung to one man sitting there having a cigarette, and it was Steaven.

It wasn't him of course, but it seemed like the man's face was temporarily over-shadowed by Steaven's or the features had shifted for a moment and he looked up and right at me with full recognition!

An excited shudder ran though me, and I knew that my friend had momentarily merged with this man and was having a quick three-dimensional look at this guy who seemed to be able to hear and see him. The man looked away as he became himself again and I had to fight the tears as I resolutely carried on to the restaurant door and went inside.

Standing in the queue waiting to be served, I was close to the ladies' washroom and idly watching people go in and out, as one lady turned and stared at me in the same way the man outside just had. A look of greeting and recognition – just for a second – and this time it was my Auntie Edith!

I hadn't had any direct contact with this younger sister of my father's yet, I knew she was very busy looking out for my father, but it was her features and her hair and her *eyes* for the briefest flash before she continued into the washroom.

It was hard to speak as my turn to order came up and I paid and left and drifted back to work in a blissful dream.

Sri Bhundari and Edna and White Feather swirled around me while I did my job for the rest of the afternoon, and sent me visions of beauty and love and hope. Soon enough it was five o'clock and time to go home. I added a photo of Shiva to my screensaver before shutting the computer down, and then I commenced the ritual of locking the doors, turning off the lights and closing the blinds on the front window.

I glanced out the window as I performed this last duty and I just froze as tears sprang into my eyes – I just couldn't credit what I was seeing. It was still light outside as daylight saving time wouldn't end for another week yet, and I robotically finished my duties and left the building by the front door, for once.

The front lawn of Positive Print was covered with white feathers. I mean covered – you could barely see the grass at all – there must have been hundreds, if not a thousand or more evenly spread right over the lawn. They were nowhere else, not next door or across the street or on the road – they were just... here.

I was astonished beyond astonishment and I gasped and gaped at this sign that was just for me and impossible to ignore, or dismiss, or rationalise.

My mind started to go down the road of logical explanation, but I put the brakes on right away – I wouldn't insult this message from God by doing that. I walked across the now white lawn trying not to step on any of them, which was impossible, and I gathered what I could to add to my ever-increasing collection of feathers. I picked up a hand-full and sniffed them deeply... they had to be seagull feathers, and I thanked the seagulls and the earth and the sky... I didn't want to leave. In another world I would have lain face down with my arms spread wide.

For some reason today I didn't have my camera with me, so I had no way to record it. Of all days to forget my camera! I saw myself racing home to get it and flying back before the wind blew them away, and then I thought no... this was just as it should be. This vision had to just live inside me somehow, and had nothing to do with photographs or records or "proof" of anything or for anything. This was this moment only and I drank it in like a kind of spiritual nectar, eventually walking around to the back to collect my bike and go home.

I slowly rode past this sea of feathers and I had one last, long look before I set my sights for home. I would never forget this moment no matter what would happen in this world or any other. I am blessed beyond anything I could've imagined – I thought, as I slowly pedalled away.

Last Quarter
Diwali and Rex

I was thinking about Hinduism and the Atman (or soul) and things such as this when I found out that Diwali, the festival of lights, was almost here. The computer at work was invaluable for bringing things like this to me that I may have missed otherwise.

That night I found myself alone in the bedroom, and I was just sitting in a dream, thinking of nothing and everything at the same time somehow.

Something caught my eye, so I very slowly turned my view towards it – it seemed delicate, and I didn't want to sweep it away with my eyes. It didn't go anywhere, and I had a clear view of what was before me for a good three seconds, I'd say. It was a flame, inside a circle – and then I noticed the circle was actually a bubble! A flame, about the size of a candle flame, in a perfect sphere, and it just slowly floated through the air.

Three seconds doesn't sound like very long, but if you time it you'll notice it's more than enough to identify what you're actually seeing. I had no doubt as to what it was. After discovering the Diwali festival earlier in the day, it made perfect sense to me how it related to that, and of course with Sri Bhundari and everything, it was obvious.

All I could do was press my hands together in gratitude and go outside to look at the Moon.

☙ ☙ ☙ ☙ ☙ ☙

By now Rex was just popping in on a regular basis and letting me know he was always here and waiting for me to "hurry up." This dog really was the best dog ever to grace the earth, but I know everyone thinks that about their own dog, and that's as it should be.

He's a cross-bred terrier, a rusty colour, and he has the temperament of a saint. When a ten-year-old me was told we were going to immigrate to Canada, I quickly said – I'm not going anywhere without Rex! –

thinking this would stop the madness in its tracks. Little did I know this had all been anticipated, and the answer was – of course Rex is going with us.

Thinking back, he really was the difference between being absolutely destroyed by this insane idea, to it seeming at least possible, or tolerable. He was my world and somehow I could leave England and still take my world with me. No rabies in England, so no quarantine or anything, and he was coming on the same ship as us, so I could see him and walk him every day on the voyage!

Whenever I looked at his photo on my wall, or thought of him at all (one thought away also applied to him), he always had something to say to me, and we quickly dealt with the issue of me taking him to the vets that last time, and the decision I made. This almost killed me. Did I ever think that one day I would get to talk to him and try to justify one of the hardest decisions of my life?

The grace of these creatures is beyond discussion and he made it very, very clear that he'd had enough of his old tired body, and *he* knew (if I didn't) that we would be together again before too long. The beings we call animals are fully aware of their own multi-dimensionality and how things work, far more than we are at this time. If there's an animal on this planet a bit slow on the uptake – you know who it is.

So once we got that bit of business out of the way, we were free to talk and be together again in a new way, now that I'd gained this awareness and realised he had never left my side.

This is critical for anyone who loves the animal kingdom and wonders where their pets go, or if they have "souls," and all that other nonsense about the differences between us. The crucial thing here is when your animal friend attains a sense of identity and develops free will from a loving contact with human beings. This exposure to love and emotional involvement in our lives creates individual identity, and short-circuits the returning to a collective animal consciousness upon death. (Of course ultimately we're all part of one unified consciousness down the line.)

Our own consciousness raises the beloved animal's vibrations, it rubs off so to speak. I remembered Seth saying that contact with friendly humans causes the animal's consciousness to be "immeasurably quickened." That sounded real good to me.

If none of this was true, well, I just wouldn't want to be around. Physical life, or any kind of eternal spiritual existence for that matter, without animals and animal spirits would be beyond tolerable. This idea of us as humans helping animals to spiritually progress, simply by loving them and wanting them to share emotionally in our lives, is for me, one of the greatest gifts God has bestowed upon us.

I know we help each other to progress too, in myriad ways, but at least I knew we were all stumbling along in the same direction anyway, and we had to have attained a certain level of consciousness and self-awareness to be operating these very complex human forms.

When it came to the animal kingdom, and this incredible contribution we can give to them, I felt a kind of honour and pride, and I hoped that in the grander scheme of things this would help to balance the debt somehow. I couldn't bear to think of the injustices done to animals on this planet every day, but I knew somehow that every bit of love and *respect* we show to even one animal in our own homes or backyards, travelled out and through the entire animal kingdom.

Not only were we spiritually advancing our own animal friends in a mightily powerful way, but we were also giving all the other creatures in the world *hope*. Hope that one day the noisy heavy people would wake up once again and know there is no separation between us.

The animal kingdom has seen it all – human beings at their best and human beings at their worst. I had to remember that we didn't have the power to destroy the consciousness of a flea, and animals currently "extinct" because of our blindness, were still flying and swimming and gambolling about – just not here. They weren't here anymore because we were no longer *worthy* of them.

So, they *are* souls, just like us, with a consciousness as valid and eternal as our own, and although I've said you must make up your own mind about everything, there's no question about this in my heart. If I'm certain about anything at all – I'm certain of this, and I wouldn't say it unless I knew. They are souls who are free to grow and evolve and become more with no limitations – just like us – and once that bond of love is there, it never dissipates. I remembered Seth again when referring to animals *and* human beings – "the mechanics of consciousness remain the same."

There was no need to worry. If your animal friend should go before you do... they wait for you. With my new life and abilities, I was living the truth of this before I'd even died, and my earthly life was turning into my kind of heaven right before my very eyes.

Thank you Rex! It only made sense – it had to be this way – and my mind flashed back to a time when I didn't know what I believed about anything at all... but I *knew* death was not annihilation for anyone. Anything else would have just been... what? Ludicrous?

Sometimes they send signs through other animals who might show up in your backyard and somehow remind you of your dog or cat. (I'm sticking to dogs and cats at the moment because that's who I know about the most.) Shortly after they cross, once they've got the hang of things, you might see unexpected colours or markings on a bird or a squirrel that just look so much like your dog, for instance. With the help of your guides on the other side, they can of course get messages across with synchronicities from anywhere or everywhere – you might see their name popping up all over – and sometimes they will occasionally merge with your new animal friend, and you'll wonder how your new cat or dog could possibly have the same unique behavioural quirk. You'll know.

If they can stay with a family member who has crossed over – fine, but if there's no one like that, there are places where these animals are taken to wait for you. There are beautiful meadows and woodlands to run and play in, with people who adore animals and gladly devote themselves to their care while they wait. With telepathy having full play, it's easy for these caregivers to merge with Rover or Fluffy, and to manifest exactly what is needed for maximum comfort and joy. Until they have developed enough to do this themselves, these animal lovers will manifest familiar environments, with the favourite cushion or chair on which our friends can rest and put their heads down... and the favourite food to eat. Like us, they will soon learn they don't need sleep or food but can still engage in these activities anytime they want to just for fun and pleasure.

No detail is overlooked by these heart-workers when it comes to the care and tending of our eternal friends. People on both sides engage in this work, and if you feel a pull to do this – you probably already are.

I have a friend from Positive Print called Ann who does this work, and a lot of children who cross-over take on this job also. Rex waited with my grandma and granddad before my mother arrived on the scene.

Oh Rex, there you were on day one with Gordon and me in the coffee shop... there you were. And yes I see you there curled up on the bed by my feet just waiting for the day... the cats know you're there too. I have your collar and your medals, but we won't need those next time will we....

new Moon

Alarm Bells

Monday at work they played "The Skye Boat Song" and I just had to stop everything as well as I could and listen. Always one of my favourites, this old Scottish song took on a new meaning when I heard the line "over the sea to Skye," and instead of traveling to the Isle of Skye, I saw us all travelling into the sky.

I couldn't help but think of "Into The Mystic" once again. There were connections with everything, and I was feeling better about the world and myself as I realised we were in for the ride of our lives. I was excited! So many things were going to change for so many people in the next few years, and I hoped all of us could flow with it and handle all the necessary adjustments with as much grace as possible.

The rest of the week was fairly quiet compared to the way it had been going sometimes, when I could barely keep my journal up to date with all the experiences and wonder. I added the Sanskrit symbol for Om to my screensaver, along with a snow-hare and a photograph of the heart birthmark.

I was all right with the quieter times now, after all that concern about maybe sliding backwards or whatever I was afraid of, and I thought to myself – do you think you're going to wake up one day and suddenly not know how to play the piano?

When it came to clutching and grasping and possessing, these were things the Buddhists had warned us about all along, and I knew it was just as applicable to spiritual awareness and knowledge as much as anything else. Attachment is one of Buddhism's favourite words, and it can only exist in a world of duality where one thing is seen as separate from another.

This wasn't something I had now. It wasn't something I'd gained and had to keep... it was something I *was* now. There was no separation. It was actually who I'd always been, and these deeper truths had been patiently waiting for me all along. All I had to do was flow with it.

Those sequential numbers were turning up everywhere. I would see 1-2-3 or 1-2-3-4 or 2-3-4 etc., on clocks or house numbers or licence plates (licence plates in general turned out to be a rich source for messages), and I thought about the twenty-three years since my mother left this reality – that was a sequential number too.

Then I realised I'd lived with my parents for twenty-three years before leaving home, and somehow this seemed like an interesting kind of balance. There were so many things to think about when it came to numbers.

On Friday, my own life was starting to feel different, and I recognised this feeling from past experience with myself. Major events in my life seemed to be decided somewhere else sometimes, and then I would find myself going through the motions knowing the real work was done, and all I was doing was catching up in a way.

It started with a client from across the street coming in, and being very upset with me because I hadn't billed him earlier, as now it was a bit more than he wanted to pay at one time. He really let me have it, and after he left I was quite upset. I thought I was doing him a favour and not bothering him with lesser amounts until the invoice was worth writing up, but I guess not. It was another one of those situations where doing what you thought was best for someone, completely backfired.

Then I thought about how I'd been elected to add billing to my repertoire after Ann had left the company and no one had been hired to take on her responsibilities. It was just one more thing I was expected to do now. It really got to me, and at quarter to four I knew I had to go home an hour early, so I told the boss I had to go. The reaction to that was one of resistance, and how do you like that? Considering I ran the show here and had never even taken a holiday for eleven years, just added to the feeling that I'd been used for too long, and I felt used up.

Getting myself together to go home regardless, I was up by the front counter when the door chime went off... and then again. Two more times it chimed, for a total of four as I was finishing up what I could before I left.

By now of course I knew it was my mother, but she was being quiet other than this, and I had a feeling she was ringing the alarm bells.

I know mum. I feel it too and I don't know what I'll do after this, but I'm glad you're there.

I went to shut down my computer, and found a note from Walking Wolf Woman regarding a couple of things we'd talked about earlier.

The day before, she'd sent me a beautiful poem and I loved it. She now told me – "George Harrison sang it in my ear." I hadn't told her I'd felt George around myself, so I was ecstatic. As if this wasn't enough, in response to a photograph of the birthmark, she'd now sent a video of the band Savuka performing "Great Heart." I quietly watched and listened as I got the rest of my things together:

> The world is full of strange behaviour
> Every man has to be his own saviour
> I know I can make it on my own if I try
> But I'm searching for a Great Heart to stand me by

I thanked Lorraine for this gift, and with tears stinging my eyes, I shut down the machine, grabbed my gear, and headed for the back door.

First Quarter
Something In The Air

The weekend disappeared into history and all I could really think about was what I was going to do on Monday morning, and whether I was actually going to go to work. Nothing had really happened other than leaving an hour early on Friday, so I was clear to go back and just continue on as before if I wanted to.

It was November 19 and quite chilly outside, so I decided to walk to work and just see what I would do once I got there.

Everything was there waiting for me, so familiar and so comfortable after eleven years, and I put my knapsack in the usual place and turned on the computer.

I had a note waiting for me from Susan, and I noticed she'd sent me an MP3 of a song from long ago that she thought I would like. She was right. "Something In The Air" by Thunderclap Newman was the song in question and I'd always loved it, but it was the title now that had my attention.

I just stared at it for a while in amazement. How could she have known?

With no access to a computer over the weekend, I hadn't sent anyone a message saying what I was thinking or that something was indeed in the air. Of course I knew the real communication was all under the surface, and that friends always knew when something was going on. It was fun to just gape though, and be amazed.

This coupled with the four chimes on Friday helped me to understand that the universe was way ahead of me, and I clicked on the song and let the melody fill the air.

> Call out the instigators
> Because there's something in the air
> We've got to get together sooner or later
> Because the revolution's here, and you know it's right
> And you know that it's right

We have got to get it together
We have got to get it together now

Oh lord, what was I going to do? I'd better get it together all right. There was a huge job coming in today or tomorrow that we weren't equipped to do, but I was somehow supposed to figure out. There were my regular customers, some of whom were old and only wanted to deal with me, and I loved helping them out. There was Roxy....

If that beautiful poodle had arrived in the next hour or so, I don't know what I would have done, but by ten-thirty I found myself gathering up my things and copying the latest additions from my secret Bardo folder to disc... and getting ready to leave.

Fortunately I'd been saving all of my research to disc as I went along, so this now stood me in good stead as it only took a few minutes to top up the disc. I told the one employee who had arrived that I didn't feel well, and by eleven o'clock I was out the door.

That night the boss called knowing something was up, and I couldn't talk but the message got through that yes, I had resigned. The only thing now was my photographs on the wall and my radio and cup still sitting there. This gave me one more opportunity to change my mind and say – I don't know what came over me. But I knew it was really over, and the next day in a ten minute whirlwind, I rolled up the photographs that were all neatly attached to green cover-stock, deleted the Bardo folder, grabbed the radio and cup and left for the very last time. I thanked the Goddess that once again, Roxy was not there.

So I left the job at eleven o'clock on the eleventh month after being there for eleven years. It wasn't until I got my record of employment form a week or so later, that I realised I'd worked there eleven years to the actual day! I'd started on November 20, 1996 and if I'd have worked one more day, it would have been the first day of the twelfth year. When I saw this, the last vestige of uncertainty about my decision was eradicated and I knew I'd put in the exact right amount of time at the company, and now it truly was time to move on. I said thank you with all my heart for this clear sign that I'd done the right thing.

I was now out of a job, with no computer, and in Ontario at this time if you resigned from a job, the chances of receiving any employment insurance benefits were virtually nil. I had no idea what I was going to do from here, but I dutifully applied anyway, and I thought to myself – if I could only talk to a female worker about this....

That night Edna touched me on the left shoulder with a firm squeeze and I knew everything would be all right somehow. I went into my tent, lit a candle and listened to the wind, thinking about the true wealth I'd somehow now acquired in my life. I saw myself running and flying through the stones at Stonehenge, and I sensed Duncan there.

I thought of the heart birthmark on my wrist and how this magical symbol now represented living through the heart to me, and it only made sense I would have this sign for this particular lifetime. I thought of Marie and "You were born with a mark...." Then I considered how sometimes things like this represented an injury from another life, a gunshot wound maybe, as I'd heard about things like that.

My vision now travelled to another time and place and I was riding a fine horse while holding an unsheathed sword pointed at the ground with my right hand. There was a mighty storm underway with booming thunder and flashes of lightning across the dark sky as I guided my horse with my left hand as we headed up a slope towards a high cliff. The rain was lashing down making it difficult to see, and it would have been so much easier guiding my mount with both hands, but I wouldn't sheath that sword for some reason.

I wondered if this was one of my too few warrior lives, but there was no one else around, and I had the feeling "he" only wanted his sword to be part of the storm. He glanced at it every now and then, being careful not to take his sight off the trail for more than a second or two, watching the rain run down to the tip and feeling the thunder reverberate up the blade to the hilt and into his hand.

I came back to myself slightly... hearing the wind in my own world, and hoping his rain wasn't a convenient way for him to wash off the blood. It was a slightly chilling thought but I saw no evidence of this, nor did I really want to, and I thought again of Sri Bhundari's admonition that I hadn't had enough lives like this with the masculine energy allowed full reign.

Back into the vision, he/I reached the top of the cliff and stopped, raising the sword high up towards the sky, and it seemed as though it could actually almost touch the roiling clouds as he turned his rain-soaked face towards the heavens and waited.

I found myself holding my breath in both worlds as only a moment or two went by before a bolt of lightning came streaking down as though by invitation, striking the sword tip and travelling down to his hand and away.

It was like something out of "Highlander," and somehow neither he nor his horse were injured in any way, but at that second I knew the lightning had left him with a burn... with a mark... on his wrist.

It didn't matter if this was plausible or not in the physical world I currently lived in, and it didn't matter if this was truly another incarnation of mine or an allegory for the magic of the birthmark. It just didn't matter, and I could check into that later if I wanted to. This was an amazing vision regardless, and I thought to myself – this just gets better and better.

I opened my eyes to the candle still flickering in the tent and watched my hands move of their own accord as though feeling fabric, as though they could touch the magic in the air somehow, and I thought of Parvati and all the things she had said to me. I had a moment when I thought of how truly incredible things had become and I hoped I wasn't putting words in her mouth somehow.

you put life in my mouth – and I put life in yours

That was loud and clear. Everything was true and it had all really happened to me. I sensed the light of my being and wondered if the tent was glowing from the outside.

Eventually I unzipped the tent, stepped out and looked up at the stars. They seemed brighter than I'd ever seen them in the city before, and they winked at me as I raised my hands up as high as I could to touch their magic.

Moon Seven
A Glimpse of Heaven

I was getting used to this new freedom of not having to go to work each day, and I was available to do things like go with Officer Jane to her dentist appointment. I looked across the street from my seat in the waiting room, and saw a huge sign for a restaurant. "Awaken your inner-self" it read, and I just had to smile.

Somehow in the corporate advertising world this had seemed a good way to sell hamburgers, but of course to me it meant something else, and who knows? – maybe some people would actually take the message to heart and think about a few deeper issues.

It seemed to me like the world was trying all the ways it could to get the idea across that it was time to wake up and take our true place in the scheme of things. I felt like the universe was just waiting and whispering – come on... you can do it.

The next day it snowed for ten minutes and I was in heaven. I'd been waiting for this and I could feel my spirit rise as I turned my face up to meet this magic from the sky. What was it about snow? Everything! It just did something inside of me nothing else could in just that way, and three friends had something to say.

First it was White Feather:

I see you've found a friend!

Then Parvati:

for you

And finally, my mother:

"Do you feel better now?"

I sure do mum! It was November 27 now, and this was just a taste of things to come. I could hardly wait until it engulfed the city and muffled all the noise, leaving only the sighing sound of it softly falling and dusting everything white. Maybe that was part of it, everything became so bright, the light increased everywhere, and just maybe it really was a peek at other side – a glimpse of heaven. It was for me.

Later that evening I saw Aunt Ciss with two relatives who had recently crossed over – Betty and George. They were all laughing, and from Betty and George I heard, "We know who you are now!" This was pretty funny, as the last time I'd seen them, at their daughter Allison's funeral, they hadn't remembered who I was, and Betty had even said to me, "Do you know Sandra?" as she gestured towards my sister!

None of that mattered now, as they were piecing things together on the other side as I was trying to do here, and I could still hear the three of them laughing as they faded away with smiles on their faces.

The next day White Feather showed up again.

how are you?

I told him I was all right, and I felt him enter me in a way similar to the way my mother had when she'd run her "diagnostic" on me. This time it didn't escape me that the word "Gnostic" was right there contained in that word.

Gnosticism and salvation through esoteric spiritual knowledge was definitely something I could relate to, although I didn't agree that matter was base and flesh impure. The physical body is very holy ground, and you won't advance spiritually at all by denying the sacredness of the physical world.

I saw White Feather nodding as he re-emerged from me, so I guessed he felt I was doing okay as he came towards me and once again, we went sailing up into the air and straight out into the cosmos together. For White Feather, nature was the entire universe.

This time we went further and faster than before, and I willed myself to remember as much as I could, but I knew most of what was happening was far beyond my ordinary mind, so I just let myself go and tried to simply retain a sense of self. This guy's way of introducing you to the universe, was to grab you by the collar and literally drag you out there. Then you seem to pass-out.

I slowly regained the footing of my rational mind as I saw the earth quickly coming into focus beneath us. We were coming in feet-first. The speed, if I can use that word, was stunning but somehow natural, and familiar.

can you make it back on your own?

I conveyed the thought "yes" to him, and to myself I added – I think.

As I plummeted closer I heard one more thought as he disappeared from me:

the atmosphere won't harm you

This was great when people knew what you were thinking... I'd had a moment there when I wondered if I'd burn up upon re-entry. But that was the physical world, and I was something else now and those rules didn't apply. I saw North America and then I was back in Toronto, in my room, and in my body once again.

I had one last vision of White Feather beside the river next to his fire, and he sent a final thought before he faded away:

that was some elevator ride!

ಸ ಸ ಸ ಸ ಸ ಸ

The next day was the sixth-year anniversary of George Harrison's departure from this realm, and as they played another one of his songs on the radio, I closed my eyes and Edna and I were on a carpet silently flying high across England.

I'd been thinking about a few things relating to our current relationship, and how it all worked, and she addressed these issues now with a couple of succinct thoughts:

*"Most of my **essence** is with you."*

And

"Don't worry about the time thing – now is now, in either reality."

She also had a comment about my current situation after Positive Print, and the last six months:

"Move into the next phase of your life with élan."

Not really wanting to leave the flying carpet, I reluctantly opened my eyes, came back down to earth, and wrote down what she'd said.

"It's quite something watching you write down my words."

I can imagine mum, and believe me, it's quite something from my end too.

I went for a walk, and as I was passing St. Anselm's Catholic Church, I saw a bird and my mind drifted along thinking about how amazing they were, and how Seth had said birds are, "God flying." Less than two seconds after this thought, a flock of birds – hundreds – came out of nowhere and circled high above me to land in the tree beside the church, all talking at once and somehow managing to fit in the same tree.

In some other life I might have said "It was as if..." but it wasn't some other life – it was this one – and those birds knew what I thought and decided to put on a show just to make sure I knew they knew, and they were ecstatic to be recognised for what they were.

Once I realised I was standing frozen on the sidewalk with my mouth open, I closed it and slowly carried on my way up the street, in awe of this tiny corner of the universe.

Last Quarter
Through and Through

It was December 2 now and six months had somehow gone by and still here! Happy anniversary to me! How could this be? Maybe I'd make it past the two year mark as well.

I was astounded and I could see Edna smiling and nodding. I'd wondered if I would physically make it this far, or if I was actually handling things the best way I could, even with all the never-ending reassurances, but now after six months I could put all of that behind me.

"We're hooked-in tooth and claw."

Yes mum we are! We really are – we did it we did it we did it! I must have said thank you to the universe a hundred times, and I felt more blessed than I would have thought possible. This was becoming a recurrent thought.

"We'll never be disconnected again."

No, we won't. We had worn this path down to the rocks now... the bones.

I was full of a new kind of confidence only time could bring, and I was beginning to see I *had* made it through this transformation – at least this far anyway. Six months and still breathing was a good start no matter how you looked at it. If the next six months went this fast, it would soon be a full year. I had a feeling they would go even faster still though.

It was my physical body I was a bit more concerned about, now I was sure my mind was intact and somewhat reliable. I'm telling you though, it was touch and go there for a while even though I understood what was happening. I thought of Marie the Yoga teacher and her saying – "If you're not prepared...."

I was beginning to think no one could be fully prepared for what had happened to me, and a line from a Leonard Cohen song came into my mind – "I stepped into an avalanche." The second line – "It covered up my soul" didn't work, so I changed it to, "opened" up my soul. That worked so much better, and I sang it aloud and figured Leonard wouldn't mind the slight variation.

An avalanche is definitely what it had felt like, and it was only now after all this time that I seemed to have dug myself back up to the surface, and could take a look around and view the new landscape. Everything had changed. The theory was now the practical, and somehow I hadn't gone crazy buried under so much so quickly, and my body had managed to stay in one piece too.

"How are you through and through?"

Through and through? Well, in all seriousness mum, I think I'm doing okay when all is said and done.

I felt her merge with me in that way again, to check the nuts and bolts for herself. I wondered how she and White Feather did this, and what they could see or hear, or effect should they find something out of alignment or whatever.

I just had to stop and say to myself – it's magic. You can't figure everything out Neli, you can't break it all down to a schematic. It's just magic. That's what everything is.

The verdict came:

"You have enough steam in your engine."

Well I'm really glad to hear that!

The rest of the week I spent looking in a few Seth books, and lo and behold, his and Jane's words came alive again in a new way now that I was a different person. These books always did this. I'd read them so many times and every time was like a brand new experience, but this time it was so completely different – even from four months ago when I'd discovered the Kundalini reference in Seth Speaks.

It was like reading from the other side of things, if that makes sense. I could nod now and say – yes that's right, I know exactly what you're talking about. What a nerve to put myself in the same boat as these two masters, but that's how it felt now, I'd finally caught up with the words.

So I came across a section about nature spirits, and I felt so blessed to have had an experience with Mr. Green that illustrated the point so well – and I would soon find out that Mr. Green was just the beginning of such experiences.

I also had many encounters with the notion of happiness coming from within. It would come from my Sikh and Hindu shows on the TV, and then it would appear from somewhere else. Over and over again it would turn up, until I just had to figuratively throw up my hands and say – I get it, I get it!

Saturday night I went outside on the back lawn to look up at the stars.

"You're on a great journey."

We all are mum, but I know what you mean.

I gazed at those countless stars, and wondered how even God could have imagined such beauty and wonder.

"Imagination is the tool of creation."

Yes, I *imagine* it is mother.

We both chuckled at the feeble humour, and that feeling, of the living and the dead laughing together, just made us laugh all that much more.

As we finally stopped our giggling my mind went back to day one and the photograph of the Stop-Caution-Go cats. Those red, amber and green glowing eyes signifying the start of something greater than I could have ever thought possible in one lifetime.

I took a step towards the house, and then stopped to have one last look at the night sky before I went inside. There was an airplane up there now, a small plane flying below the clouds and barely making a sound as it travelled to its destination.

All I could really see were the three flashing lights, rhythmically pulsing to announce its presence in the dark windy sky. Red – amber – green.

New Moon

The Orbs Begin

On the Wednesday of this week it was December 12 and I knew Vera would call. It was my mum and dad's anniversary, and Vera never missed it. Nor did she ever miss their birthdays or any other particular days of note. Death-days had been added to the list over the years too, which is just what happens if you end up being one of the people "still alive." Any reason to talk to Vera was a good reason, and that's the way I felt about it.

Since Edna's departure, I looked at her sister walking and talking in this reality with a kind of awe and wonder. At the risk of repeating myself, if you add that to the immense love I always had for her right from childhood, you can get some idea of the way I feel about her. Oh and she's my godmother too.

We had a nice talk like we always did, but it was when she was signing off that really got me. "Say hi to Edna for me!"

Vera was just taking it all in stride, and it was at this moment I knew she really did believe me.

I've known her since I was born, I know the way she talks, I've seen her happy and I've seen her sad and I think I can read her by now. She really wanted to make sure I said hi to her sister, and I must have stood there with the dead phone in my hand for a minute or two, before I slowly put it down.

Thank you Vera. I almost don't care what anyone else thinks, and you have no idea what those six words meant to me.

Following on the lines of this, the next day I received an e-mail from my sister Sandra with the line "I totally believe." Okay this was all going better than I could have expected and I breathed a sigh of relief on so many levels.

That night I was at the kitchen table when my mother had another request.

"*Get your camera and tripod – go outside and take some photographs.*"

Photographs of what? – I wondered, but I knew better than to ignore this and at the very least I would be out in the snow and I could take some shots of the yard and my tent. It wasn't snowing at the moment but there was quite a bit on the ground and everything was crisp and beautiful.

I got my gear together and went outside, and plunking my tripod in the snow, I commenced to take photographs of nothing, essentially. I pointed the camera here and there, following no particular plan but just going by impulse and I took about twenty-five photographs and then came back inside. Sometimes I make a point of not looking at the photographs right away, but this time I went upstairs and connected the camera to the TV, marvelling at how photography had come to this point where there was no developing of film, no waiting unless you wanted to, no waste and you could just delete anything you didn't particularly like.

There was the tent, there was the fence, there was the composter and there was the...? My jaw dropped... Are you kidding me?!

In one photo there was the most beautiful white Orb just floating there above an old pedestal that used to hold a birdbath. I couldn't believe my eyes, and again I remembered Gordon asking me if I'd seen any Orbs yet on day one in the coffee shop.

Well, I guess I have my first Orb – was about all I could say. I have to send this to my friends! I looked at it and the way it was positioned above the pedestal... suddenly I got it. My mother's sense of humour came shining through, and I understood the visual joke she was sending.

It didn't take a genius to figure out this particular Orb was her, or at least created by her, and she knew how impressed I was with the way she had broken through and re-entered my life. She also knew that if I ever did write a book, she would certainly be the star of it, as far as I could tell.

Putting all of this together, I could plainly see the photograph was – Edna on a pedestal! This realisation completed the photograph perfectly and I could only laugh and shake my head.

On Saturday it was twenty-eight weeks and day one hundred and ninety-seven, and I sat copying out Seth quotes from "Seth Speaks." I casually sat back for a moment and quietly said out loud – I love Jane Roberts.

I love you too – Seth sends his regards

I can't believe this! Will I ever meet you?

you betcha! – carry on with your quotes

I was reeling – oh sure... I'll just carry on Jane. You enjoyed doing that didn't you?
She'd already gone, and I was left sitting like a statue and thinking – no one's ever going to believe this.

The next day was the snow storm of the century... seriously. It was the biggest snow storm since 1944, and one of those rare ones that included thunder booming across the sky. I had to go outside, and once out there I looked up and could have died right there and then. It was thick and the sky was full of those magic sparkles swirling in the wind. I felt blessed by every one of them deciding to land on my head or my eyelashes.

I love you! – I said inside and out loud.

we love you too!

The snow was answering back and it made perfect sense the snow would know how I felt... it made perfect sense. Life was a sharing of feelings, and every time you focused and paid attention to something, there was an exchange of energy. Snow had been around a lot longer than the human being and like everything else, was just waiting for us to catch up. And the "we" part... of course, of course....

we are part and the same

It wasn't the snow saying that – although it could have just as easily been.
There was that sing-song Irish accent. She was sharing this moment with me and I could see Gwen twirling around in that way she had, with a long scarf and a floppy hat.
It was nice of her to dress for the occasion.
I knew she meant we were part of the same soul as different incarnations, and I knew she also meant everything... everything in creation.

I thought of the word – apart, and I laughed as the snow entered my mouth.

We say apart, meaning we are not together, but just look at the word! A part. We are all a part of the same thing, and even when we are apart... we are a part! The secrets in words if you just look!

I was elated beyond measure and I couldn't think anymore... there was no need to think, feeling was better. I put one foot in front of the other and trudged forward to let the snow engulf me in this brand new world of white, as Gwen flitted to and fro to return every now and then to take my arm in hers.

First Quarter

The Church

I was in the drug store and just happened to look at the condoms all neatly hanging there.

"In my day, they were hidden away."

Yeah I guess they were weren't they? Well, you seem to be back anyway mum.

"It's clear I'm here my dear"

I carried on with my shopping, and then we were outside and walking down the street. A gas truck passed by and I noticed the name of the company on the side – Direct Energy. There were messages everywhere and I thought about everything being energy, vibrating fields of energy, even though it looked like streets and houses and people – people being perceptive energy if you like.

I spent the afternoon at the library looking at books to take out and using one of the computers available for people like me who didn't have their own as of yet. This turned out to be a saving grace, as I could carry on with my research and e-mails, and for the millionth time I thanked the universe for libraries.

I needed to get a few other things at the mall, so later on I walked over there and did what I had to do, thinking about the direct energy truck as I was walking around looking at the eternal beings going about their business. Sending energy out from my heart, I felt like a beacon.

I "just happened" to look at an advertisement on the wall for an energy drink and I stopped and stared. "Guru" was the name of the drink, and if that wasn't enough, the rest of it said – clean energy for a thirsty world.

Was I a Guru now? Some people would probably think so because I knew what it meant – a spiritual teacher or master. Oh my, had all this really happened to me? Was this me now? Then I thought of my day five, and the moment of realisation – God realisation – and I couldn't deny what had happened on that day. I couldn't deny that Parvati, or God, spoke to me, and I couldn't ignore all that had happened in the last twenty-nine weeks. Not to mention the journey I'd been on right from the start in this life... and many others. I knew this life was a continuation and a culmination of everything I'd ever done.

I still couldn't think of myself as a master, it just sounded too grandiose and self-important, but I would not refute what I knew was true about me either, and it seemed like this sign was helping me to accept the irrefutable. I had to step into my own shoes now, and I had to do it with as much grace as possible and without the ego getting in the way. This didn't seem to be much of a problem. I was just Peter Nelson from Bolton in England and no one could have had more humble beginnings. Everyone was on the same expedition whether they knew it or not, and this time around it was my turn to finally reach a certain place on the way.

How many times had I said – we're all on the same train, some people are in the carriage ahead, and some in the carriage behind. A million times! My friends were probably sick and tired of hearing it, but I knew it was true. And we graciously accept help from those ahead, and then turn around to lend a helping hand to those behind.

Students and teachers... all of us... we are teachers and students, and the learning never stops, the becoming more never stops. What did Seth say – "Always in a state of becoming." How is it he always put everything in just the right way? I don't know, but for me, he and Jane Roberts always did – without fail.

I came back to myself and I was still standing there. I'd better get a move on, but not before I thought about that thirsty world, just waiting for that clean energy of knowledge. I would do the best I could, and many will think I'm crazy by now, but I won't let you down Gaia... I won't. I will help your children find their way, and I am honoured to be walking on your surface – proud to be a child of this earth...

Holy crow Nelson! Put that bag in your knapsack and get going will you? Before you save the world, you'd better go home and feed Henry.

༄ ༄ ༄ ༄ ༄ ༄

That Sunday it was the Winter Solstice, and I was compelled to go into St. Anselm's Catholic Church in the afternoon after the services were over. I was surprised to find the door open, and upon entering I dipped my finger into the holy water and ran it from my forehead to the tip of my nose. I'd been doing this gesture for as long as I could remember, usually with my index finger and thumb pressed together, and for me it was a sign of composure and serenity.

(Later on I concluded that in a Native North American life it was the first move I made when painting my face. I could feel the paint or a kind of chalk between my fingers, and after this realisation it was so obvious, but of course everything was obvious once you'd figured it out.)

Then I thought I'd perform the sign of the cross as I'd seen countless times, but never actually performed. Forehead to chest, and then left shoulder to right shoulder... was that right? Yes, I think that's the way it goes. It seemed quite a natural thing to do, and it wasn't such a stretch to imagine various lives as a Catholic – forced or otherwise – along the way. I stepped into the Church proper.

There was absolutely no one there and I first looked at the pulpit. It wasn't elevated but on floor level, which I thought was unusual. Are the priests on the same level as us now? And there's the altar, and the candles burning, and the stained glass, and a beautiful high ceiling, and... Jesus on the cross.

This was the part I really couldn't cotton to. The crucifix to me was a torture scene, and somehow it didn't belong. It has always bothered me and this one was big, it must have been twice life-size.

I thought back to my childhood, and I could still feel the first shock I'd felt upon gazing at this depiction of torment – the nails, the blood, the wound, the crown of thorns. It was terrible. I was a child back in England now, and again I could feel my initial reaction when my mother explained how they gave Jesus vinegar to drink when he had asked for some water. The whole scenario was debased and vulgar and mightily upsetting, and I decided I had to do something about it – right now.

I took an aisle seat in the back row and put my head down as the tears started to well up, but that wouldn't stop me now. I closed my eyes and went to work, looking like someone who was simply praying, but I was into my vision now, and I needed to do this for me... I needed to heal this psychic wound that I'd obviously had since I was a child. I had to fix this somehow, and I had to do this for Jesus.

I walked up to the huge crucifix and floated up to face level. His head was to the side and down in a gesture of despair and resignation – Father, forgive them for they know not what they do.

I had a moment where I was aware of my body in the back row with head down, and I thought – okay, I'm safe there, and then I was back face to face with Jesus.

I said – please come down from there – as I slowly removed the "crown" from his head and threw it away with force. It wasn't worth another glance. I reached for the first obscene nail in his hand and drew it out easily... then to the other hand as he slumped forward and I took his light weight on my shoulders. Slowly down to his feet and the last of the nails... and then he was free and we floated down to the floor and I gently set him down on his back.

I had an ointment with me, a salve of some kind with the power to remove all pain instantly and to heal one moment later. I applied this generously to head, hands, feet, side, and then as his eyes opened a river appeared and he slowly, lovingly bathed himself and washed away two thousand years.

There seemed to now be a robe on the bank of the river, and it glowed with a life of its own even before he pulled it over his head. He tied a simple belt woven from grasses of some kind around his waist, and turned to look at me.

I knew at this moment what Love looked like, as the ecstasy hit me with a force that took my breath away, and I was sure I heard my physical body draw in a sharp dart of breath. Jesus raised both arms out from his side until he *was* the cross, and I was imbued with the sanctity of the human form as he smiled for the entire universe and slowly rose up to the ceiling of the church and through – free forever from being confined to a building and an idea when he was really inside everyone.

It took me a few moments to open my physical eyes as my eyelids fluttered and then finally opened and I wiped them dry. I looked at the crucifix and was there a slight smile now upon the lips?

My eyes were suddenly drawn to the left as I now saw a blue light twinkling about ten feet from the floor to the side of the altar. It appeared to be about the size of my fist and was easily visible as it winked and blinked to finally fade away a few seconds later. Oh my.

I got to my feet feeling a little shaky, and walked outside to slowly make my way home feeling a new lightness inside me. Tomorrow would be Christmas Eve.

Almost home now, I passed a beautiful old tree and as I looked at it, a face became clearly visible on the side of the trunk. There was bump or gnarl the size of a baseball, and it was a face for all the world to see. It was so obvious!

I'd passed this tree many times before but never noticed this. Maybe with the appearance of Mr. Green I was just more open now – or ready. I stood and stared at the face and then I clearly heard two statements in my mind.

we have lots of energy to give – we have been waiting

I forced myself to start walking again, and as I passed by a house with Ivy covering the wall, I heard the Ivy giggling!

All I could do was giggle myself now, and as I got to the front door I turned to look at the street and the outside world for a last moment – nothing would ever be the same as it was before... there was magic everywhere.

Moon Eight
Christmas Pigeon

I woke up the next day thinking about that thickening air I'd seen once again in the doorway of the bedroom the night before, and hearing the song "Once In Love With Amy" that I was sure my mother had placed in my mind as it was a Frank Sinatra song, and she just loved Frank, as she called him, but it was Christmas Eve and there were a few things to do and I wasn't sure where to begin.

After six months I'd stopped crying every single day as a matter of course, but I still felt like I could barely keep up with everything that was happening. At least I didn't have to go to work on this day for the first time in eleven years.

"You're all over the show."

I know mum, I'll just do one thing at a time and I'll be okay.

I viewed Christmas with a bit of trepidation lately, as I'd experienced a few that had been terrible. One year I'd barely been able to walk with sciatica until acupuncture saved me on Boxing Day, and on another Christmas morning I discovered my nine year old dwarf rabbit Roger, dead.

Anyway, the day went fine and all the preparations were made and before I knew it, Christmas morning had arrived. So far so good until I heard a very loud sickening thump on the bedroom window and I somehow knew what had happened – I'd heard that sound before.

A pigeon had slammed into the glass, and I ran downstairs to find the bird stone dead on a drift of snow in front of the house, with a patch of red already spreading on the white. I'd just buried the Blue Jay in September and here I was again with another dead bird and another death like Roger's on Christmas day.

The ground hadn't frozen solid yet, so I buried the bird without too much trouble, singing my dead pigeon song and thinking about death always being here. It wasn't until I went back upstairs to check if the window had cracked with the force, that I saw the impression left on the glass.

It was a perfect pigeon shape with wings spread open, body, legs with head and beak off to one side. Death must have been instant from a broken neck and that bird suffered no pain at all – she had come straight-on at full speed. I thought about the bird just flying on without even noticing she was now in a different world – transitions don't get quicker than that – and she died with the wind in her face.

I realised I was looking at a work of art. The feathers were all there. You could see the ring around her neck and the smaller ones giving way to the larger feathers further down. It was beautiful. It was awful... but it was beautiful. With her last act in the last millisecond of physical life, this bird had left a stamped impression that was a precise etching.

I had to take a photograph, and I reverently did so, feeling a little odd but wanting to preserve this gift somehow. The universe was a very strange and mysterious place and if nothing else, I knew this was important, and here was something else I would think about forever. Christmas went on without any other incidents, and gave way to Boxing Day and the day after.

On the Friday I decided to go for a walk in the dark and the snow. Walking was even more fun than it used to be now, as I silently blessed people as they walked by and kissed them on the cheek or hugged them in my mind's eye. If there was someone visibly ill, limping or in a wheel chair, I would send them healing energy, which I saw as green rings. I would run the rings up and down their limbs or just large ones working on their entire bodies, and I sent love from my heart in any way I could imagine.

In the local grocery store there was a tank of live lobsters, and I had a real problem with this on many levels, so I had a ritual here too. I would stand with my back to them (I couldn't bear to look), and send love and hope and a cessation of pain or discomfort or fear. I would use my healing green and also pinks or whatever felt right, and I would do this every time, even if I couldn't stop and I was just walking by.

I didn't feel silly or out of my mind and if there was one thing I knew without any kind of doubt, it was that All That Is, or God, or whatever you want to call it, knows everything you do and think.

These guys couldn't even open their claws (can you imagine?), and if they could have, I'm sure they would have mercifully dispatched each other. It was all too terrible to contemplate, and other than knocking over the tank and running off with them to take them... where? It was the best I could do.

On this day though, I had nowhere particular to go and was simply walking down the familiar streets, enjoying the night and the Christmas lights decorating the houses.

As I went passed a street lamp it suddenly went off right as I was underneath. I stopped, looked up at it and wondered... did I do that? I remembered this happening before June 2 but I hadn't thought about it too much. Street lamps just went out sometimes didn't they? This time, as soon as I walked off and carried on my way, it immediately came right back on! Okay, this was really cool! I would keep this in mind and see what happened in the future.

The next day I went to the library to pick up a crop circle DVD I'd requested, and I ended up with The Bhagavad Gita as well before I left for home. Later on I had to go to the mall, and on the way I noticed a familiar shape attached to the window of a building. I wouldn't have normally walked this way but I saw my former/recent boss, and I didn't feel like that confrontation right now so I was led right here.

It was another wasp's nest built in the wrong place, and upon inspection I found several wasps frozen to it. They died going about their sacred business, and you could barely tell they were dead except for them being static. I got the camera I didn't go anywhere without now, like I said, and took some shots. They reminded me of a cat I'd come across years ago while walking in a winter field – just frozen upright in mid-stride.

I sensed Parvati with me as I took the photographs, and I was feeling more upset all the while.

Thank you for the wasps – I thought to Parvati.

as you wish

But dead?

they are the same – aren't they as lovely?

No. May I say No?

of course

It's a little sadder.

should we not be happy – they are cold no longer

But they're....

I started to crumple here and Parvati put her finger to my lips.

a cup can still be beautiful when it's empty...

Last Quarter

2012

The New Year was here now and things were getting back to normal in the regular world, and calming down a little in my own. I'd reached another plateau of sorts, but this time there was a quiet reflective feel in the air and I found it difficult to keep notes. I needed to put the journal down for a day or two.

That being the case, everything pointed to this being the perfect time to review Bardo, specifically the Ascension folder. If I was taking a break from the incessant writing, I didn't think it would hurt if I finally attempted to organise the files into some sort of perspective that worked. That would still be taking a break wouldn't it? Somehow that made sense.

As I started to go through it all piece by piece, I was thankful for the opportunity I'd had to print out so much, and I arranged things in order by date and relived what I was feeling on those days. These printed sheets were a time-lock in the same way the photographs were, the date I'd accessed these sites was recorded on them, and it was easy to go back to those moments and somehow see my own eyes opening all over again.

My inner reality had shifted cataclysmically, and the more I decided what I agreed with and what I didn't, the more I saw how my view of the so-called outside world would never be the same from here on either.

The beauty of it all once again, was that in my heart, I could feel something was brewing. It wasn't a matter of being convinced as much as finding out exactly what was being said... and there was a lot being said.

I gathered more and more material together, and one thing was for certain, something was definitely going on, and it was going on now. It all made sense to me – a leap in evolution on a universal level, a shifting from one dimensional state to another, a dissolving of barriers... and here's where it all began to combine so perfectly with my own personal situation and I realised they were one and the same, if I hadn't already.

There was no question about it, my own transformation was intimately connected to everything transpiring now, and I was glad to be no less punctual, there didn't seem to be a lot of time to spare from what I was learning.

What a perfect time for all this to happen to me! I was caught up in the same sweep of eternity as everyone else and we were all just opening up like flowers to the light flowing into our corner of the universe – and everywhere else.

There seemed to be two issues that were intricately interwoven together: what was going to happen exactly, and when would it occur. Only an idiot would try to separate the two and approach the subject in such a way, so I decided to separate the two.

I was thinking about events not just happening in time, but forming time in physical reality somehow. I was thinking about intensities impinging upon time and it occurred to me that 2012 was a marker – a marker of intensity.

If there is a point, a threshold, an event horizon, or a peak intensity of some kind, we can look at all the different sources that specify December 21, 2012 as that moment with truly remarkable parallels and similarities. Throw in for good measure the solstice is slated to happen at 11:11 a.m. Universal Time and things begin to get very interesting.

One other idea is a twenty-five year period (as opposed to one spectacular date), starting at the harmonic convergence in 1987 and ending in 2012. Another notion is the three decade span from 1987 to 2017, and there's another one from 2012 to 2032 as the period to watch – there are theories galore.

I believe there's definitely a time period involved, whenever it may have started, it only makes sense – a change like this doesn't happen like the flip of a switch, does it?

On the other hand, I also believe the winter solstice in 2012 to be a wild card of sorts, and I think the closer we get to the singularity, or the nanosecond, or zero-point, or whatever you want to call it, the easier it will be to manifest anything we may dream for ourselves.

In other words – anything can happen... or nothing at all, and the X-Factor is probably us.

When it came to the various prophecies, I realised the agreements between these disparate sources was far more significant to me than the individual prophecies and what they may say – they all say very similar things in different ways, and the clincher is they all agree that now is the time.

There have been enough forecasts seemingly fall flat, so from the universe's perspective of trying to seriously get our attention, what better way than to have all of these prophecies converge on one moment and one idea. On top of that, have many of these notions coming from indigenous peoples who the world have only now come to realise are the keepers, the holders, and there's no one who can fail to sit up and at least notice the odds if nothing else.

There's something in the air. We're restless. The sky looks different. I thought about all the people alive on earth right now, and how they knew all about this before they got here this time. This potent universal synchronisation would be a major reason for anyone's presence and participation, if not the main incentive.

This was why there were so many people on the planet right now.

2012 is the end of a chapter. This was all about cycles – in the universe and in our bodies – and the more I learned, the more I understood that they were as ancient as the wind, but this particular gust was different, this had never happened in quite this way before.

We were in the fast lane heading for a new world, while at the same time streaking towards complete destruction, and there appeared to be a number of options available between these two variables. At the same time – however we were going to handle this singular moment would cascade and echo throughout eternity. It became clear that whatever we did at this juncture would have profound significance in many if not all realities – all eyes were on us and bets were probably being made.

This seemed to be what was going on, and the universe was excited!

I'd been absorbing these ideas for months now, but by creating physical folders for the printed material and taking the time to organise my own feelings, things fell into a fuller perspective. Where was the old world I'd inhabited only a short while ago?

Trying somewhat vainly to stick more to the when and why of things for now, I looked at some of the cultures that point to 2012 or thereabouts as the time to hold on to your hat. Right now I just wanted to list some of these cultures, and I figured I'd get to what they actually had to say later.

The Maya and the Hopi come to mind right away probably because they're mentioned in the public media but there are so many more, including the Hindus if you look at the Vedas, and the Tibetan Buddhists with their Kalachakra teachings.

You also have the Egyptians, the Kabbalists, and the Essenes. Then we have the Qero Elders of Peru, the Navajo, Cherokee, Apache, and the Iroquois confederacy.

There's the Dogon Tribe of Africa, Australian Aborigines and the Maori of New Zealand, not to forget the Christian prophets who believe the rapture is not too far off.

The Mongolians and the tribes on Boa Boa also apparently agree about a golden age coming right about now, and there are more, so we have all these unrelated cultures saying the same thing in their mythology and you have to wonder. It would be amazing enough with everyone pointing to the same time period regardless, but add to that the overall agreement as to the possible events themselves, and it becomes a mysteriously divine adventure.

I was feeling butterflies in my stomach.

So what was going on in the galaxy anyway? There was no way you could really think about any of this without tilting your head back, and having a long hard look at that black mystery with the wishes of our entire race hanging from every star.

It seems to have started with the Harmonic Convergence in 1987 and the beginning of our sun's alignment with the super-massive black hole at the centre of the Milky Way Galaxy – this would be when we entered the Photon Belt. What we're heading for is the moment when the earth will be in exact alignment with the sun and the centre of the Milky Way, and there was agreement on this point for the most part, but opinions varied in the chronology.

I found some people believe this galactic alignment, or the grand crossing, will occur exactly on December 21, 2012 and others believed it had already occurred in 1998 depending on your vantage point. Even the end date itself seemed to be in question, with the "true" date being October 28, 2012 in some people's minds who know a lot more about the Mayan calendar than I do.

Once again, I didn't find these discrepancies upsetting at all – did it really matter?

I just stepped back and looked at the big picture – and came to the conclusion that in terms of the universe and for me personally, these slight variations were inconsequential. Here we were again, three-dimensional humans applying linear time to what could be called a quantum event (in this sense unprecedented and fully multi-dimensional), and considering *that*, it was amazing there was as much agreement as there was.

According to the prophecy of Quetzacoatl, after the ninth hell would be a new age of peace, and with the convergence beginning on August 17, 1987, hell-on-earth officially came to an end.

All of this was beginning to sound really good to me.

After this, the cycles culminating on or around 2012 start to pile up like they all have the same ticket to the same dance.

The 26,000-year Progression of the Equinoxes is a main consideration because we move through the twelve constellations of the zodiac like a birth cycle, and I thought about the crop circles and my feelings at the start of this, that they were signifying the birth of something. This was also known as the cycle of evolution.

Other cycles coming in to swing past home at this time are:

The end of the 2160 year Age of Pisces, and the beginning of Aquarius.

5,125 years – The Great Cycle of History.

A 78,000 year earth cycle.

A 25 to 26 million earth-year cycle – this is one complete rotation of our Milky Way Galaxy and evolution ties-in with this cycle.

A Grand Cycle of 225 million years – this is called the Grand Procession or the Galactic Year, and is the duration of time required for the solar system to orbit once around the centre of the Milky Way galaxy.

Then there's the movement of the Milky Way Galaxy around the Grand Central Sun of the Pleiades, called Alcyone, which apparently occurs every 20 billion years.

You could carry on if you wanted to, dividing the larger cycles into smaller sub-sets, and I was sure you would also find larger patterns the further out you went *into* time – into the past... and into the future for that matter. We were in a tighter and tighter spiral towards this event, like a penny on those roulette coin-donation vortex funnels, going faster and faster until... through.

I saw the same shape on the other side, as fresh probabilities – new trunk lines – exploding from there and it seemed like we were on the central point of an hourglass, which I thought was an appropriate vision as I just let myself go and got out of the way.

I noticed how natural it was to absorb some cold hard facts, and then let the parts of yourself sort it out as you went about other matters. I would stop and play some music, like an Armenian piece I'd learned and couldn't stop playing, and I would just forget about it all for a while. I wondered how much organising I was doing in the dream state too, because it was getting easier and easier to wade through opinion after opinion and know what felt right for me.

It was about letting things fall into place more than anything else, and I found myself pacing about in my room giving lectures to no one (that I could see), and feeling I was discovering the treasure I was always meant to find. I had no problem believing in this at all, and everything seemed to just fit into place in that comfortable way it sometimes did when the pieces made a sensible whole.

Better keep your voice down a bit though Nelson.

The most interesting thing though, was all these various cycles were slated to close simultaneously on December 21, 2012 at 11:11 a.m., and all of us are here now to eventually tell the tale. Everything that had happened to me on a personal level slid tailor-made into the grander vision, and I felt that elegance again engaging my heart and my inner-knowing. This all felt right to me.

I carried on. Plato and the Greeks called the end of this current age the Suntelia Aion and it was symbolised by the Ouroboros – the snake eating its own tale. This image referred to cycles also, especially in the sense of something constantly recreating itself, and of course I couldn't think about serpents now without immediately considering Kundalini.

My mind drifted off somewhere and I saw myself riding a powerful female Dragon up into the sky and beyond....

Coming back to myself, I learned the myth of the Ouroboros refers to a serpent of light residing in the heavens. How not surprising! The Milky Way galaxy represents the serpent, and apparently when viewed from a central point, it appears to eats its own tail! Of course the date the ancient Greeks gave for the Suntelia Aion is December 21, 2012, and on this day the sun is said to rise out of the mouth of the Ouroboros.

There was no getting away from serpents and there was no getting away from light. This reminded me of the Photon Belt, which we'll get to in a minute, and I decided to take a little detour from 2012 for a moment, and just think about light for a while.

Spirituality and light are inseparable. "Let there be light" virtually starts the Christian Bible, and go "Into the light," is always the advice when one finds oneself dead isn't it? You can look at spiritual art with the halos and sparkle and brilliance – holy people radiating an internal light with rays of gold streaming down from heaven – and you can also consider the first thing ever worshipped on this planet. It has to be the sun I would think.

I knew that on the light spectrum, the frequencies we can see with our physical eyes are stunningly narrow, next to nothing really when you get down to it and have a good look. That's funny!

I decided to take a minute to find a nice clear chart of the spectrum and see what we knew about light so far – at least what we knew from a third-dimensional aspect. I somehow knew light was so much more than what we saw here, and so much more than what we were aware of, whether we could see it or not.

I found a colourful chart and it was a revelation for me, not only was our visible light miniscule – tucked-in between Infrared and Ultraviolet – but I found out something else I'd never really appreciated. On the low end of the spectrum where the frequencies were the lowest, sat radio and TV waves, starting off with AM radio, and then shortwave radio, TV signals and then FM radio.

These everyday signals were made of light! Why didn't I know this?

Next came microwaves, used for radar amongst other things, and then we were into the Infrared followed by our tiny band of visible light. Finally, as the frequencies continue to increase, we find Ultraviolet, X-rays and then Gamma rays. It was all various frequencies of light!

I don't know why all of this was so surprising, because I already knew light was an electromagnetic wave, but I'd never really connected it to all of this before.

These types of electromagnetic radiation all travel at the same speed – the speed of light – and they only varied in frequency and wavelength, like colours. This would all tie-in to the higher spiritual realms of light and sound, and to our light-bodies.

Was everything light? I was beginning to think it was.

With a name like The Photon Belt, it was pretty obvious this high-energy band was composed of light. You could say electromagnetic energy in a fundamental or quantum (smallest particle) state, or you can just go the more spiritual way, and say light.

It is considered to be a ring 760 trillion miles wide by the people who actually believe in its existence, others of course don't believe it has any basis in fact at all, and is merely new age nonsense. Still others believe our space agencies and governments know all about it, and are keeping quiet – as with many other things. In the early 1980s there was a report on American radio about our solar system penetrating an electromagnetic cloud in the near future, but the story seems to have started and stopped there.

Another theory is that the photon belt (also known as the radiant or golden nebula) is not really anything "exterior" at all, but the leading edge of our collective consciousness coming up against frequencies that are not yet synchronised and aligned – once aligned, we will burst through and make our transition. From the point of view that there is no outside without us, this makes perfect sense, and we would be projecting this psychic event out into physical reality to manifest as this loop of multi-dimensional light.

Assuming it's "out there" for the rest of this discussion, this particular light seems to be able to stimulate the evolution of everything everywhere, and streams in from the centre of the galaxy with us passing through it twice in every 26000 years. We discovered this with satellites in 1961 according to some, but The Maya actually *refer* to this field of light, and believe it's from the creator – Hunab K'u.

This reminded me of another Jane Roberts book – The Afterdeath Journal of an American Philosopher – which had long ago supplied a wonderful description of God: An Atmospheric Presence – A Knowing Light. I loved that – Universal Love of the Creator in the form of a supportive, encouraging light.

God and light have been working together for a long time.

ᘒ ᘒ ᘒ ᘒ ᘒ ᘒ

We were entering further and further into this band as we got closer to the alignment, with full saturation on December 21, 2012. The date was everywhere, but so was the idea that this light was raising our frequencies and changing our DNA and we were well into it at this point. This light was *exciting* everything, and there was a notion that all the planets were warming and getting brighter as a result. In my own tiny world I remembered thinking the Moon and stars were brighter than I'd ever seen them before.

I also loved another idea that all the black holes in the universe had started to emit light and a particular tone – a new song for the universe. At times like this it didn't matter to me whether it was possible for anything to *emerge from* a black hole, physics was being turned upside-down anyway, and somehow it made sense to me the black holes of the universe might have started to sing. I'd always thought of them as dimensional connectors anyway, places where energy was exchanged and balanced, so it wasn't much of a stretch to imagine them participating in a trans-dimensional clarion call. Sound created shape and geometries, and I wouldn't be surprised if sound was an element in the construction of the crop circle formations.

I noticed I was combining ideas into a fabric that covered everything nicely for me, and it was a matter of feeling around until something gave me a jolt and fit with the way I was feeling. I'd recently come to realise that I physically felt this jolt and had to close my eyes for a second and shake my head a little, when I "remembered" something very important.

The science of it all was fascinating and absorbing and coupled with my own experiences for the last thirty weeks or so was easily elevated to a place where the theoretical just didn't need all that much more to justify itself. Destiny unfolding on a universal level really didn't seem all that hard to appreciate these days.

As long as I stayed centred and in the magic, I didn't mind finding out about the third-dimensional mathematical details, even though my overall feeling was that everything is alive and growing and changing and it's as simple as that really. It seemed like getting a few external facts straight was a good idea though, from the point of view of passing the information along from whatever angle worked the best.

I remembered years ago learning that the earth is a sentient being – Gaia – and at the time it was easy to believe considering the breathtaking variety of life in the skies, seas and on and within the surface, but that wasn't the point, the planet is actually alive... regardless of that. Maybe that's why we say planetary *body*.

Life takes many forms and I remembered Seth saying, "Consciousness creates form – It is not the other way around."

The heavenly bodies themselves are conscious and alive, and I went back to my experience with the sun on day one – there was a presence there – and saw how we have to open up to a new definition of life within us, because you could feel the totality of the universe if you wanted to. I had a feeling the definition of "life," was about to burst open like a seed pod.

Okay, so this was happening right now with the Photon Belt, and I thought maybe I'd see what else was currently going on before moving on to the big picture and where we might be going with all of this.

Well, the frequency of the planet itself was rising, and the magnetics were falling.

Did I even know what the frequency of the planet really meant? I'd been talking about vibrational frequencies from the spiritual point of view for so long, it was incredible to find something like this manifesting on the physical level.

The earth's vibration rate or heartbeat-pulse is called the Schumann Resonance and was at 7.83 cycles per second until the harmonic convergence in 1987 when it suddenly started to rise. Currently around 11 cycles per second, there's a belief that 13 is the magic number we're headed for.

It was all making sense to me and I was in a kind of bliss with papers all over the place and highlighters and markers strewn around. I just sat there for a minute and my attention was drawn to a small folded piece of paper down by the floor and stuck between the drafting table and the wall. I had so many things going on with open folders and books that it didn't take a genius to figure out it had just flown out of something and landed where it had. I fished it out of its hiding place and opened it...

Summer 2006
The frequency has changed

There was nothing else written there, and clearly now, I remembered being at work when I'd written it down a year and a half ago. I'd stood stock-still for a moment, grabbing a sheet of paper, and I recalled writing without looking and breaking the spell. It had been one of those jolt moments, and I'd folded it up and tucked it safely away somewhere, only to forget all about it and have it fly out of nowhere right now.

My lord I knew! Look at that! I didn't even know what I was talking about, but part of me sure did! This note was the assurance I needed as once again, I'd come to a conclusion or feeling about something, only to have the details fall into my lap afterwards. And this time I'd even forgotten what I sensed!

I stared at this note for a long time thinking about the elegance of everything again and feeling confident now about what I was doing at this stage in the proceedings.

I thought of the me who was compelled to stop everything and write this down in 2006. If I wasn't doing this research today, would he have written that note to be found right now?

Shaking my head at the wonder of it all, I decided to call it a day and head for the bath and then dreamland.

ನ ನ ನ ನ ನ ನ

Next on my agenda was the magnetic field strength of the earth, the decline of which was a possible indication of a pole reversal. The idea was a drop to zero at the same time the hertz frequency made it to 13 – this would be December 21, 2012.

If different frequencies open us up to other dimensions, and if the magnetic structures are a managing system, it made sense to me that we were moving toward heaven and barriers were dissolving at the same time. These were the kinds of things I chose to dwell on.

There was another way to go though, with all kinds of things to be afraid of if you wanted to go down that path.

The earth could slow down and possibly stop rotation at this point, and then slowly start to turn the other way. Magnetic, then geo-physical pole reversals would follow – or just happen on their own anyway without the rotational feature – and here come the dire consequences. All kinds of up-heavals would occur on the earth with life seriously affected everywhere, and this geo-physical pole shift would take only twenty hours.

I decided again to just think positively about the whole thing and concentrate more on the spiritual aspects – fear was the last thing we needed at this point.

Solar pole shifts involving the sun's magnetic field happen every eleven years in a sunspot cycle as a matter of course, and it just so happened the next solar maximum was scheduled for 2012. There was talk of more activity than normal for this one and possible untoward consequences, but even adding this to the other calamitous possibilities, I still couldn't feel any fear inside of me, it was just another probability and there were too many other things to be over-the-moon about than to get bogged-down with the worse-case scenarios.

We were going for a ride and I was sure the transition wouldn't be particularly easy, but it was what everyone was waiting for, even if they didn't realise it yet. We were in a time of cleansing and transformation.

The other thing happening already was the earth changes. Earthquakes, tsunamis, volcanic eruptions, floods, fires, hurricanes and tornados were seemingly on the rise. I knew consciousness affected the weather and gloomy people help create dreary days as much if not more than the reverse, so I couldn't help but think that our own psychic emotional imbalance was severely affecting the earth. The upheaval of the earth was a reflection of the chaos occurring on her surface, thanks to the disharmony of the human beings who have lost their connection to Source. Disharmony? More like complete pandemonium. What a mess. I'm sorry Gaia.

This all tied in to the cleansing of old energies, and it was occurring now so I included it in my 2012 pile and then brought myself back to the subject at hand and discovered the crop circles from August 2004 and 2005 that were Mayan calendar formations. These crop circles were obviously trying to seriously bring our attention to 2012, and I wondered how many more of these glyphs would reference this as the years flew by.

I placed another article in order and read about Terrance McKenna, who had studied the I Ching and applied numerical patterns to the hexagrams coming up with a graph depicting times of change. The I Ching or the book of changes is one of the oldest Chinese texts on earth, and I remembered trying this divination technique out years ago – I felt comfortable with it so I read on.

The Timewave Zero concept, presents graphs with peaks and valleys corresponding to historical highs and lows. The correlations with great civilisations are interesting enough, but it's what happens in the future that really makes one pause.

McKenna saw time spiralling tighter and faster until reaching the Omega Point where all potentials would occur and everything would happen at once.

All potentials *do* occur and everything *does* happen simultaneously anyway, but this seemed to point to a peak saturation of magic-in-time somehow, and the funny thing was, this time-line of our history culminated from the I Ching, stops dead in its tracks at the end of 2012. How not surprising.

There was more, and my head started to swim with spirals and cycles and octaves and cadences and beginnings and endings, and then of course there really were no beginnings or endings in the grander scheme of things, and I just had to stop and feel.

Something magnificent had happened to me, and something magnificent was happening in the universe and the two were one and the same. My own transformation made it so easy to believe that the magic had burst free somehow – or was about to.

I looked at all of this information spread out on the floor and knew I'd only scratched the surface really. You could have taken any one of these articles and gone deeper and deeper in that direction, but it just wasn't necessary. Seeing everything arranged like that reinforced what I'd thought right from the start – the discrepancies are nothing, and the similarities are everything.

As the week continued, I added to what I'd already discovered by plugging into the computers at the library and getting myself as up to date as possible.

There was one area of all this that obviously attracted my interest, and that was what the mystics, psychics, sages, prophets or just anyone whom you really respected had to say. I found there were so many people channelling and receiving messages in every conceivable manner, that after a while the information fell into the same feeling of so many sources saying the same thing in infinitely different creative ways.

Lo and behold, there was an agreement you could see – from the psychic channelling an entity to anyone with half a brain who looked out the window and truly saw the degree of trouble we were in.

It seemed like there were two ends of the scale – on one end, the purely pragmatic observation that we have almost actually destroyed the planet we live on/with, and there's really nothing you can think of more serious and unbelievable than that, and on the other end, the idea that we will have the opportunity to be swept into heaven.

The big issue here of course, is not what happens on this date, but what happens after. All the indications point to us already being in the middle of an incredible transformation of spirit and maybe 2012 is a check-point or a point-of-no-return.

It was fun to have a date, like a fire to dance around, and the concentration alone from so many millions of minds would have a profound effect on reality regardless of anything else going on, and when all is said and done – what was wrong with hoping for some spectacular cosmic fireworks and a reality-shattering event anyway? Let's hope for that regularly.

However you wanted to look at it, we were at a crisis-cross-roads and you could go with it on the one level where everything was fear and politics and power-struggles and greed, or you could join another vibration where there was something far grander going on that made you want to close your eyes and consider the mystery of it all.

New Moon Ascension

By now I had a good idea about what I thought was going on and I haven't made a secret of it – no matter where I was lead, or what I found, it was all coloured by my mother's unique reference to evolution and DNA using her name Edna.

I went back to the beginning to find out this happened on day nineteen, basically right at the start, and it made sense that she would get straight to the point as soon as possible. She'd basically waited until I was fairly sure I wasn't dead, and then went right to the subject at hand. Yes I now knew, as I approached making sense out of this material, that it truly was all about evolution and DNA, just like she'd said, and it was starting with planet earth, with Gaia, who was ascending now whether we went along for the ride or not.

I don't know how many times I came across statements like, "This has never happened before," and I wondered how anyone might actually know about that, but the fact was, we were still here in a third-dimensional reality and there was a distinctive excitement in the air, so did it matter whether or not this had happened before? Not to mention that every single moment or now-point is totally unique and original anyway.

However, according to some, planetary consciousnesses like our earth *had* done something like this before, and the planet, along with whoever else was going, had just merrily gone on its way and this wasn't particularly unusual, but the difference this time was one of scale. Apparently we had some catching up to do. We were about to take a much larger leap than normal, and from what I was gathering, there would be no reality untouched by this. The rubber-band theory came into play here, and the idea was that the further we had descended or been pulled down into the darkness, corresponded to how far we would subsequently shoot up into the light.

It was the sheer magnitude of our transition that had the neighbours talking, and the fact that we were a third-dimensional reality had a remarkable side-effect going for it. From the point of view that the so-called higher dimensions "depend" on the previous ones, the idea is – when the consciousness of planet earth is lifted up, so will the consciousness of all creation.

This is where the really big deal part comes in, and why it's in the best interest of the universe at large to support us and help us in whatever way possible. Our situation was of great interest to beings all across the galaxy – we are anything but alone – and I liked the idea that everyone was waiting for us to take our rightful place in the far grander picture. It wasn't frightening at all that we were surrounded... it was a blessed relief.

Unfortunately, not everyone *was* ready to start living through the heart instead of the head-mind-ego, and this couldn't be more obvious if you just took a look at where we were and what we were doing as a species. Controlled or not, we were out of control.

And people still scratched their heads and wondered why we weren't being openly visited by other life in the universe. This idea of us as a race being quarantined from the rest of the civilizations out there, started to make a whole lot of sense to me.

We were still fighting over skin colour, and nationalism, and who *owns* what, so how on earth could we accept races from other worlds and dimensions? Would *you* land here? Maybe we were in the boondocks of our galaxy for a reason.

Somehow, thinking of us all as some kind of cosmic castaways locked in the back room until we figured a few things out, just made my heart burst to aching all that much more for humanity. For some reason, I felt blessed and honoured to be a part of this rather less than stellar group of beings, who just seemed to want to fight and destroy and... didn't know any better.

The manipulators were looking for controlled responses and had found a "what luck!" situation much to their delight. Imagine an entire race of human beings who didn't know their sweeping divine power. Imagine them thinking there is actually no other life in the universe. Imagine keeping them in the dark forever if possible and using them... and imagine the moment when it all comes crashing down and the human race *remembered*. This was epic!

It didn't matter how lost we'd been... it *did* matter of course, it had made us who we are, but again I felt my love for all of us outweigh anything else. We made sand-castles on the beach and put silly hats on our heads just for fun... some of us have died trying to save our dogs and cats. This was who we really were.

The earth was holding more and more light, and heading for the fifth dimension, and all of us with sympathetic vibrations would be going with her – the animal, plant and mineral kingdoms were all signed-up and ready to go – and those who weren't ready, would not. So how was this going to work?

Well, some people were going to simply check-out and die in the normal way and watch from the wings, or not watch at all if it wasn't in their purview. There was a great deal of consensus regarding a large portion of the population going this way before during or after whatever was coming. For some people, the overture is enough and the rest of the concert can take care of itself.

Some people would be ascending along with Gaia, and some people would be remaining in a fear, power, greed-based third-dimensional reality on an earth indistinguishable from the one we have now. This is where the notion of a separation into two worlds comes in, and it all happens right here.

Gaia was going whether you were ready or not so you'd better get ready but if you're not – you wouldn't think anything at all had changed. Events would unfold further to their logical conclusion in the world you've always lived in, and people would continue to grow and evolve at their own rate. For those in tune, they would ascend with Gaia and become caretakers of the Promised Land.

This seemed to be the general consensus from a number of different sources, as fantastical and astounding as this idea is.

I kept thinking – no one gets left behind – but this didn't seem to be very realistic from what I was learning, and for a moment I despaired.

Would the people remaining in 3D be aware that certain others weren't around anymore? How literal was this? What *would* the awareness be between people on the ascended earth and people remaining in the third-dimension? No one wants to lose friends anymore.

As a third-dimensional human being right now I can't see the fifth-dimensional level of existence with my physical eyes, and it seemed to me that this ground rule would remain. Third-dimension was third-dimension. Thinking of this, it only made sense that if a sudden phase shift should occur... oh, say like in 2012 or something, the end result may indeed be people suddenly shifting out of frequency range right before your eyes... and disappearing.

The Christian Rapture might not be as crazy as you think – I thought, but I couldn't get past this idea of separation (here come the sheep and the goats), and hadn't we all had enough of that with death?

It made sense that a desire to break through barriers and say I love you would always be possible in the same way it was now at least, and I decided to take some solace in that, knowing all systems are open and it would be up to the third-dimensional personality to awaken to these realities, as is the case now.

As grand as it all was, I knew it would actually unfold on an individual basis as to who was going where, so I decided to leave it at that and keep the mystery there. If I wanted a blueprint, it was mostly for passing on some reliable information to others and as a back-up to what I already sensed.

Some things sounded dicey but an ultimate nature was behind all this, and I felt safe when I thought of being in the hands of the universe – or the arms of the goddess. I also felt a "we're in this together!" relationship with the earth herself, and I could sense my being penetrating to the heart-centre of the planet.

There were so many questions. I'd seen so many miracles by now I knew anything could happen, even at the last micro-second, so I decided to just hope for the best and to accept that everyone had their own beliefs and visions steering their course... and their own time.

༄ ༄ ༄ ༄ ༄ ༄

It was all so astonishing and immense. It was more than I could've ever hoped for, and it was almost strange how so much of it was easy to believe and understand.

Thinking of the cosmos and all that majesty surrounding us, my thoughts flew back to day five and the pinnacle moment when I had my appointment with the Creator, and felt my oneness with God and all of existence.

The bedroom had turned into outer space – anything could have happened at that moment, but it was planets and moons and nebulae whizzing by – and when I relived that moment as I would continue to do forever, nothing seemed impossible and I realised I was also being prepared for ideas such as these. I saw the universe unfolding, but you could just as easily say I saw cycles and evolution.

I wasn't just *reading* about evolution either. I thought about day five again, and the moment when I'd physically felt my head move, and I had to laugh as I thought about a T-shirt I'd seen thirty years ago – "Why wait? Mutate now."

A short-story I'd started years ago and never continued with came to mind, it was called "The Mute Room" and was going to be a science fiction story based on a room that caused physical changes and mutations (don't laugh, it was many years ago). Holy smoke! I hadn't thought about that in years... how not surprising! These ideas had been coming out in one way or another.

Association took me back to another time when I realised cats were evolving. This had started so many years ago when I noticed more and more cats looking at me right in the eye. I knew they hadn't all done that before, as I remembered Mao Mao being one of the few cats I knew who did so, and it was an amazing and noticeable thing. I loved it when they did that and really *knew* you. They had started to see themselves in mirrors too, and I remembered how many times I'd just blurted out – cats are evolving!

This tied-in perfectly with what I was discovering about the Ascension and animal consciousness being elevated to near-human qualities as we make the shift. The idea was that they would fill the void we left behind, and my heart jumped for joy at the thought of this.

I squeezed my eyes shut on the tears and remembered again the dreams I'd had talking to animals, and of course I thought of Rex. Once again I had the ongoing experience of Rex chatting away all the time, and Brandy's comments on day one through Gordon in the coffee shop, to lay the groundwork for all this. I thought of Henry saying "I could fall into you." We were going to be able to talk to the animals! If nothing else happened at all, this gift would be more than enough for me.

Nature spirits would also be advancing in the same way, and after Mr. Green and the face on the tree who spoke to me... well, it all made sense.

It was time to pull it all together and decide what I believed and what I didn't, but I had the luxury of what I'd been living for the last seven months as an undeniable backdrop to the notion that something was definitely going on, inside and out.

No sir, with what was going on with me, none of this was particularly difficult to believe, and I didn't find it too hard to feel my way through the material. This sorting through and just knowing what was true (for me), was easy enough once I learned to trust myself and my initial reactions, and I knew there was a phrase I was looking for that I hadn't thought of yet.

From the universal to the cellular, from the Multi-verse to the Omni-verse to the whatever-you-want-to-call-it verse, we seemed to have come up against the opportunity of the ages. Evolution sometimes goes in spurts – have you seen those grasshoppers turn into locusts overnight! And it seemed that we were on the verge of turning into light... if we didn't destroy ourselves first. It would be that feminine energy justly restored that would save the day – I thought.

The timing was now, as we found out, and the event was evolution – a giant leap.

Okay... let's see exactly what some of these cultures have to say here about 2012 being an appointment with destiny:

By now I was so familiar with Hinduism and considered it part of my home base, so I knew it was the end of the Kali Yuga – the Dark Age when people are as far removed as possible from God. Coming up from the Goddess Kali was Kalki, who will end this age of darkness and destruction. For the Buddhists, it was Maitreya, also referred to as the Second Christ – the idea of a final world teacher and master appearing had already started to develop.

I tended to think more about the master within, our own inner-selves and guides finally getting through to us, but if an actual physical visit (or manifestations) from someone like this was in the works, it wouldn't surprise me at all. Whether physical or not, I was sure many other Ascended Masters were here now to help us during this most auspicious time.

Considering who had said hello to me so far, and the magic I'd witnessed, none of this was difficult to accept or understand. I wondered what I'd think of this material if nothing out of the ordinary had happened to me personally, and thought I would still find it all quite credible. Something *had* to happen and we couldn't go on this way – that was for sure. I went back to my list and started to add a few details.

The Australian Aborigines say it's the end of the 40,000 year dreamtime as we leave one dimension to dwell in another, or both.

The Aztecs call this the Time of the Sixth Sun – time of transformation.

I found out the ancient Cherokee calendar also ends in 2012 when all is reborn. Rebirth was to turn up over and over again.

With the Christian Rapture, it seems that millions of the righteous will simply disappear and zoom to heaven a little earlier than expected.

The Dogon Tribe say that visitors will return in the form of a blue star. My lord! And the Hopi have a Blue Star Prophecy don't they? I'll get to them – I thought. This was what I'd already suspected about the incredible similarities, but this was... incredible!

The Celtic Druids also had their thirteen-moon calendar and I knew they were involved in all this – along with everyone else it seemed. The prophecies of the Merlin indicated a possible pole shift, so do the predictions of Edgar Cayce.

I next found out that the stone calendar of the Great Pyramid in Egypt, records the present time cycle as ending in 2012.

Organising things alphabetically, I came to the Hopi next anyway, and sure enough, the Blue Star Prophecy talks about a Fifth World emerging – The World of Illumination – after the Blue Star Kachina appears. (In late October, just two and a half months ago, the comet Holmes unexpectedly erupted and became visible to the naked eye. By November, the coma had expanded to a diameter greater than the sun's and appeared as an enormous blue star.) This would be the day of purification, and here was something else that would turn up over and over again – the idea of cleaning house.

The Incas call this "the age of meeting ourselves again."

The Maoris say the veils between the physical and spiritual worlds will dissolve.

The Maya talk about the end of the fifth and final age and also the End of Time, with a portal materialising within the dark rift at the centre of the galaxy.

It was funny, the Pueblo Indians of New Mexico were of the opinion it was the *start* of the Fifth World, but it didn't make any difference – just look at this! It was just different names for the same thing.

The Tibetan Buddhist Kalachakra teachings that we mentioned earlier, actually call it the Coming of the Golden Age.

The Zulu are one of my favourites and simply say the whole world will be turned upside down.

You could keep going if you wanted to and include The Sybil of Cumae, a Roman Oracle who wrote her prophecies on oak leaves, and Mother Shipton, a seer from Yorkshire in England during the late 1500s.

The dreams and visions of Black Elk, the Dakota Sioux Shaman, point to this time of transformation also, and there's also a theory that Nibiru, (Planet X) swings into our solar system every 3600 or 4200 or 6500 years (depending on who you believe), and of course if it's not a myth, the next appointment is 2012.

For those who believed in the non-interference directive, the quarantine was to be lifted on December 21, 2012 and open contact with our galactic family would move forward untethered.

And we can't forget – This is the dawning of the Age of Aquarius – and if you remember the song at all, and if you want a supreme example of divine synchronicity and humour, you might also remember the name of the group – "The Fifth Dimension."

I mean... seriously.

Some scenarios felt right, and some things didn't. We are all final arbiters within ourselves, and I held certain ideas close to my heart... and others I discarded.

I remembered a line I'd read that added to what I was saying earlier, about not believing anyone else about anything, unless it struck a chord deep within you – learn from everyone, and follow no one.

ॠ ॠ ॠ ॠ ॠ ॠ

2012 has to be the ultimate synchronistic event of... what? The last 20 billion years? All time? It wasn't just a synchronizing of the heavens, but also possibly, of consciousness. The people who were thinking along similar lines were linking up with the earth and each other psychically, as well as in the external world through books and seminars and the usual things, with the internet now as that final connector.

Was the Mayan Calendar about measuring cycles of consciousness more than anything else? This made a lot of sense when you thought about it.

It was these indigenous peoples with whom I felt most at home with, along with the psychics channelling all of this amazing related material, and for a moment I digressed and gave myself a short lecture:

"How do you get to Heaven without dying first? Well, you increase your vibrational frequency here and now. Everyone has a unique vibrational signature and no two are the same – this is like your own personal song in the universe and it is inviolate – this is what we are, vibrating fields of energy. So is everything else.

Upon normal death when we separate from our physical bodies, our spirit bodies, or astral bodies, or dream bodies if you prefer, vibrate at a higher rate and are therefore invisible to physical eyes. Generally, we can't physically see those particular frequencies at this stage of the game, but of course there are always exceptions as some people *do* see, and sometimes there are bleed-throughs. As an aside, we are therefore surrounded by invisible spirits who are vibrating faster than us, but they are there nevertheless and inhabit the higher dimensional realms.

Once you've learned you can leave your body consciously, and you've zoomed around your bedroom or neighbourhood even just once, you'll never doubt this again. Of course this release also comes along naturally all by itself during sleep and at the time of death.

We come back to this again... you must *believe* you can do this, first, or you'll never be able to – the proof comes after. Things are the opposite of what we've been taught. It's not – prove it and I'll believe it. It's believing it right now, (faith), and the proof will *then* show itself to you. It literally *will not be possible* for you if you don't believe it is, for now you will immediately inhabit a universe where such a thing is indeed impossible – for you. We are that powerful.

You have to decide what you believe, all by yourself, and this is worth repeating.

The point is – we are already spirits, souls. It's just that at this moment, we are temporarily enmeshed with our physical bodies. The physical body and all matter is energy vibrating at a very low frequency, and we don these bodies like space-suits or diving outfits so we can exist in this particular third-dimensional physical reality. So if we can raise our vibrational frequency while still in a physical body, we open the door to the fourth dimension and beyond."

I laughed at myself and then I got down to the business of looking further into what was actually going on with all of this.

I came upon terminology describing the fourth dimension as an octave above the third, and the fifth being an octave above that, and I couldn't believe my eyes once again.

What had I been going on about right from the start? That word had come up for me on day five. Octaves! I was ecstatic.

I tried to calm myself down a bit – but it was difficult. Was all this really happening to me? Am I still saying that? I had to go for a walk. It was the second week of January now, and a walk in the winter air would be invigorating and bind me to the earth – I said thank you to the universe beneath a sky full of twilight.

༄ ༄ ༄ ༄ ༄ ༄

The fourth dimension is generally regarded as being the astral realm or the first non-physical reality we find ourselves in after death, with the fifth dimension being Unity Consciousness and the dissolution of the usual ego. Obviously you can't approach that infinite expanse with the psychological approach you've been used to.

I read about some of us having had a taste of this from a third-dimensional perspective, and people reported a sensation of flying apart at the seams. Holy smoke! Wasn't this more or less what I was trying to describe on day five? To look at things this way, it seems I'd temporarily entered this fifth-dimension on that day.

This is something that saints and masters, or certain accomplished ones like shamans and highly evolved cultures like the Maya no doubt, have been able to achieve consciously for millennia, but now there was a kind of accelerating opportunity available for anyone to utilise on their personal spiritual journey.

For me, I felt I'd lurched and stumbled and barely managed to fall into the Goddess' arms, and I wished everyone else a safe journey through their own obstacles.

The baggage and drama was bobbing to the surface to be dealt with quickly now, and we needed to attune ourselves to these new wavelengths as well as we could.

It was the people who knew nothing of any of this, (like me not long ago), and people who thought they were flesh and blood only, who concerned me the most.

We were getting a boost from All That Is, from God, from The Great Spirit, in the form of this new light coming in, and I just sat back for a minute and realised once again that I'd learned more, and become more in the last seven months, than I had in my entire life as a whole. My life suddenly had purpose and meaning beyond anything I could have imagined previously, when my main concern had been simply to develop my own abilities and to practice and rehearse for the day I died. How selfish that seemed in a way at this point.

Becoming a *good person* was what it was all about: living by higher principles and caring more about others than yourself, revering all life, and respecting everyone's beliefs and opinions no matter how far they may diverge from your own.

Feeling gratitude, compassion, forgiveness and Unconditional Love towards everyone was the way to go. Not just family, friends, certain neighbours and maybe some acquaintances... but everyone (especially yourself or nothing works). These powerhouse emotions were the ones to cultivate, and with everyone you forgive, and every stranger you send love to, and every lost soul you feel compassion for, and every sunrise you thank the creator for, your personal signature rises and becomes a more pure tone.

These emotions come easily and naturally once a few things are pointed out – such as us all being sisters and brothers in a more profound manner than any simple blood-relation could ever be... such as us all being a part of the same overall consciousness.

True joy only exists when everyone is laughing.

It wasn't about doing what benefits *me* the most (looking out for "number one" was the old distorted energy that had gotten us into this mess), it was simply living through the heart and doing the *right thing* – for the good of all.

If we could stretch a bit further and include in this love all the life in the universe, then we were ahead in leaps and bounds as the universe is full to bursting with life, and we are a part of it all. To go along with that, is reaching a centre of balance within ourselves by releasing all old negative energies and karma, just like the earth was doing with the weather changes and the upswing of earthquakes and the like. There was also the notion that we as a planet were the chosen instrument to transmute all negativity for the entire solar system, and rather than feeling put upon by this, I hoped it was so.

Everything simply falls into place with an open heart instead of a closed mind, and we turn fear into love, greed into generosity, jealousy into acceptance and anger into inner peace and joy. There was no place for these negative debilitating corrosive emotions where we were hopefully going, and it all started with the intent to think and behave differently.

There was also talk about this new energy offering a kind of karmic amnesty, where lifetime's worth of built-up fear and negativity could be summarily left behind like a worn-out coat, and we could enter into this new world all nice and clean.

Other than the obvious, was this what "cleanliness is next to godliness" meant?

ಽ ಽ ಽ ಽ ಽ ಽ

I came across the idea that a dimension was a state of consciousness, and this didn't seem to be that hard to understand either, considering that *everything* was consciousness in one way or another when you got right down to it.

DNA was everywhere I looked, and the so-called "junk" DNA was anything but that, and was being encoded by this new light and activated. We had been operating on two strands only and now we were heading for full twelve strand activation – and there was that number twelve again!

The Russians had already proven this possibility scientifically, transforming frog embryos into salamander embryos by transmitting DNA information from one to the other using sound frequencies, or vibrations of you prefer, delivered simply by using laser light. I got the distinct impression the universe was now doing the same thing on a far vaster scale to say the least. It was astonishing.

Before I went any further, I had to back-track a little to find out just how much DNA we had in our bodies. All I really knew was that it was tucked in there somewhere.

I was in for a revelation or two.

DNA is in every single cell of the body, and depending on the source, there are anywhere from 50 to 100 trillion cells in the human body. A typical cell size is 10 microns or micrometres long and a micrometre is one millionth of a metre, or one thousandth of a millimetre. To put this in perspective, approximately 10,000 average-sized human cells can fit on the head of a pin.

It gets crazy and amazing when you consider that there is 1.5 to 3 metres *actual length* of DNA inside the chromosome package in the nucleus of every cell! If you took the total length of DNA in the human body, it would stretch from the earth to the sun and back something like *seventy times*, and we are ninety-three million miles away from the sun. This really put things in perspective for me, and I realised for the first time that we are veritably riddled with DNA. It's everywhere.

At the same time as this, as an aside, I learned the mitochondria and magnetite in our cells, pointed to a scientific basis for our electrical-magnetic natures, even on the physical body level. I was astounded.

This idea of the photon belt energies reprogramming our DNA with its magical light now took on a whole new significance for me, considering the sheer extent of this God-material inside of us.

Each one of us is over thirteen billion miles of DNA just walking around!

I had to just stop and think about that for a minute and let it really sink in. Then I had to check my sources again and redo my calculations. This was truly staggering to me.

It is a thirteen billion mile receiver/transmitter interface with the divine, and this was the image that made the most sense to me – spiral antennae – and blended easily with the serpent-spiral drawings, depictions and visions throughout history.

I knew our emotions affected it also (and this was ground-zero for health and healing), but in this case, it seemed new instructions were being given to the body from the universe, or God.

Our DNA was being changed to a crystalline structure from its usual carbon-based form, and this was allowing more light into the body. Also, our physical molecules were vibrating faster as our frequency increased and therefore moving further apart. This would also create more space or room for light to enter if you wanted to think of it that way. On our way from these dense physical bodies to pure consciousness and light, each subsequent form was more refined than the last.

There were comparisons to ice becoming vapour with the addition of energy (heat in this case), and when you got right down to it, it was still water whether in a solid, liquid or vapour state. The chemical composition hadn't changed at all... just the form (phase) and the properties. It was a great analogy – if you considered solid ice to be the third-dimensional state, and water and vapour to be the fourth and fifth respectively, it really worked. It was incredibly interesting, and I thought for a moment about atoms and how they themselves were mostly empty space as it was.

This was how the physical body ascended in theory, and if anyone was really sure about anything, it seemed to be the light. We were becoming light-beings.

Now I knew why we were seeing references to DNA, as well as the Mayan Calendar, in many crop circles. In August 1991 there was a broken DNA formation, which happens before a cell divides, and in June 1996 we had the double helix formation. These were followed in 1999 by a triple DNA pattern in June, and then a blossoming triple DNA in July. In the August 2001 Chilbolton formation, there was also reference to DNA in the "reply" to the message we sent in 1974 from the Arecibo radio telescope in Puerto Rico.

The crop circles had somehow transcended the exquisite solution to communicating from a non-interference perspective, and gone on to become not only mandalas of sacred geometry and inspirational beauty – each meaning something unique to the individual – but also a means of support if you were looking at things a certain way.

Looking back at these breathtaking geometries in order over the decades, I had a feeling the circle-makers could barely contain themselves now, and I felt there was excitement on the other side of the circles to match our own.

If you were one of the people who felt the Ascension and 2012 were the same thing, the references in the crop circles were piling up, and I thought – now that's reassurance I feel comfortable with! The circles were connecting the universe to the earth, one wanting you to pay attention to the other and notice the new dawn.

Could people not notice? It all seemed so blatant now, but I knew it was just one way of looking at things and some people would always see what they expected to see: crop circles were just people fooling around, channellers and psychics were fakes, personal "religious" experiences were madness, and the Hindus and the Maya didn't have a clue as to what they were talking about – they were old and done and not civilized. So no new fifth-dimensional crystalline light-body for you! – I laughed, then on a more serious note I realised the body, whatever it may turn out to be, would be just a reflection of the changes experienced within.

I was to learn more about this light-body later on, but for now, I concentrated more on the DNA aspects and I considered something stupendous – we were being upgraded.

ॐ ॐ ॐ ॐ ॐ ॐ

Ley lines, or Dragon lines, really fascinated me, and I knew about these pathways all over England and how many crop circles seemed to favour them, but I hadn't realised they were all over the earth and by some estimates, eighty-three thousand sacred sites were located on them. Where they intersected were vortices or places of additional power, and I thought of Seth and the Coordinate Points he had talked about so many years ago – subordinate, main and absolute. I remembered him saying the four absolute coordinate points intersected *all* realities. It was incredible, material I'd studied over thirty years ago was now coming back to be integrated into what was coming out now, and I considered how fortunate I was to have discovered Jane Roberts right at the beginning.

It was a natural progression to go from the telluric (earth) energy currents of the ley lines to the new Unity Consciousness Grid that surrounds our planet and was in the process of being activated with crystals and ceremonies occurring on the earth at this very moment. Plato had talked about this cosmic grid of consciousness, and it also related to Jung and his "collective unconscious," only this time, the feminine and masculine energies would be balanced and working in harmony, and the "unity" factor would allow us to understand and experience that we truly are all one. This was also referred to as the Ascension Grid – how not surprising!

In the meantime though, the old world was already falling apart. You didn't have to look too far to see the rocks being turned over and all the secrets and corruption being exposed to the light. That's funny! Yes, a sense of humour would definitely be a good thing to hold on to at this point, and fortunately cosmic humour was a reality in whatever dimension you found yourself in. As we used to say in England – sometimes you just have to laugh.

Instant karma was already happening as far as I could tell, and that was good. The last thing we needed now was to accumulate more baggage, and I had the feeling we weren't really being given the chance to do that anymore. (As I'm writing at this moment, I have to tell you that Instant Karma by John Lennon just started to play on the radio – okay, something's telling me I'm on the right track... I pray I am.)

Our own personal wounds and shadows were also coming to the forefront to be dealt with *now*, and especially in our intimate relationships, the need to seriously sort things out once and for all – or to move on – would not be ignored for very much longer. There was no place for hypocrisy where we were going.

At the same time, our divine essence did appear to be leaking out, depending on what you looked at and concentrated upon – depending on what you *see*.

There were so many different ways of looking at the world and you were creating it every time you looked at it. Never was there a more important time to see only the good, and to acknowledge without a doubt in your heart that we are all magnificent divine beings of light assuming our roles as young gods and co-creators, establishing a relationship with the universe that has as its starting place – intimacy. As we learn more, we step further in.

We were becoming fully conscious beings, and it was time to take full responsibility for our thoughts and behaviour. Ultimately, whatever we *believe* is going to happen will be what we personally experience – just like now. The stakes were just a little bit higher coming up in a minute or two.

Already I'd experienced people open to these ideas, and others who thought it was absolute nonsense, but I figured now was the time to bring it up because if the things we've been talking about did come along, there would be a lot of people who only saw the old world imploding, and would not have the comfort of knowing it was all leading to something glorious. I had to try, and figured the worst thing that could happen would be people gently indulging me as an eccentric or even crazy person, but basically harmless.

No one left behind? Maybe that was indeed naive of me, but I decided the people who were on the same path at this time would appear if they needed support or something I might hopefully have to offer, so I had to trust in divine forces – I had to trust God – and from what I'd seen and experienced in the last seven months or so, this wasn't difficult at all.

Things were getting quite interesting – All will be wondrous well – would be a good mantra right about now.

So we were ascending... one way or another. For the ones going this time around, it seemed like you either went straight to the higher realms and stayed there, or you maintained a physical presence on the earth in your new light-body vibrating at a higher dimensional frequency.

It would seem that the fifth dimension (sometimes called the Angelic dimension) is the highest vibrational level where we still take on a physical body, albeit a new and refined one.

If you were vibrating too high, your essence wouldn't be contained that way at all, it would be too much to be actualised in a particular system, and you would have to take on a form such as the light-body by stepping-down your frequency rate in the same way our own souls do now to assume a three-dimensional physical form.

Either way, it didn't seem like "dying," in the usual sense of the word was even in the cards, and the incarnation cycle would definitely be over, with full awareness of all your other lives.

For those staying with the new earth in one fashion or another, the idea was to return the earth to the paradise she always was, to usher-in a world based on love instead of fear – to help co-create heaven, right here at home.

I realised I didn't really know what I would be doing. It seemed like I had the vibrational thing going on and yahoo for me, but these decisions were not the kind to be made by the conscious mind, and I would have to rely on the more knowledgeable portions of me to make those discernments. I hoped Malcolm, or Neli-Two, knew what he was doing.

Years ago, my young nephew Steve had asked me, "What's your favourite thing?" just waiting for me to get my answer out of the way so he could tell me his – "Ninjas!" Without even thinking, I'd answered, "Planet Earth," and whenever I thought about that as the years went by, I was always happy with my answer.

Wherever or whatever I may find myself to be in the "future," earth would always be the legendary home, and was I just going to maybe zoom off to heaven now as fast as I could – given half the chance – or was the entire reason for my being here, to help sort through the rubble, (metaphorically or otherwise), and lend a hand after the shift? Could I do both?

It would be so easy just to bail-out, assuming I make it that far, but somehow this didn't sit quite right with me. What had I signed-on for here? One day at a time, I decided – just take one day after the other Nelson, and try to be the best "you" you can be, whatever happens.

ᘛ ᘛ ᘛ ᘛ ᘛ ᘛ

The final thing I wanted to check into here concerning the Ascension, was what people thought the new light-body earth-walker might be like. There were so many opinions as to what the new person would possibly be capable of as an evolved human being vibrating at a higher level, but still on the planet - embodying the transcendent. Moving from national to planetary to galactic to Universal or Infinite Consciousness was bound to have some benefits, right? We were already infinite consciousness, but at this stage we would *know*.

So how might that go?

Well the first thing would be accepting our role as conscious co-creators, and being fully aware of the power to create with thought. Our intention would have to be clear now, and our awakened psychic abilities would be a normal natural mode of operation. Our thoughts and desires would manifest quite instantly at this point, and compared to the time-lag version of manifestation going on now, it'll be a wonderland of magic... as long as you know what you're doing – I reasoned. I hope everyone's been practicing in dream land, because a focused steady mind is going to come in extremely handy.

I'd been concerned about this part in the past with simply dying in the old-fashioned way, and I'd always wondered how anyone could cease all negative thinking once there, but after my vacation in Nirvana I knew how easy it was.

I recalled telling Marie that all negativity was gone, and it was so effortless and natural because it was just the feel of the place and you really understood the ramifications. The feeling was along the same lines as having just... grown up, of having attained an inevitable level of maturity.

Consequences begin with thought.

People are also very fast learners when reality flies back in your face faster than a mirror – I thought, and it wouldn't take long to sort that one out I'm sure.

Welcome home... you'll get used to it and remember.

Love would now reside in our hearts, and fear would be left behind as a dim memory of when things were "wrong." The twin master-illusions of time and space would be clearly seen for what they are – simply a manifestation of a third-dimensional reality and not the way things *really are* at all.

It was starting to sound exciting! And I decided that feeling excited and even eager, was definitely the best way to go considering the other options available. The best thing would be to drop fear right now, dwell on the divine aspects, and to understand that not everyone gets to go through something like this. We had chosen to be here at this time and to experience this mystery, it was a privilege – yes, but we were also brave souls indeed.

I laughed when I thought about something I'd read regarding this decision to confront the unknown – it would look really good on your spiritual resume.

I got back to the "Homo Luminous" as some were calling the new human being, although that sounded pompous to me in a way, and I tended to think of it all as unimpeded magic more than anything else. Nothing weird was going on... this was all *natural*, and it was also just in time – I thought.

I decided to think it would all be fun, no matter what happened.

Flying was something I was, of course, supremely interested in, and there was no consensus on this at all. People have been levitating throughout history so it didn't seem like much of a stretch to me, but it certainly wasn't a common thread or anything like that. We went from yes, we were going to fly – to no, we're not going to fly. I was holding out for magic carpets at least.

It was funny but for me, the image of flying is one of the most holy – and the most exciting. Whenever I envision anyone from a ghost to an angel to a spirit to an ascended master to a saint to an Orb to the fair-folk, to God, to a being of light I always see – first thing – a complete disregard for gravity. That's probably the first sacred or other-worldly special effect I ever latched onto and I never got away from it. Would I still have to wait until I left any kind of physicality behind to finally soar like I did in the world before this?

Okay so forget about that for now. There seemed to be enough other ideas going around that there was a great deal of agreement on, and the obvious one when you come to think of it is the telepathic abilities. That's funny!

If you hadn't started to do so already – which was unlikely if you were open to these ideas – you were going to go on-line with the universe, and you were going to have to figure out the difference between thinking and listening. I had to laugh when I thought about that, and lesson number one a lifetime ago.

So whether you started off talking with dead friends and relatives or went straight to, basically, any other consciousness in the universe – including The Creator once you got the hang of it – you were going to be plugged-in. Your consciousness would simply expand and you'll end up laughing at an old term like "Cosmic Consciousness" realising how appropriate it really is. Clairvoyant, clairaudient, and clairsentient abilities and so on, would be standard. Easily sensing the eternity of your own being must be a level of safety and security that in itself would be an underlying ecstasy.

I came back down to earth and thought of how merging was blending with other aspects of yourself, or you being a human was merging with you being an eagle. At the same time, the creation of individuality was probably the greatest gift of all and we could have *friends*.

Yes, we are all ONE, but the funnier thing was that Prime-Creator had the incredulous ability to assure us we were also capable of being... one. You could have as much individuality as you wanted to. You would be aware of all your other individual dimensional aspects, like your incarnations at first, or I'm sure you could consolidate everything into as tight an individual statement as you felt like. Does that make sense?

The other parts of us were *aspects* of this identity we were now, and from our perspective we were the flagship, and that would never change.

The ramifications of consciousness were endless and this was only scratching the surface of the surface.

It was time to get back to the fun.

Projections or Astral Travel or Out-Of Bodies or whatever you wanted to call it would be conscious and standard for those still walking the earth. Seth's three types of projections would come into play here, or maybe just the last, unhindered one – I thought. I also started to think about Seth's Inner Senses and would get to that in a minute.

Changing the form of your new body would be a natural ability from the looks of things. You could be younger, or older, or take the look of one of your other incarnations or possibly a fresh look altogether. Don't worry, "you" would always be recognised as you.

Becoming aware of your extra-dimensional activities and becoming able to hold the awareness in both "places," (bi-location), or maybe even more (omni-location?) would be possible.

Another promising potential would be a kind of teleportation of your main focus *with* your new body on and around the earth, and my mind went back to the Castaneda books once again.

The Yaqui Indian shaman-sorcerer Don Juan Matus had talked about his own ability to astral project but with a remarkable twist. Upon arriving at a destination in his astral form, he had the amazing ability to manifest his physical body at the new location. In other words, he could project and also take his physical body with him, dematerialising it at the starting location, and then rematerialising his physical form at journey's end.

How many years ago had I read this? It was so long ago, and now these same ideas where being discussed in regards to the Ascension. This was incredible!

Getting back to projections of consciousness alone, and considering the new light-body, travel through the entire universe with no boundaries or restrictions would also be on the table. You would be your own "light-ship."

That would be Seth's "True Projection Form" wouldn't it? And I really must get hold of that material in a moment or two.

I guess this would all be best-case-scenario type situations though wouldn't it?

Some were of the opinion that there wouldn't really be much happening in the way of amazing abilities, just a vastly expanded awareness, and again I thought – does it really matter? At least *something* was happening – at least the universe had noticed we needed help in a profound way and boy... here it comes.

What made the most sense to me were people transitioning to whatever level based on the frequency they were already putting out, with one commonality – our sense of separation being summarily blown-away.

Some people would be better equipped to deal with it than others – meaning some people would already have a closer idea as to how the universe actually worked. This was accelerated growth with a blast of universal wind and you would move through it accordingly, you would go with it the best way you could. There was no judgement involved, but if you could understand what was happening from your accumulated spiritual work, you had a better chance of holding on rather than being knocked off your feet.

I also thought there would be people who would simply "get it" at the last minute (if there was a last minute) and align with everything. They'd just sail forward with a smile, knowing they had chosen to do it this way.

I wondered if this related in some way to accepting Christ at the last moment of your life and still being "okay," in the Christian tradition. I coughed a laugh when I went back to an old idea and wondered if those lifetime-worshippers might be a little annoyed at that.

How *drastic* would it be on whatever level? That would be one of the core questions whether referring to the physical or etheric worlds, and it all seemed to depend on exactly who you *are*... as a person.

Who you are as a *being*, is someone who can create realities with your thoughts – and your thoughts follow your beliefs. Knowing this with every fibre is your stepping-off point and everything that happens from here on in will make a whole lot more sense. Three-dimensional earth is a tough university for emerging gods, and this is really the one and only lesson. Once you realise that all life is sacred, and all is *you*, then you can take full responsibility for this divine gift of infinite measure, and create accordingly.

Everyone will be exactly where they're supposed to be on the planet, or going to exactly where they're supposed to be going, based on simply their personal signature. There would be no masking or mistaking the music of your heart as the engaging navigator.

When I thought about the magnitude of what I was actually calmly considering like it was a topic around afternoon tea, I could only reason that without the last seven months as a foundation, I would probably still be talking about it if I knew, but more as a lovely dream or as a really good science-fiction-fantasy story. A probability for certain, but – what are the chances... you know?

After all the beyond-imagining experiences though – and I had to think of that obliterating ecstasy – I knew we were on to something here. When I thought of the note from 2006, a full year before all of this had begun, and "the frequency has changed," it was the equivalent to something you would feel in your bones.

If you decided to interpret the events unfolding in this way and open yourself up to the new melody being played in the universe, tuning yourself to these new dimensional harmonics, you could go somewhere beyond your most profound dreams.

Time would be *looser*, and I thought of my after-the-fact déjà-vu and the looping and not knowing if I'd already said things before or not. It would probably be easier to accomplish more time-travelling types of adventures in consciousness too – I wondered. I thought of my mother's reality and how time went so much slower there, which is one way of expressing it, and this correlated to the notion that time compresses and reality opens.

Instant access to universal knowledge would be normal. Direct information as we need it performing in full operational mode, and the drop-in-your-lap factor will probably be hilarious.

This would be the true internet, of which the physical version is but a third-dimensional rendition with crystals and magnets and electricity but with a wonder all its own nevertheless, and a true liberating factor during the time when everything happened at once somehow. This unfolding evolutionary dance would not be following the same lines at all without the web of our own creation – the internet has allowed for an immediacy of shared spiritual knowledge and a focusing outlet for this fountainhead of awakening energy.

Seeing energy in a more natural way would be another reasonable conclusion, or the energy that *is* everything will be more obvious than ever before. Seeing auras was the start of this. This would also lead naturally to enhanced healing abilities – tuning imbalances in someone's frequency vibration with colours and sound directed by thought, or some people might dance you to health. It would be a safe bet to conclude that any comparison of this to our current medical mechanical health (not healing) system... would be impossible. There just wouldn't be many "sick" people anyway. Illness, the way we knew it, would be gone in shame.

ૐ ૐ ૐ ૐ ૐ ૐ

The three bodies, The Astral, the Mind Form and the True Projection Form were as I'd remembered, with the capabilities of each one increasing, but what struck me was they matched the particular frequency of whatever reality they found themselves in – they were a natural configuring dimensional garb in the same way as our third-dimensional bodies now. It was like dressing appropriately to walk into the crisp winter world. Consciousness took on appropriate forms in the same way as it travelled from one reality to the next, and this would be automatic as we tuned-in to the vibrations of a particular dimensional field. I would come back to this.

I finally got down to Seth's Inner Senses, after having been unable to stop thinking of this material as I made my way along. Internally, I was always checking with my home-base, but I had to have a good look now as so many things were pointing in this direction and was that Jane Roberts peering over my shoulder? She wasn't talking, but I sensed her presence and a joyful interest in what I was doing and how I was *using* the material. I was being left alone.

It was being outside of a camouflage reality with the active illusions and ground-rules, and getting the full panoramic multi-dimensional view that was the really interesting thing, and this was where the inner senses came in.

These were the root senses when all of the illusions have been stripped away, and the playing field is seen to be open, infinite, and almost unfathomable but somewhat navigable relying on a finely-tuned intent. When these basic, core inner-senses are operating in all their transcendence, there's disentanglement and a direct experience of unveiled reality. These inner senses are our true methods of perception, and operate regardless of form – these were the senses of the inner-self.

Seth listed nine of them but listing them didn't matter right now, they operated together the same way our outer senses did anyway and you could separate them if you wanted to, but as an overview it was all about merging, inner knowing or direct comprehension, changing form, and changing realities. It was about mobility of consciousness. These natural senses of the soul were involved right from the beginning in lucid dream states, projections, and were in operation during any kind of psychic adventure.

The outer senses don't deal with what is actually out there, they create a world inside of you that you think is outside. They focus and narrow down attention to bring a particular reality into view and it's unique to the creature witnessing. A cat sees an entirely different world to my world, or the world of a butterfly – it could be a different planet for the way our individual senses arrange "reality" for us. Even from one person to the next, the world can be a completely different place.

I thought back to "realm" meaning "real dream" to me, and returned to an even older thought when I was just twelve, about the illusion being real. This was when I began to think that reality and illusion may not be mutually exclusive.

Our definition of real was crazy. We'd narrowed it down to a three-dimensional speck in the universe, and even then, our speck was still just a dream like everything else.

To assume "real" means a third-dimensional reality, is like saying I only speak English so no other language exists. Whatever affects you on any kind of psychological level is very real to your soul – a dream can affect your day more than any physical event. The dream world is another dimensional reality we are all intimately familiar with, and is a first indicator that we already inhabit many different worlds.

All the various dimensions and realities were psychological constructs – they were all illusion in the bigger picture, but they were also very real within their own spheres. Falling off that bridge will definitely kill you.

When all is said and done, the only true reality is infinite consciousness – infinite unconditional love.

ꕤ ꕤ ꕤ ꕤ ꕤ ꕤ

Looking through the very early Seth Sessions, where so much of this information on the inner senses is located, I almost fell over when my eyes hit upon the term – Fifth Dimension. This material was as familiar to me as the back of my hand, but the words hit me as though I'd never seen them before. There was a slight feeling of disappointment, along the lines of – how could I forget something like that? But at the same time, I knew *that* was the strength of the revelation. It was now, it was right now at this moment that I had to connect this, and another circle was completed.

Seth linked-in and locked-on and seamlessly blended with the new information on people's minds, or no, not new information, currently circulating information. The information itself was anything but new – it was ancient. It was "as old as the hills" – I could sense my mother in my mind, but she was leaving me alone as well and enjoying the adventure of my discoveries.

This material was from the sixties, and there was also fresh material here because of Jane Roberts' death-bed request to "Publish everything."

The early sessions were now complete unto themselves, and as I went through them looking for references to the fifth or fourth dimensions, I found both... in Seth Session number one. I was stunned.

He started early when it came to these things, and if I was unsure before about being led to this place – I felt a rightness now. Seth had started *and* completed the outside of the jigsaw puzzle for me, or it was more like the information was a circle or a spiral. This knowledge was timeless and alive somehow and really had no beginning or end, I now felt. I saw the snake with the mouth saying hello to the tail, and I felt like I'd walked around the planet and met myself still standing there wondering if I should get going.

I felt a sensation of completeness somehow, even in the eternal incompleteness of existence.

On a much larger scale, this feeling would have been an apt description for day five – I decided, but I wasn't going to go back now and add it in. Everything had its order and I wasn't going to cheat by pretending I'd thought of it on that day. I couldn't stop looking at that line though, and wondering if that was what it was all about really – trying to somehow feel complete when you never are or ever will be.

I decided there was no contradiction between feeling a completeness within yourself, and also always and forever becoming more. We're used to growing – that's what we do here.

By session 259, after Seth had established dream exploration and out-of-body projections as a natural way to embark on a spiritual journey, he states, "It is training for fifth-dimensional existence...." Okay that was it! It doesn't get any more succinct than that. Lucid dreams and out-of-bodies naturally resulted in a far wider view of reality and a glimpse at the nuts and bolts of how it all worked.

I realised that preparing for "death" had only been the preliminary, and Seth had been thinking in much larger terms right from the start.

The astral body is the structure the self takes in the fourth-dimension with certain limitations as to range and abilities. With the Mind Form, things expanded further until our psychic structure attained the True Projection Form, and I was now convinced this was the same as the fifth-dimensional light-body. It was all just different terms for the same thing.

I felt a warmth with the feeling that everything was okay now. It was like your best friend coming along at the last minute when you didn't think they were going to show up. I'd read so many different things over the years and I always remembered Seth saying to follow no one other than yourself and your own inner journey – at the same time, this body of work had become a part of me, and I couldn't help it now if it felt like home. I couldn't help that at all... and I took a moment to thank Jane and Rob and Seth for everything.

༃ ༃ ༃ ༃ ༃ ༃

Everything was as it should be... things would unfold the way they would and in the truest sense it was all natural and wonderful.

Graduation day was coming and we were being pushed into the examination room whether we were ready or not. I thought about this divergence, and it hit me the shift would be like a psychic centrifuge in a way. I could see us as consciousness-bubbles being separated using a kind of spiritual weight. It wouldn't have anything to do with worth or value – in the universe, such a thing is inconceivable – this was simply a cosmic shake-up and sorting-out, and when the dust settled, we would truly be where we *belonged.*

In the meantime, the idea was to help as many people as possible to awaken, and this was happening at a rapid pace all over the world from what I could tell. It was amazing and I would simply never have believed it just a few short years ago.

I was seeing tossed-off comments between people on the internet that brought tears to my eyes, as I realised the younger generations were arriving with a lot of knowledge already under their belts. They were talking about dimensions of reality and esoteric teachings as a matter of course, and I thought if enough of us as individuals started to see who we really are... that in itself would have an effect on the rest of the world as a kind of tipping-point or threshold was reached. The hope inside of me grew.

Being psychic was our natural spiritual state all along, and the universe had turned out to be a fantasy magic adventure. Myth and reality were merging, and I considered a world where the concept of a stranger would never be the same, and there would be no such thing as an enemy.

The stuff of the universe was *alive,* vital and not inanimate at all, far from it, and emotional feeling was the cohesive through everything. Love breaks through all barriers, right? I'd found that out for myself in a most personal way, and all you had to do was believe. Doubt seemed to be a natural thing so far, but an unwavering certainty was in the wings, and magical events were happening to people all over the world. What we dream for and yearn for and "know" was all but on our doorstep.

This transformation to unconditional love and ecstasy is our birthright, and the time for us as addicted, possessive, dominating and dominated human beings was all but over as far as I could see. The dream and the dreamer are not separate in the pureland, and that was where we were heading as we got closer to the unity of the Godhead.

I'd sorted things out enough to move on now, and to selfishly get back to the no less incredible events in my own life.

I felt connected to all of these major universal goings-on and it didn't make me feel like what had happened to me personally was any less stupendous because I'd had the benefit of this added new energy. It crossed my mind though, and then it just didn't matter. If this boost had made things possible for me, all I could say was thank you for allowing me to help, and overall there was a feeling of spontaneous precision with the way things had unfolded. It was a dance.

We are in for quite a ride I'm sure – just know where you want to go.

And as we head towards our unfolding destiny as a race – think your best and grandest thoughts, feel the earth breathing beneath your feet, raise your arms up to eternity, let love flow through your heart, and dream your most splendid dreams.

I can't help but think this is truly the best advice of all.

First Quarter

Believe

I received a DVD from my sister consisting of all the home movies my mother made with her 8mm movie camera, and watching these silent movies of my mum and dad on holiday in Florida and Las Vegas after three decades, was a wonderful but wrenching experience.

I remembered these old films of course, and I also recalled my mother with her little editing machine, cutting and splicing and assembling the whole thing onto a large reel. It was like a lost world now to see my parents walking, waving and laughing, and it was about as surreal as it gets with Edna watching the whole thing with me.

After all these years my nephews had assembled the whole thing on disc, and of course it couldn't have been more perfect for it to have come along at just this moment in my life. There was about two seconds of me on the compilation. I remembered how I wouldn't allow my mum to film me when I was a teenager, and I thought to myself – what an idiot I was spoiling her fun like that. I was so serious and deep and... miserable.

I hoped I was making up for things like that now, as I also remembered performing at the auditorium in Bramalea (with Lorraine and songwriter Jane) and insisting my mother and grandmother not go to see me. At that time it was easier for me to perform in front of a hundred strangers than it was in front of one person I knew well – especially my mum and grandma. How I regretted that for so many years afterwards when everyone was dead and gone, and they never did see me play and sing in front of an audience.

I felt a wave of emotion from my mother and knew it meant I had far surpassed that performance with the one I was now engaged in, and with *this* act, she was a co-performer. I finally let all the regret go, as I considered how gracious the universe was to somehow give me this unbelievable opportunity for redemption.

Along with the disc, Sandra sent a note ending with, "Tell mum I love her!" which proved that yes she really did believe, and I hugged myself with joy, feeling my ribs. I was a hundred and thirty-three pounds now which was a step in the right direction, but I still felt pretty fragile.

"You're as weak as Willie's wee."

I couldn't help but laugh at this even though it was actually kind of serious. It was something my mother used to say in response to a really weak cup of tea.
Don't worry mum, I'll be okay as long as I don't drop dead.

"Don't be a fat-head – you're not an old codger yet."

That night, I went for another walk around the neighbourhood, thinking about what I'd learned and how much more there was *to* learn. It seemed the further along I went, the more obvious it was there was so much more to realise and remember. Parvati dropped a sentence into my mind:

perhaps your mantra should simply be – I know

Yes, I knew what she was talking about. All the answers were definitely within, but it was hard to find them sometimes, and you just had to listen to yourself, there was no master who could do it for you.

I was thinking about everything that had happened up to this point, and how to accept it first, and then integrate it. I turned up a street and saw a bright living room window with the curtains still open and I could see their fireplace mantle. On top of the mantle in the centre, was a large carved wooden word, and the word was – BELIEVE.

Oh my lord! Nothing else needed to be said and nothing else needed to be thought about. That one word said it all, and there it was, just for me. I was enraptured and carried on walking and walking until I'd made it to Bayview and turned around to make my way back.

I came back a different way, just letting my feet do the navigating, and up ahead there was one dark street lamp, and once I got to it, I stood beneath it looking up and it was completely dead – no flickering or any sign of life at all.

I felt Parvati still around, and I spoke to her out loud.

"Okay, come on then. It doesn't matter if you do this or not, but there's the lamp... and if you could just... you know... turn it on...."

"You really don't have to... I won't feel any less sure if you don't, and I feel kind of embarrassed, but..."

At that second the street lamp came on with all its glory and shone down on me. I was speechless, I was flabbergasted, I was elated, and I squeezed my eyes shut and said a massive thank you and I really didn't want to leave. I could've just stood there staring at that light for hours with my heart bursting, but after one more thank you to Parvati, I got myself going and headed on down the street.

ॐ ॐ ॐ ॐ ॐ ॐ

By now, I was re-reading books I'd read many years ago, such as the Tao Te Ching, and I let myself go wherever I was led. Sikhism still fascinated me and I read more about Guru Nanek –"There are no Hindus, there are no Muslims"– and everything opened my eyes just that little bit further. With the freedom I now had from work, I found myself spending hours and hours at the library and reading there, as well as coming home with my latest treasures under my arm.

Before too long I'd just about gone through the spiritual and psychic sections of this fairly small library. I made sure I interspersed this with periods of not reading or researching at all, and tried to find a balance between the two – it was a glorious time.

It seemed like I was actually making it through after all, and even when I still felt that some new synchronicity or event or miracle was too much to believe, something told me to *dare* to believe it. It just wouldn't be contained somehow and spilled over everywhere. My mother was always there to help and instruct and sometimes just to throw one-liners at me:

"Peter – this is for real."

It was normal now to catch a glimpse of White Feather smoking, or to hear a voice or to follow an impulse, and there was nothing else to do but to go with it. I generally felt excited like a child most of the time, and I knew this joyful innocence was a type of strength. It felt like I was playing in God's playground now, which I always had been anyway, but now I knew it.

"You'll be okay, you crazy coon."

With lines like this from my childhood in England, my mother knew the best things to say at just the right time, and I couldn't help but have faith, and believe and accept. The world had turned upside down but somehow, I'd managed to hold on and regain my footing, and every day I would go for a walk, no matter what, and let the universe speak in whatever way she wanted.

On this day it was the full moon, the first one of 2008, and noticing a large advertisement on the side of a passing bus, I read – The event that will be felt, long after the night is over.

I couldn't have said it better myself.

Moon Nine

Merkaba

I'd ended up getting a call from employment insurance and lo and behold, it was from a very friendly lady who sympathised with my plight. "Let me see what I can do for you, I have discretion in these matters." She'd been particularly interested in the lack of a raise in pay for five years or so, and I think my benefits being rescinded years ago also really helped to tip the scales.

The end result came on January 23, day two hundred and thirty-six, with the arrival of two cheques and then another one a day later. The outcome of this long delay was an amount of money at one time that I would probably never have been able to accumulate otherwise, and a laptop computer was now in sight.

I decided I wouldn't spend more than a thousand dollars, and began researching various models based on the music studio program I wanted and the connections it would need and so on. With any luck, I'd be able to start recording again as well as being able to possibly start a book. I was really excited about the prospect, and having a few dollars in my pocket also made me feel a lot freer than I had in the past two months.

In the meantime, I carried on with my new life and during one more period of reading about the Ascension and related subjects, I came upon a most interesting subject that connected to something I'd been drawing for a long time.

As far back as I can remember, one of my most recurrent doodles when mindlessly playing with a pencil has been two triangles – one inverted on top of the other. In this case, it turns out that "mindless" means bypassing the mind, and going somewhere deeper and more profound, as I found out that this image is the simplest representation of what is known as the Merkaba.

I couldn't believe it, I'd found drawings in my sketch pad as recent as 2006 depicting triangles inside of each other, one upright and the next upside down, sometimes fitting inside of each other by getting smaller and smaller until they disappeared in the centre. I'd been doing this without thinking about it for years and years, and like so many things lately, it was about to start making a whole lot of sense.

The Merkaba was a three-dimensional Star of David, a Star Tetrahedron. It related to the Kabbalah, and Egypt and the Hopis and... everyone it seemed. Once you started to look for it you found it everywhere, and this to me was the best evidence for something of profound significance. And as usual, I'd come to it myself first somehow, and then found the backup information, which for me, was the best way for things to work and gave me the most confidence.

But there was more, it was also found in the heart chakra, and I had another look at the Hindu Sri Yantra I mentioned earlier, and without even thinking about it before, the central portion of this sacred geometrical image was nine interlocking triangles!

It turned out Merkaba meant Light-Spirit-Body! I felt that jolt again. Now I'd found a name for what I learned about during my concentrated burst of study about 2012 and the Ascension. This was incredible! Everything was coming along at just the right moment for me, and I'd been drawing renditions of this thing for years without any idea of what it would one day refer to. Oh thank you and once again, I had the sign I needed to feel secure that I was on the right track.

This divine light vehicle consisted of rotating fields of light that could carry one's consciousness directly to the higher dimensions. This referred to a journey inwards, and a reconnection to our source or God.

Oh my, this was starting to sound familiar by now.

It was also known as The Chariot of Ascension! The Hopis called it The Chariot of the Star People. It manifested as a saucer-shaped field about fifty-five feet across, and could be activated through breath-work and meditation or, as I suspected, spontaneously if it was your time. I was to also learn another term for this – the DNA Field!

I was elated – another circle was completed in my mind, and I stopped and stared at my hands for a minute. They had drawn those little sketches and punched the keys on the computer, and even though I knew the knowledge had come from somewhere else entirely – I thanked the universe for my beautiful hands.

Upon further reading I discovered this field could affect various electrical systems, and sometimes street lamps were known to have been turned off and on just by walking past. I also found references to electrical field interference in further research on Kundalini, regardless of the Merkaba.

As electrical beings none of this was particularly surprising, but it was fascinating how the knowledge slotted into place. The pieces of the jigsaw puzzle were fitting together in a perfect elegant way which made me feel I was really coming into my own, and I just sat in amazement as I considered that even the scribbles I'd done for years had now attained a significance I could barely have imagined. Revelations were occurring before me and inside of me with a rapidity that made my head spin, and I truly was in heaven.

I'd known all along I couldn't continue the way things had gone those first few months, and no, I didn't feel quite as delirious and emotionally obliterated the way I had during that time, but it had been replaced by these steady miracles and I knew this would never end. I was in the lifetime all my incarnations had been waiting for somehow, and I wouldn't let them or myself down. Whatever I learned here would be passed along to all the various portions of myself and I knew this particular life was the fulcrum of them all.

ꙮ ꙮ ꙮ ꙮ ꙮ ꙮ

After the situation with my glands and gums I wasn't overly concerned when my jaw began to really hurt, and then the pain travelled up to my ear. I could feel the track of it on my face and now I had ear-ache. It was all part of the Kundalini cleansing purging process, which had been humourously referred to as a cosmic makeover, and I calmly jotted it down in my journal. Actually, a part of me was happy when anything relating to the Goddess occurred, and I welcomed the pain as an indicator of my transformation, but of course I would keep my eye on things.

I remembered having severe ear-ache as a child and my mother rocking me all night long. It had been impossible to sleep and is the type of pain I would wish for no one to experience. This wasn't as bad as that, thank god, but my mind went back to that time and I thought about mothers and what they would do, or wouldn't do, for their children.

"It's okay Peter – you're not on your tod."

Oh hi mum! Yeah I know I'm not on my own and you would rock me if you could. That would look pretty funny these days with me being bigger than you!

We both had a good laugh at the vision of that, and chatted away until I went to bed, quite able to sleep despite the ear-ache this time around, and in the morning it was gone.

Last Quarter
Look Back with Affection

It was Friday and another snow storm had blanketed the world in wonder, and it wasn't over yet. I put my boots on in anticipation of a walk in the magic, and after getting my camera and bundling up I stepped outside into the pure white world.

It was at times like this, when I felt truly alive and blissful, that my spirit friends would easily join me and share in the miracle of life on the physical earth and this energy called the weather.

Gwen was the first to come along and let her presence be felt.

it's a fine and beautiful thing Peter

Oh yes it is Gwen, just like your Irish accent – I thought to her as I walked along, stopping every now and then to slowly turn in a circle for a full three hundred and sixty degree view.

I felt like I was trying to fit myself together but there was always more and more pieces, and I knew the process would go on and on as I simply became more than I was a moment before with every breath.

I still sometimes missed the intensity of the first few months, and I remembered once again the comment my mother made about having fun with the beginning time and that I would relive it with great affection. I did, just as she predicted, but I also missed it too. I remembered the first time I heard her voice and the depth of the incredulity as everything tilted, and I started to slide off the old world and right over the edge. Like everything else in life, there was only ever one "first time."

Gwen had skipped away as fast as she came, and Edna was here now.

"Look back with affection – but not loss."

You always say the perfect thing mum, I'll remember that.

*"What you have now is so much stronger.
That was the foundation – then the firming – now the layering."*

Okay, I'm listening.

*"You're still in the world, and you have to deal with it.
You're less shaky now – more controlled."*

Well, that's good. I still feel pretty shaky sometimes though.

"You asked for it, and it knocked you senseless."

Yeah, you could put it that way all right.

*"I did put it that way.
Gather your things around you – your instruments and books and such.
A computer would be good."*

I think I'll have a computer soon.

"Good. Be as comfortable as you can. You're never alone. We're a team."

Then the other member of the triumvirate, Sri Bhundari, appeared for the last word.

we're very good at what we do

This was a line from another favourite movie of mine – Millennium.

They were gone now. I pulled off my gloves and fished some paper out of my pocket to write the exchange down. Here I was in the middle of all this snow swirling and flying around like silver faeries and I had an open line to the spirit world. I couldn't imagine anything any better than this. I thought this must be paradise right here, as my vision soared into space and I could see myself standing here on this little blue planet as she spun around and flew through space herself.

I love you Gaia. You're *my* planet. I'm a child of the earth no matter what. We're part of each other.

I love you too my child

By now the earth herself had spoken to me a few times, and here was one of those times. For some crazy reason, a Carole King song came into my mind and I found myself singing – I feel the earth... move... under my feet....

I always know where you are on my surface

I had no doubt about that – no doubt whatsoever – and as I started for home I could see Duncan the Druid in my mind with his hood back on his shoulders this time, and he looked very much like me!

only better-looking

That's funny Duncan. I'm so happy you've spoken to me! I must be progressing along okay – I thought.

Out came my note-pad again, and rocked by the wind, I wrote down what had happened with the snow lifting my hair as it flew back up to the sky.

༄ ༄ ༄ ༄ ༄ ༄

On the Monday my granddad visited and we talked about music. I just knew it was him before he even said a word, and I was amazed at how everyone had their own specific signature. This was the unique vibrational frequency we talked about earlier, and in practice it was like recognising someone's face, voice or scent.

Later on it was Allison, the relative whose funeral I'd attended not that long ago.

thank you for the feather

This was because I'd quietly slipped a feather onto her coffin before leaving after the service. What an incredible device the universe had for distinguishing one person from another – it was mind-boggling when you thought about it.

I went on to think about those first thirteen days, and by now I considered them to have been a kind of siege – in the nicest way of course. Then I considered all of our current lives on earth, and how we played the parts we had agreed to play under these difficult conditions, what with the built-in amnesia and everything.

"Roles and regulations."

That's hilarious mum – it's perfect!

I repeated the words slowly to myself that night as I drifted off to sleep – roles and regulations...

New Moon
Steady As She Goes

On the Saturday I saw Gordon for two hours and attempted to fill him in as well as I could. It was basically impossible even with the notes I had with me, but I did the best I could and it was becoming more evident all the time that a book was the only hope of keeping it all together.

In the evening I visited with piano student Jane and decided to tell her about Steaven and a few other things to go along with it. She had no problem accepting this, and casually told me she saw and spoke to him herself! This was wonderful, and I wondered how many other people were psychic in one way or another but simply kept their mouths shut most of the time. A lot more than you would think I suspected.

I would visit my mother too, in her house on a rough cliff overlooking the ocean in Lancashire, and we would spend time sitting at a long transparent table in what I called the kitchen area. It was a long table, but like most things in her house it seemed to have the ability to be whatever size was required depending on the number of people there and the meaning of the gathering.

Sri Bhundari quite often joined us and we would have business meetings and talk about the serious issues regarding my current life. At other times there were more people, and I felt it was a delegation of some kind. I seemed to be more of an onlooker at these times, and I had the feeling that no matter what stage I was at, there was always a bigger picture unfolding and some things I wasn't ready for yet. I never felt left out though, just respectful and almost embarrassed that there was this much caring and concern about me.

No matter who was or wasn't there at the table, one thing was always in attendance without fail – a single silver rose. Long-stemmed and shimmering with a life of its own, my mother now kept this symbol dead centre in a beautiful shiny-black vase in the shape of a crotchet, or quarter-note as they say in North America.

Of all the shapes to choose for a vase, this could not have been more perfect or appropriate – a music note. The glistening black of it setting off the silver rose in a manner that only accentuated both of them to an astonishing level of beauty. It always rendered me speechless and when discussions were on a level I couldn't follow, I would stare at it and become hypnotised not only by its reality here on this table, but because of what it meant. If I was to die today, this home would be where I would find myself – just as she'd promised.

Back in physical reality and walking up the street, things generally seemed clearer now, and I decided I really liked this new feeling of assurance. It felt like another stage had begun, a new era of relief of sorts – a comfort zone.

My mother popped in and wanted a description of the feeling as well as I could describe it. I told her it was like the breaking-in period for a new pair of shoes being over, and the stiff newness and sparkle had given way to comfort and familiarity. Not the greatest example perhaps, but she thought it was quite an apt description.

A new psychological season had begun and as I crossed the parking lot to the grocery store, I had a vision of a ship calmly sailing along on tranquil seas... steady as she goes – I thought. Suddenly it got dark – the sea was churning and the rain was lashing down upon the deck as the wind howled. What the...?

I heard Edna laughing now and knew she'd bumped my vision with one of her own and was laughing herself stupid.

"Would you like a Sou'wester to withstand the weather?"

Nice one mum! It was hysterical, and we shared the laughter and the memory of me having one of those particular sailor's waterproof-hats when I was a kid in England.

I don't think I wore it very often, knowing me.

Mostly this moon phase, I scrutinised this strong, new grip I seemed to have on things, and I spent time at the library on the computer. I was learning a lot about laptops, and narrowing down the ones I was interested in.

Coming home from there on Thursday, I went the long way and took photographs of St. Anselm's church in the snow, and I would never look at that church again in quite the same way after my experience with Jesus and the blue twinkling light. It had attained a mythical status for me now and I said thank you to the statue of St. Anselm himself before I continued on my way.

My mother suggested we play with the TV captions when I got home, as we hadn't done this for a while, so once inside, I went upstairs, put my things away and clicked on the TV. The second it came on it said – "She's... dead!"

This was altogether too much – It was the same as on that first day with the captions!

We both burst into laughter, and then as I kept looking at the screen, the next line was like a directive from the script, and it read – "both chuckle."

This just made everything all the more hilarious and we hooted and howled.

First Quarter

You Will Be All Right

The street lamps were going off and on all over the place now – far too much to just be the lamps naturally burning out or having intermittent electrical problems. Every time I went out for a walk it was an adventure, and I thought about our electrical and magnetic natures and how this illustration with the lamps was just the slightest indication of the fields we generated.

Thinking about our infinite power, I decided to try spoon bending. That's funny!

I remembered seeing Uri Geller so many years ago now, and I'd read about people currently having spoon bending parties with a great deal of success. There really was something happening on a mass scale, and even though it seemed trivial and was just the tip of the iceberg to say the very least in terms of what we're capable of, I thought I'd give it a try anyway.

I chose a spoon that was fairly thick and sturdy, and gauged how much effort it would take to bend it in the normal way – it was really hard to bend. Satisfied that I would really have to put some strength into it, I took another spoon from the same set just in case I'd weakened it, and decided to not only try to bend it, but to also twist it around in loops.

Not really knowing any particular techniques but knowing the entire issue would be dependent on my belief, I stared at the spoon, rubbing it a little as I'd seen people do, and I imagined it becoming soft. Belief and imagination are as supremely powerful as it gets, and from here it was a matter of eliminating all vestiges of doubt. I closed my eyes and concentrated.

At the right moment – however that moment came – I opened my eyes, and holding the bowl with one hand, I took hold of the handle with the other, and started to bend. It was like putty! With all but no effort on my part, I bent it over and then wrapped it around and around until I had a bent spoon with three tight twisted loops!

I was incredulous. I stared at it in wonder, and as you would in a situation like this, I tested the strength I would need to try and straighten it out. A lot, it was stiff now and I would probably need a vice – it was a strong spoon. Holy crow! I took a photograph of it for my friends and as a record, and I laughingly imagined eating my porridge with it tomorrow morning.

The spoon bending thing is not a trick folks, but if you don't believe you can do it, you can't – just like everything else.

The ear-ache had gone the day after it had started, to be replaced by shooting pains from my thyroid gland to my head behind my right ear. One of these pains was excruciating and felt like a hot, tiny bolt of lightning. I'd had to squeeze my eyes shut and grimace at that one, but fortunately it only lasted for three or four seconds. It certainly got my attention though.

Now the right side of my head hurt exactly as though I'd been struck by something or had fallen – I hadn't. It really hurt and I also felt that sensation of being hair-sore as we called it in England. Five days later, the pain moved across the back of my head to the left side, and after staying there for about a week also, it travelled to the top. I could actually feel it moving, staying in place, and then moving on again. It seemed methodical somehow, and now my entire head was just – sore.

It was painful and tender to the touch, and feeling around to check things out, I now noticed my head felt *different*. There were ridges where I was sure there were none before, and I got the distinct impression my head was actually changing shape! This was disquieting until I really sat down and thought about it, and tried to put everything together in a way that would make some sense.

The fact I'd been cutting my own hair for decades came into play here, and because of that I knew I was fairly familiar with the shape of my skull. Once again, something as innocuous as that became a reason to be confident I actually knew what I was talking about. My head *was* changing shape!

I connected it to DNA and the rewiring and encoding that was happening to us as human beings, and again I thought back to the beginning when my mother had said "Edna" meant – Evolution DNA. I just couldn't stop thinking about that – she'd prepared me for developments like this right from the start.

There was no doubt about it, the bone structure of my skull was evolving/mutating into something else, and I decided I was okay with that. I had visions of turning into some kind of alien being and I laughed out loud. Good, as long as I could still laugh I was all right, but I would definitely have to follow this development carefully, and for the next little while I always seemed to be pushing and poking with my fingertips. I noticed the crown of my head where my hair swirls seemed to be moving around too.

Things had gone about as far into left field now as they could, but then again I'd thought that before and another startling development had always come along.

Just hold on tight Neli, that's all you can do, and keep that sense of wonder about you.

ৎ ৎ ৎ ৎ ৎ ৎ

It still felt as though I was out of focus in a strange kind of way. There was nothing particular and I was confident within myself now, but everything just seemed weird sometimes. I was moving from one dimension to another and talking to spirits just by thinking about it, and I felt like I was neither here nor there.

I had to stay grounded or I would float away, and the earth always stepped in with another vision of beauty and awe to captivate me and hold me down. The cats continued to bring me back to myself as well, and always sensed where I was emotionally. Then there were the nightly baths which were still crucial, and other than that there was music.

As much as music has the ability to take me far away, it also has the ability to bring me back and I followed my feet to the music store and bought Enya, Seals and Crofts and "Chants of India." Ravi Shankar produced by George Harrison was a combination you couldn't go wrong with, and I found myself listening to this music and feeling all was right with the world and myself.

On Tuesday it was my father's birthday and the next day was a total lunar eclipse followed by the full moon the day after that. So many things were happening so fast and I experienced waves of tears, but felt them purging and washing away lifetimes of ignorance and blindness.

My mother was always there, being my mother.

*"You **will** be all right."*

I know mum... I know I will.

Moon Ten
Learn to Discern

I was thinking about the Hindu Vedanta, the end of the Vedas. "The point where no sacred texts can help you anymore" – as expressed by Deepak Chopra, and I was beginning to dare I was there.

I couldn't worry anymore. Oh I had my concerns like everyone else, but it wasn't the same. God was everything and everywhere and I was surrounded by miracles. Every breath was a gift from the divine and I marvelled at how my eye-lids blinked.

I thought of day one which was two hundred and sixty-five days ago and "Open unto yourself," and now another phrase dropped into my mind – learn to discern. Discern is an interesting word and means two things – perceive, and distinguish.

I was on my own now and the line just struck me as perfect. It reminded me of trying to separate the voices in my mind back at the beginning, and of trying to feel what made the most sense awash a sea of information and conflicting opinions depending on who you read or what you heard. Learn to discern – was simply following your heart. This was the phrase I was looking for earlier! I now had my sixth T-shirt.

I felt like some kind of infancy was over, and I was finally growing into the new me.

"I get to bring you up all over again."

Hi mum. So you've been listening have you?

"I wouldn't miss this for the world."

No, neither would I.

I caught myself giving flying lessons in the dream state, and I woke up one morning with a line in my mind that I must use – "Imagine yourself there, then 'notice' the journey." This really made me laugh, and I was happy to be useful and busy in the dream world.

I decided this was one of the reasons I was so tired no matter how much sleep I had, that and all the changes going on in my body. It turned out to be a very good thing I wasn't working now – in the conventional sense anyhow – and in retrospect, I wondered how I'd managed to carry on for so long, but at the same time I knew I would have fallen apart without that glue of normalcy.

It had been three months since leaving my old job and when I thought of my former workmates I sent them love and hoped they didn't look ill upon me for leaving the way I did. Whenever I did imagine a finished book, I thought of giving them a copy and hopefully they would understand some of what had happened... or think I was completely bonkers and good riddance. I couldn't bear to even think about Roxy.

I knew I'd have to re-enter the world at some point though, and I thought of the African proverb – when you pray, move your feet.

I did feel I'd be able to start actually writing soon, maybe when I got closer to a year under my belt, and in that regard I'd decided on a particular model of laptop to buy. I went to the store on Sunday ready to take the plunge, but was informed the model was out of stock. That was okay. Maybe I would decide on something else or maybe I would go to another store. It didn't matter, I knew there was a reason for everything and I had no issue with waiting another few days or so. I was interested to see what would happen next as though it was someone else's life.

I received a CD I'd ordered called "Native North-American Chants and Dances" and was completely taken in by the rhythms and voices. There were recorded thunder storms and wolves howling set to chanting, and it stirred ancient memories in my blood. The sound of the wolves was particularly appropriate at this time, as Walking Wolf Woman recently told me she'd sent me a wolf to accompany me on my spiritual travels.

This was Telinka, a female wolf whose name came to me as soon as she arrived, and she always walked on my left now, with my dog Rex on the right. Henry was on my left shoulder either in the flesh for the time being or in spirit when I was out of the house... or out of my body. My rabbit Roger sometimes joined us too, and on occasion I would sense Tony on my head.

Tony was our budgie when I was a child, and the first animal companion I could remember in the house. My mother would spend hours at his cage saying – "Who's a pretty boy," and it was always a true miracle when he would say it back. He lived to be fourteen years old and now here he was saying hi again.

So I never went anywhere without my entourage of beautiful creatures accompanying me, and this gave me a kind of strength that filled me with deep gratitude and humility. This, plus the rock of Master Sri Bhundari and the undeviating companionship of my eternal friend and mother Edna, put me in a condition where it really didn't matter what happened now. All would truly be wondrous well, and I was to never be alone again.

"We are solid."

Like Gibraltar mum.

༄ ༄ ༄ ༄ ༄ ༄

Back at the library and looking into Judaism, I found out the first tenet is that there is only one universal God. By now I wasn't surprised. Underneath all the great teachings we find this starting point, and it seemed to be more and more amazing that there were ever so many discrepancies about the Creator in general. When you got right down to it, the only differences seemed to be in the various names given to this singular force.

I decided Love really was the best description for this living energy that created everything and was everything. It's the *feeling* that makes everything real.

I think... therefore I am – is an intellectual statement of existence that worked in a way on the level of the mind, but you don't have to think to exist. I feel... therefore I am – would be much closer to the truth. My truth anyway, but don't listen to me or anyone else, just listen to yourself for everyone's truth is unique.

It seemed obvious now that the idea of controlling emotions (don't let your *feelings* get in the way), or eliminating them entirely for the sake of "getting on with things" was denying the natural flow of the universe. Men particularly – especially in the world I grew up in and even more so in my father's time – to be taught it wasn't "manly" to cry was a crime against nature, and in another sense was a restraining tactic to stifle the innate knowledge of our magnificent power, us as Gods – Co-Creators. Better not let them know that, right?

You might know God is there intellectually after reading a thousand books, but you can feel God immediately by gazing at a flower. Men *have* to start crying now – they can't be half a person anymore.

God isn't just within everything, but *is* everything. The seeker as well as that which is sought and also the very act of seeking itself.

How many saints and masters have simply said – "Know thyself?" Weren't these two words inscribed on the Temple of Apollo? And now I realised that you and I seeking to know who we really are and becoming more in the process, is also All That Is seeking to know whether or not "it" is actually all there is and becoming more, and yet if God is really all there is or ever will be, how can there be any reason to search?

It was another one of those paradoxical dilemmas that always made me feel I was on to something. The universe would always look to find another universe or more of itself even though it already was the entire universe, and it would do this in the most creative way possible – by having all of its creations search as well.

Always more – never less.

I left the library with all this swirling in my head and then decided to just forget it and be at one with the day. It was the end of February now, cold and beautiful and I decided to walk to the mall and back before going home.

On the way, I saw a billboard advertising Point Zero clothing, and I couldn't help but think of Zero Point energy as it related to quantum physics' ground state and also to the spiritual aspect of things with 2012 being a crescendo. I was thinking of this living light coming in to be of the "anything goes" kind, with potentials inside of potentials. Every single thing was leading my thoughts in a certain direction and Edna and I laughed with abandon as I trotted on to the mall.

Half-way there I noticed a falcon high up just gliding along and I followed this majestic sight as he tilted and wheeled to finally land on the electricity tower. There seemed to be more power in that bird than in all the electrical generators on earth.

༄ ༄ ༄ ༄ ༄ ༄

The next day I decided to call the store downtown and upon finding it available, I went to buy the laptop. This was a major step and I came home to load the sleek new machine with the music studio program I'd already bought, and the word processing and photography programs I had on hand.

After this I was ready for a walk, and I also figured I was ready to do some work now. Once I'd learned the music studio I could record again, and I now had a place to view and organise my photographs. I was also ready to maybe even start writing a book now if I really decided to take on this huge project.

What if I'd really just gone nuts though and a book simply *proved* that beyond a shadow of a doubt? What if it became the diary of a madman, the day by day colourful descent into paranoid schizophrenia by Peter Nelson? Even the people who were keeping tabs on me only knew a fraction of what had actually gone on so far. What if I started to write and then my mother disappeared and I was left with a kind of sham?

> *"You write this down you.*
> *Remember all that I said.*
> *This conversation will **never** be broken.*
> *We will decide our unfolding together.*
> *You know you're going to write it.*
> *You've known that all along.*
> *You've just got the jitters."*

I obediently got the ever-ready pen and paper out of my pocket and wrote down what my mother had said. I felt better already, not just because of the words, but because it was all working so well and I could hear and feel her so unmistakably. No, this was all true and real and the last nine months were a spiritual tour de force I couldn't deny.

I headed home eager to get back to the new computer and it began to snow. My heart jumped at the sight as it slowly started to flutter down, and my love for snow burst from my chest.

> *we melt in your arms*

That was the snow talking to you again Neli, with a pun no less... no you're not crazy at all!

I laughed out loud and then thought of the Native Americans and all the other indigenous peoples I respected and admired. They said everything spoke to them too. I was in good company.

Last Quarter

No Time to Hurry

Today was thirty-nine weeks and I decided to do a diagnostic on myself.

Well Nelson, how do you feel?

Well, I can tell you that I still feel pretty darn peculiar to say the least, and my head hurts.

What do you mean peculiar?

I mean like I've never felt before. I feel reassembled but weightless – amorphous.

That's not too surprising, and tell me about your head.

It still hurts on the outside like I said before, and there's a strange kind of pressure on the inside. If I was in the regular world I would think the stroke my mother mentioned was about to occur, but I know what it really is.

Anything else?

Well, I'm not crying every day now, so that helps as far as functioning in the world goes, but I still have these waves of emotion that feel almost orgasmic in nature.

You've always been that way on a lesser scale Neli.

Yeah, I guess. All in all though, I feel I'm in a place of glory.

That doesn't sound too bad does it? Is there anything you would have done differently?

I would have liked to maybe have had a bit more confidence in myself and what was happening along the way, but considering the sheer intensity, I must say I think I've done okay.

You have.

ᠵ ᠵ ᠵ ᠵ ᠵ

I decided my Pineal Gland had a lot to do with the feeling in my head, and I read all I could about it in relation to the third eye or sixth chakra, Kundalini, and spirituality in general. There's a lot of information about it and a lot of history behind it. It tied in to the specific pressure I was feeling, and as usual I was led to the right information at the right time to make me feel secure about what was going on.

As a case in point, I found a Kundalini support website on my new computer and ended up in the testimonials section where people were sharing their experiences. From the six stories available I just happened to choose number three first and lo and behold, there was a testimonial from a man who had lost 90% of his sight ten years earlier and who had recently experienced a Kundalini awakening. If that didn't make it fascinating enough, about halfway through the dissertation he started to describe what he called the most "bizarre" and "remarkable" thing that had happened to him... his head changed shape.

I couldn't believe what I was seeing! It was only two weeks ago I'd come to the same conclusion myself, and I must have read that paragraph about a dozen times over. It was too incredible for words. He described feeling ridges, he talked about a pulsing pain, he mentioned it feeling as though the bones in his head were moving.

I was absolutely dumbfounded, not just by what he was describing, but by the fact it had only taken this short amount of time for this information to fall into my lap and reassure me. Thank you! He also noted it took about three and a half months for the whole thing to calm down, which forewarned me not to be surprised if this kept up for a while, although of course we would all have our own variations.

Knowing I wasn't the only one experiencing this, I went hunting for more information along these lines, so I chose my search-words carefully and went to see what I could find. It didn't take long before I found four more references to exactly the same thing and I couldn't deny feeling better about the whole thing even though I'd known what was happening to me.

One source mentioned the head becoming larger to accommodate the growth of the pineal gland. Another stated feeling pressure in the crown of the head and having a sensation of the skull becoming oblong. One other talked about a ridge forming and the skull changing shape, and finally, the last simply said – the head is enlarging.

I also felt that my tailbone or coccyx was larger than it used to be, and at first I'd thought – well, how often do you check that out Nelson? After finding the head information though, I figured I'd have a look at what people might be saying about it relating to the Ascension process, and sure enough, I found references to the tailbone and other chakra centres becoming painful or sore for some people. It also didn't surprise me the coccyx was attached to a large triangular bone called the sacrum, which means sacred.

It was enough to allow me to realise I wasn't imagining things even though I hadn't felt pain, and when you considered this was the "home" for the sleeping Kundalini serpent... it wasn't too surprising. I also had to consider all the other goings-on with my body, and in the end, I considered it to be yet one more change I'd noticed.

The information flying my way was amazing, and with the aid of the new laptop and continuous trips to the library I was finding out about ancient civilizations like Atlantis, the Lemurians and the Sumerians. I was reading about people channelling Thoth, the Pleiadians and assorted Ascended Masters – I felt like Rainbow Warriors were flying around in my head. When I thought of the Pleiades, which I found had a powerful attraction for me, I couldn't help but think – play at ease.

I noticed there were pyramids all over the planet and it became clear we didn't know who we really were or what our history was, and things were about to change in that regard, our true history was being rediscovered. This followed my own long-held belief that the truth will always come forth one way or another and I could feel barriers crumbling.

Who would have thought the Internet would turn out to be this critical spiritual tool? The timing of it was so perfect, and there were people all around the world waking up to who they really are, and sharing their revelations with each other in real-time.

It was funny, it had been feared people would stop socialising or knowing each other in an intimate way with the birth of the Internet, but people were finding their true kindred spirits right across the world as well as next door, and coming together in a way no one could have suspected.

Unexpectedly, my reservations about any kind of world-wide spiritual awakening were completely destroyed once I'd started to really see what was going on in cyber-space, and I couldn't have been more overjoyed to have been so wrong.

If only I'd had my own computer years ago... but no, the timing was perfect, this was how things were meant to go for me and I knew better than to think otherwise.

"Gee willikers, I'm glad you think so."

I do mum – I'm learning.

I still had to step back and stop the research sometimes, but I also felt I really couldn't waste any time so I tried to strike a sensible balance.

"Waste not – want not."

That's funny coming from you and the eternal now where you are.

*"Yes, I have **no time** for waste – or haste!"*

I burst out laughing again – it's a good job I'm alone here – and I remembered how my mother really never did waste anything. That was another lesson I'd learned from her all those many years ago.

She also now made me aware that there really was no need to hurry. Everything would unfold in its own way and in its own time.

I remembered an old guy from Newfoundland I'd seen on TV one time, and I never forgot what he'd said as he went through his life like a peaceful steady stream, "I ain't got no time to hurry."

New Moon

Orbs and the Red Crystal

I'd been seeing Sri Bhundari meditating with a red crystal for weeks now. It was big, the size of your hands clasped together, and I would catch him sitting with it before him – his eyes were closed. I knew better than to disturb him so I simply watched and waited to see what he was going to do next.

In the meantime I took a lot of photographs, either just in the backyard or while out for a walk, and I truly could hardly believe what I was getting in them. The Orbs were now coming on so strong it was astonishing.

I would take five or six photos seconds apart, and the third one would have a glorious Orb just sitting there in the air – there'd be nothing unusual at all in the other shots. I would take one shot with nothing in it. The next would have one Orb, and then the next would have two or three until the last photo would have a flock of them.

They seemed to know when I was looking and hoping for them, and they did everything possible to deny the usual explanations like dust, rain, fog, snow or digital camera artefacts. It didn't take too long before they'd convinced me of their reality.

I went back to the photos I'd taken before the first Orb, and there were eight months of shots with no Orbs at all – it wasn't the camera. Since the first one when my mother told me to go outside with the camera and showed herself that way, they were everywhere, and I had to create a separate folder on the computer to keep them organised.

There are so many theories, but in light of what was happening in my life it was obvious this was simply the next development, and considering what had been going on with my camera already, well... it wasn't much of a stretch to accept this.

I was still critical though, and I did a lot of test shots in the rain or fog and while it was snowing so that I knew the difference and didn't fall into the trap of thinking absolutely everything was an Orb. It was true there were a lot of effects you could get this way, but I quickly became confident I knew what I was doing and could tell the difference. That plus the last nine months of my life and I was sure something really big was happening. This became even more evident when we started to interact and when they eventually spoke to me. Along with the Orbs, some other astounding photographs were to follow, and of course they made the Orb photos even easier to accept, if I still needed any reassurances by then.

I would get the same recognisable Orb in a slightly different position from one photo to the next, and if you alternated quickly between them you could see an animated motion. You could actually see how it had invisibly zipped from one place to the next. Sometimes there'd be three of four photographs like this, and then in the last one it would be gone.

I tried meditating first or chanting. I would hold the camera to my heart or against my forehead or on my head, and check the results. These sometimes produced the most startling shots. Maybe they just thought it was funny.

I ended up coming to the conclusion that it wasn't any particular chant or technique. It was the attention itself that made the difference. They liked to be thought about and talked to and it was about as simple as that – they wanted to be *believed* in, and as I mentioned earlier, the belief comes first and the proof comes after.

So now I would get a beautiful green one in front of the tent, a liquid blue one above the garage, and a violet one by the cedars. I made a point of asking for one by the tent and there they would be.

There were just too many times when they knew what I was doing, and then one day I asked them why they didn't just talk to me.

would you not put on a display first?

Yes I guess I probably would, come to think of it. Who or what are you?

we are gentle and loving

I absolutely loved the answer and I couldn't have thought of a better one if I'd tried. It suited me, and like most things in the spiritual world I felt the answer was tailored to me in a way.

They were trans-dimensional I was sure, and telepathic most definitely, and they had a spiritual *presence*. However, when you realise that everything is spirit manifesting in a myriad of ways in infinite dimensions, you tend to come to the conclusion that *everything* is spiritual. How could it not be? When God is everything then... well you get the idea.

So I suppose what I mean to say is, they felt *alive.* Then again, everything has consciousness and is therefore alive so... oh forget it. They felt friendly! So either single Orbs or in groups, and sometimes other shapes I simply called faeries – they came.

In the house there was a swag lamp of Mum B's and underneath it was Steaven's ashes, so it seemed like a logical place for at least the two of them to maybe show themselves in a photograph. I hadn't tried for Orbs inside as of yet.

Sherrie, Steaven and Mum B were the first three people to come to me at the beginning under Edna's supervision, so they were always grouped together in my mind and I thought possibly Sherrie might join us too – and maybe even Edna if she felt like it.

I thought of the four of them and hopefully radiated the love and gratitude I felt for them still being in my life as I took the photograph, with the lamp and the wicker box of the ashes visible in the shot. This photograph I did decide to look at right away, and oh my, there were three Orbs around the lamp with another one off to the side.

It was breathtaking! And it didn't take a genius to figure out that Mum B, Steaven and Sherrie had gathered around the lamp, and my mother had kept herself over to one side – I was elated.

After more photographs outside over the next few days, I came to the conclusion that since the sphere was such a basic form, not only were they dead people or various spirit beings never incarnated here, but they were many other things too. Maybe the different colours were an indication of some of this, or the inner patterns, but I didn't put too much effort into trying to decipher it all, as I quite enjoyed the mystery of it actually.

One thing I did notice, some of the inner swirls or designs looked like certain crop circles I'd seen. Somehow this didn't seem surprising in the least. Maybe the same kind of sacred geometry was at work here.

I also began to get wispy spirit smoke, a nebulous material appearing in some photographs around trees or just on its own. I did tests with my breath and cigarette smoke and it wasn't either of them. I discovered some people called this material psychic mist, life-force mist, spirit mist or fog or vapour, and it turned up whenever it felt like it.

After one of these photograph sessions out in the back yard, I came inside wondering what I might find and sat down at the computer. Not wanting to look at the photos yet, I carried on setting up my new computer just the way I wanted it and added an image of Krishna and Radha to my screensaver. I would look at the photos when I felt the time was right, and I had no doubt my thoughts at that moment would affect what I would find, the same way my thoughts at the time of taking the photographs would have. In a real sense, there really wouldn't *be* any photograph, until the instant I looked.

I was in a great mood after being out in the snow, and my heart was open with gratitude for all the wondrous mystery unfolding in my life. It was at this moment when I became aware of Sri Bhundari and the red crystal, as he came forward with it in his hands and placed it into my heart – the heart area of my subtle body. The word "installation" came into my mind but I couldn't determine where the word had come from.

I closed my eyes and with complete faith and trust in whatever he was doing, I thanked him for this gift. I was entranced and kept my eyes closed knowing I would feel when the ritual was over, and a part of me observing nodded with a kind of knowing.

I opened my eyes, not being aware of how long they'd been closed, and I saw Sri Bhundari smiling. He'd been working on this for a month and he had a look of satisfaction on his face. Good – I thought, whatever he had done I would have been really concerned if I'd have seen a panicked distress on his face with his hands holding the sides of his head. That probably would have been something White Feather might do for a joke!

I thought of the foundation, then the firming, and I wondered if this was part of the layering my mother had recently mentioned. Then I clearly heard Sri Bhundari's response to this thought as he faded away with that look of contentment still on his face.

the tuning...

First Quarter

The Crow and the Crystal Serpent

we don't feel the cold like you do

I like the feeling of the wind – you would call it sensual

This was my favourite tree speaking and I loved the alternating between "we" and "I."

This particular tree had been important to me for a quite a while, so of course what with the new developments, we just shifted our relationship forward and now had conversations. Sometimes I would be stuck on an idea and just couldn't put the right colour on it when my tree would say the most appropriate line or word and everything would feel better. I just accepted this when we passed each other now.

Later in my room I heard a crow outside the window, so I opened it wide to witness the crow heading straight for me at a top speed only to veer-off at the very last moment and swoop past my face. That happened for a reason whether I figured it out and understood it or not. It wasn't even necessary to look any further into it than to know it was a sacred event.

In the bath I thought about those ants again, and felt the presence of the ant queen who spoke for all of them it seemed. I called her the Ant Goddess and I didn't feel crazy.

I found out talking ants make an appearance in the Qur'an, and I remembered Psyche when the ants came and helped her sort the grain. It also didn't surprise me when I discovered that biologists classify ants as a special group of wasps, thus tying the whole thing up nicely with me and the wasps.

I couldn't and wouldn't deny my visions and conversations, and loving everything didn't seem like such a bad religion anyway. Everything is alive and everything wants to talk too, but I couldn't just tell anyone all of this stuff could I? I think I knew by then how far I could go on a person to person basis, and if there ever was a book... well, it would only end up in interested hands I would think.

I sat down at the computer and turned on the radio. Gordon was being interviewed on talk-radio and as I listened, I added a few things to my screensaver: Jesus, Archangel Metatron, the Mayan Calendar, a crop circle, Archangel Uriel, more lightning striking water, my grandma and granddad, and a white buffalo calf. With the appearance of the White Buffalo, something else mystical and wonderful was happening right here and now.

All I could do was just carry on as well as I could, and know when *not* to say things like - well Sri Bhundari's working on a green crystal now... since the red one's installed and everything....

The thing is, he *really was* working on a green one and he was doing the same thing with his meditations as he did with the red one - I had to wonder if it would stop at two. I thought of that red crystal and the crystal skulls and the evolving crystalline structure of our DNA and I thought about a dream I'd had many years ago.

If I had to remember when it was, I'd say about twenty years ago and I called it the three-way conversion. It was a connection dream - I knew that as soon as I woke up. Three realities were involved somehow, coming together in the dream, and the main gist of it was the meeting of my other incarnations.

It was a receiving line of people and I went down the line greeting them one at a time. We would shake hands and embrace and I remembered one old guy lifting up his hair at the front and showing me his high forehead as an act of identification. He got me with a conspirator's wink that seemed to say - don't tell them, but we have the same forehead!

I remember a lot of those faces, and at the time I knew it was a very important dream. The point is, after I'd gone down the line and met everyone, I was presented with a crystal and there was an interesting reconciliation everyone had made within themselves, because they knew I couldn't take it back with me, not fully into my world anyway. It was given to me with a reverence as to its worth, but with an "oh well" attitude because this was the dream world and it wouldn't be in my hand when I woke up.

The crystal was shaped like a serpent now I come to think of it. For years I've thought it looked like various things, but now the obviousness of the snake/shape is too much to ignore. My own crystal serpent!

So it's taken all these years for the true meaning of the crystal in the dream to become clear, and the more I think about it... of course, and it would also mean DNA and a time in the future when the serpent would uncoil and I would be recalling this dream for a book about Kundalini.

There was a summing up going on. I felt things were coming together with bold strokes of magic, and fitting this dream into my current life brought time and space and the dreamtime together in a perfect way and blended them.

I was meant to remember this dream now and fit it into the larger perspective, and if I'd been making these arrangements I would have done it just like this.

I looked around and saw my own handiwork. I saw clues I'd left for myself and thought – oh yes, I would have done this.

Moon Eleven
What a Song and Dance

I was seeing things. Flickers of light and small black holes where common now and I would see them here and there and say – I can see you! I thought it was important to say that and acknowledge them, and sometimes I would describe what I saw so whoever or whatever it was got some kind of feedback.

I knew for a fact it wasn't my eyes adjusting to light levels or something like that, and I marvelled again at how there was always an answer for the sceptics out there.

The universe would provide everything necessary no matter what side you were on, and I thought *that* was probably the most interesting thing. By saying, "My thoughts don't create anything," you get a world reflecting exactly that, and you get it because *your thoughts are creating it!* I thought this was just the funniest thing when you thought about it.

On this day I saw a small white flicker and then I saw the green astral nose-shape for just a moment, but this time it was with my naked eye. I felt like things were coming full circle now, and it made sense when you considered that one year was coming up fast.

I didn't know how that could be possible, but today was the first day of spring and June would soon be here. I was glad I could still be calm with everything going on in my head, but it just seemed to be so easy – being calm was actually a natural state of being.

it's good not to have a lazy mind though

Hi Mum B! That's true of course. I don't mind a busy mind – I just want to be calm at the same time. Thanks for dropping by!

It was always so nice when Mum B showed up, and again I thought of the feeling that indentified people when they came along – it was so interesting.

This was another week where things had been relatively quiet, but there were always one or two things I had to jot down and that was good. If I wasn't constantly writing, sometimes I felt like I was ignoring some essential work, but I had to find a balance and the slower weeks were good for me.

Overall I was just spending too much time scrutinising the details so I had to relax, let it flow and take me with it.

"What a song and dance!"

Oh I know mum... don't even listen, okay?

"How many times did you say – am I going to make it through this?"

I know.

I knew things would be okay because they had to be didn't they? I mean after all this, surely to god I'll be able to carry on and go out there in the world and get some work done, right? If I can't take my place wherever that may be and help people in whatever way possible, I might as well have died and moved on... what would've been the point of staying?

It was here when the first person who needed some help appeared on the scene. Seemingly out of nowhere and through one of my newly rediscovered cousins in England, I now had someone who was experiencing a transformation of her own, and needed some idea as to what might be going on. I was overjoyed to be able to help and was also pleased that the universe at least, considered me ready to take on this task.

Dealing with someone's state of mind is a tricky business, and I laughed to myself about being placed in this position already, but I was as ready as I was going to be, and if I could help even one person during this mass-awakening going on, then I figured the real work had begun. For the good of all, right?

I also had a laugh when I thought about day two and becoming a celebrated psychic, sitting there imperiously and with full ego in operation while the querents asked one thing after another as I closed my eyes to find the answers for the poor little things.

When it came to psychics making predictions of future events, it showed a complete lack of understanding about the way reality works, and the fluidity of time. The future was being created in every moment, with every thought, and to make a prediction for someone else was doing them a grave injustice by denying them their own awesome power to create their own future with every breath.

What did people think free will actually meant? How could any psychic worth their salt go along with the charade that the future was set in stone and just waiting for you to catch up?

I saw myself looking into someone's eyes and saying – the future is entirely dependent on your every thought about it... I'm sorry but it's up to you.

This is what people needed to know and it was more difficult than thinking you were a feather in the wind and had no control, but it was time for people to accept responsibility as creators.

You were doing it anyway, you were creating your own tomorrow moment by moment as it was... why not *know* and accept you are, and take it from there?

You chose your parents before you even got here, you were in control before you arrived... it was time to remember all the good stuff!

The only desire now was to elevate anyone who was interested to their own full inherent abilities, to help someone contact dear Uncle Charlie themselves for a start, and then to do everything possible to inspire them to go further and to awaken their own Kundalini and their own passion to explore the mystery.

I would always pass a message along, if I had one to convey, but once people start to believe in the natural magic of the universe and get to know themselves a bit better, there'll be no stopping them. We couldn't be more divine.

I thought – I am God being Me – would be perfect for my seventh T-shirt, (with possibly – You are God being You – on the back), and maybe I should just hand them out on the street corner.

This was really what it was all about and I remembered a line I'd read recently which stated – the only desire of a true master, was to create more masters. This was where the true fulfillment came into it, not seeking deliverance for oneself, but becoming a deliverer for others.

I wouldn't be calling myself a master – that was for sure – I wouldn't be calling myself anything at all, except Neli or Nelson and possibly a teacher.

I thought of my granddad again and his "little old piano teacher" and I thought yes, I can be a little old teacher too of sorts, and I pray I do so with integrity and enthusiasm because the universe is so full of wonder and joy and play.

I considered the words "pray" and "teach," and I wondered if that was where the word "preach" came from. I decided I would do my best never to preach, because in the grand scheme of things I really knew nothing except – we are eternal. I'd bet my life on that! – I laughed. That's all I really knew.

I finally came to realise that *we* are the Ascension, *we* are 2012 and *we* are the alignment of the heavens. Jane Roberts couldn't have been more correct when she said – there is no outside.

It certainly seems there is, and that's where the fun comes in, but when it comes down to this reality we're in, hanging by a tenuous thread, there won't be any liberators charging over the hill other than ourselves. It was time to grow up and know our only salvation will come from within.

No, we don't really need the second coming of anything. We need the first coming of mankind or in this case womankind, because we need that feminine energy now like never before.

We really are the ones we've been searching for all along, and when you recover yourself – you find everything.

Last Quarter
Be Like the Wind

Sri Bhundari had chosen his moment carefully and then simply walked up to me and matter-of-factly inserted the green crystal. Now he was working on a blue one. The green crystal had been placed into my chest area also, so I figured it was just the way in, and not a crystal for each chakra for instance.

I'd received the information that "the tuning" consisted of stabilizing certain frequencies and enhancing them all. The crystals were like fine-tuning dials and could also dampen static and help to maintain centre. All in all it sounded good to me and I felt safe that he knew what he was doing.

It was a teary day today, just like old times – I thought, and I sat down and looked at my current journal. I was on the fourth now and there were still places where I just couldn't spell and words were crossed out over and over until the best guess won the day. Even the simplest words were sometimes impossible, and I would stare in amazement as my left-brain short-circuited.

I looked at the journal and then took my pen and wrote – book title: The Magic Is Real –Thirteen Days and Eleven Moons. I knew the title might evolve along with everything else, but it was April Fools' Day and it seemed the right day to come up with one and decide to actually sit down and try to write about all this. I didn't know exactly how to begin, but like my mother said, we just start and see where it leads us, and a title was a start.

I began to go through the first couple of journals and was astounded they were talking about me and not some other lucky guy who was living a life I'd always dreamt of. No this was me all right... through and through, and once I got going I seemed to have written a lot of stuff down. Good for me! I could barely believe it – I was going to write a book.

My head was still doing acrobatics and now a cold had come along. I rarely got colds so it was always an event, and this was the first after all the changes so I wanted to follow it closely. It felt like another type of purging and cleansing, and after a day or two it was well on its way to being gone. I noted in my journal that I could still get a cold and then laughed at myself. What did I think – that I would never be ill again? Well, actually it had crossed my mind but anyway... just write it down and make note of the new head bump Neli.

My sister called on the Friday and we made arrangements to meet on my birthday for a walk and a talk. I had it in my head for us to go to Blackthorn Avenue down memory lane together and my birthday was on a Saturday this year so it was perfect. This would be the first time actually seeing Sandra since all this began so I was really looking forward to filling her in on some of the developments, and this was in just eight days. This was going to be fun! I just hope she doesn't think I'm truly crazy.

"I could brain you!"

Well if you do that, I really will be crazy mum.

I found a photograph of a stone statue from Indonesia around 1300 AD, and here was yet another divine mother, a Bodhisattva in female form and she was beautiful.
There were so many when you went looking: Quan Yin, Green Tara, Isis, and Mary of course... the list went on and on and even Persephone showed up as the daughter of a divine mother – Demeter.
I was happy to see Persephone there considering my life-long fascination with her, but it was The Goddess Kundalini – Shakti – Parvati who had arrived on my doorstep to capture my heart and I couldn't stay away from her.
Maybe I just have more Hindu lives than anything else – I thought, and when I considered how old Hinduism is and the way it connected so well to Buddhism, it all made sense to me. I laughed – underneath it all, I'm just a Hindude.
Now was the time to leave all religious systems behind and to rediscover our own intimate connection to God of course, but it was still more fun to talk to Parvati than an energy field.

I went outside to take some photographs and I was visited by a fly just as I was hoping I might see one. The synchronicities were off the scale now, and it was a case of maybe just writing one or two down now and then because they were so relentless. This wasn't an event to write about in my journal now, it was normal life and the background flow of everything.

It was the same with the voices. I had to remind myself it was still impossible for some people to even *believe* at all, never mind what was now standard for me. People can get used to anything, no doubt about it. It was the same with the lights and shapes I was now seeing too, the more you could believe, the more the universe would supply whether live or in a photograph, and the photographs were mind-boggling.

There seemed to be so much to do, but there really wasn't. I would carry on as well as I could and somehow I would end up where I was supposed to be. Everything would be okay.

A line popped into my mind – it takes no effort for the wind to blow.

I would try to be like the wind.

New Moon

Passport to Eternity

Head manoeuvres – that's what I called it now, and I could feel the new painful bump moving. I really was having an interesting life considering the head factor here and the crystals Sri Bhundari was working on and plugging into me.

I could feel everything evolving around me and inside me and I had to shake my head at the sheer scope of events unfolding. If it hadn't happened to me just the way it had with all of my personal history ready to help, I don't know what I would have thought or done.

But here I was, reasonably intact, and on this day I started to work on the book in earnest. This was a good idea on so many levels and now it seemed as though events were happening from yet another perspective as I went back to the pages of those days and tried to sort it out.

It wasn't such an easy thing to do even though I had the days all laid out before me in order, there were so many angles... but I plunged ahead anyway and the next thing I knew, I had some large Bristol boards with point-form ideas written large in black marker. I made four or five of them and felt much better with some things written down where I could look up at them on the wall. This would be the best time to try and pull a book together and I knew I would never have the time quite like this again – not in this way anyway, not with this open space before me.

At that moment, constructing a book became the one thing I really wanted to create out of this particular time. I knew how fast everything could change and so I thought – come on Neli, get going while you have the chance. I wanted to be stable enough to actually think straight, but still close enough to events for them to be clear and vibrant, and at ten months now, I thought this was the time.

If I stuck to the plan of eleven moons as the span for the book, that would mean I would be starting it at about the same time it would be ending, if you know what I mean. I found this to be so interesting and some kind of indication by itself that beginnings and endings occurred at the same time, and I saw another circle completing itself.

I knew the book already existed, but still I had to actually sit down in my reality and... start writing! Okay, let's do that and try to figure out the music studio program at the same time if possible.

I felt like I had a mission now anyway, and if the book could help anyone in the "you're not going crazy" department – that would be good.

You're not going crazy – would be T-shirt number eight.

ॐ ॐ ॐ ॐ ॐ ॐ

The next day I received a message from Mars. This is what I always called it anyway when suddenly the high-pitched noise in my ears would crescendo to a startling level and then slowly dwindle away back to the standard whining that had been there for decades.

At times like this it would sometimes sound like a jet engine, and if I was near the piano or another instrument, I would find the note just to see what it was and if it was the same as last time, or if it was maybe going up or down in pitch. Quite often it was B or B-flat, but there didn't seem to be any rhyme or reason to the particular pitches as far as I could tell, and sometimes it was another note entirely.

This one was loud. The loudest I'd ever experienced in all the years since this had been happening, and like I said, this has been going on for a very long time.

I'd learned over the years that this background zinging sound was the sound of the Nad, also known as Naad, Nada, Anahad Naad, Anahata Nad, Sukhsham Nad, Prana, Qi, Ki and so on.

This life-force energy runs through the Nadis of the subtle or astral body, and the Nadis can best be described as channels. Other descriptions are: lines of force, tubes, pipes, conduits, or subtle nerve channels, and this network of filaments correspond to the acupuncture meridians of traditional Chinese medicine and the chakras. In the Upanishads there are said to be seventy-two thousand or more Nadis.

After my own experience with acupuncture and the almost instant cessation of the terrible pain of sciatica, I was certainly ready to attest to the existence of these fine etheric nerve channels, but after my experience with the Goddess... I just knew.

I now realised that this energy had been the Kundalini primordial evolutionary force all along, and I read a description of the sound being akin to love-mad bees. I could hear what they meant.

In Sikhism this "solemn music" is reported as being inseparably connected with the Kundalini, and is only heard by the spiritually evolved. Oh my.

I cringed a little at that and thought – this can't really be me they're talking about can it? It was still difficult sometimes to accept, but everyone was going to reach this place one way or another so I relaxed a bit and thought – it's just your time Nelson.

This vibration/motion/stream has also been called: cosmic sound, vibrations of the cosmos, cosmic life-force, cosmic music, the cosmic symphony, the music of the spheres, primal sound, supreme silence, the word, life-force energy, inner-sound, sound of the origin, supreme sound, the un-struck melody, vital force, psychic currents and soundless sound. The Sound of Silence wasn't just a really great song after all.

People who had never heard any kind of ringing in their ears, reported it right away after Kundalini rising, and for someone who was already familiar and used to the sound, it increased dynamically and was even more relentless – if there can be such a thing as "more" relentless. It was tenacious, persistent and unyielding.

I hoped the people needing this knowledge would find it instead of rushing off to the doctor's office, but I knew it would fall into their laps when the time was right.

This was the multi-dimensional sound of creation, and for me, if Parvati wanted to whisper and sing in my ears forever, I had no problem with this at all.

ॐ ॐ ॐ ॐ ॐ ॐ

I was thinking about England again and knew I really needed to go back there even if for just a holiday (Holy day). I excavated my birth and baptism certificates, being the first two documents that represented me, and had a long look at them.

There was Vera and my Uncle Bill as my godparents... and then I noticed I was born in the Haslam Maternity Home and I gaped for a moment as I realised that Haslam is the second part of Officer Jane's maiden name – North-Haslam! I always thought I'd been born in Bolton General Hospital but I couldn't have been more wrong, and another synchronicity from the day I was born came flying into my current reality.

I closed my eyes to see myself at Stonehenge and wandering around in crop circles and I could almost feel the sensation in my feet from just thinking about standing upon that sacred ground.

There was nothing to be scared about anymore. I always said I'd never go on another airplane as I hadn't really enjoyed the experience the first (and only) time, but none of that seemed to matter now, and I noticed how the word "scared" could so easily be changed to "sacred" with the switching around of just two letters.

All I needed was a passport, some money and the opportunity as well of course, and maybe one day I would be back where I felt truly at home on this earth. I thought of my mother in Lancashire on the other side.

It didn't really matter though, things would go the way they would and I had nothing to complain about – nothing at all.

I thought to myself – don't dwell on it too much Nelson... at least you have a passport to eternity.

First Quarter

Sandra and the Golden Sparkles

So my sister Sandra and I finally got together on Saturday, April 12, 2008. It was the best birthday present. We parked the truck on Blackthorn Avenue, got out and surveyed the scene. There was number 86 where we used to live - a new house now like I said, but close enough. We had a good look at the house and reminisced, took some photographs and then it was time for our walk. I turned to Sandra.

"Okay listen... before we start, I want to tell you – something is going to happen."

She looked at me.

"I don't know what, but something will happen, we'll see something or other.

If I don't say anything and it does happen, I know you'll probably believe me when I explain it, but that could never be the same as telling you first, and believing it *will* happen. I'll take my chances."

"Okay." She put up her umbrella, hopefully not to protect herself from me.

"Maybe a truck will go by with – Sandra and Peter's Plumbing – on the side, or we'll see a sign or something somewhere. We'll know when we see it. It'll be a message just for us. Just remember I said this, all right?"

"Oh, okay."

So off we set, on our stroll back through the decades on a good solid rainy day – very English and just perfect for us. We rounded the corner and passed my old school General Mercer, just chatting away and trying to remember what we could of those first years in Canada. What fun!

We went to the end of the street, turned around and headed back. No more than fifteen minutes had gone by as we came to the corner again.

"Well Sandra – there it is."

"There's what?"

My god! I couldn't believe what I was seeing, but I was starting to. Thank you thank you thank you.

"Right there, parked across the street – that white van." It was about twenty feet away.

"Oh...!" She froze on the spot.

And there it was. A white van, parked in front of the house where the guys were working, I guess.

"Peter's Appliance Repair Inc." – would be the sign on the side of the van.

"Well it's only *my* name, but holy cow! And I said a truck! Sandra, are you okay?"

"Yes, I just..."

"I know." I do know, I really do – come on Sandra... make the leap.

"You're freaking me out."

"I know."

We continued walking along in the beautiful rain and I found myself holding my breath as she was silent for a while. It didn't take her long to absorb what I'd been telling her and to put it together with this physical event right in front of her.

"So, you're *really* talking to mum?"

"Yes San, I am."

Nothing compares to a little demonstration, no matter what – I thought.

This event coloured the whole time we had together and said more than words ever could. I stayed with her as she drove back to Brampton, and then I took the bus home.

ౚ ౚ ౚ ౚ ౚ ౚ

Five days later I received an e-mail from my sister that read, "I can't get over the way I feel since I last saw you. I am feeling so... different – I don't know why. Love you, Sandy."

Well I had an idea or two about that. Things were changing in Sandra's world for many reasons I was sure, and there were a lot of things going on with the planet and the universe, what with all this energy coming in, but after our experience together with the van, her internal world had been shaken up regardless. Something had shifted inside of her and all in all, I felt good about it and hoped the difference was a feeling she was happy with. Her vibrational frequency had increased and she was feeling some of the magic.

The next day I went to the grocery store to get a couple of things and once outside, I placed the items in my knapsack and looked up to the sky. It was a beautiful sunny April day with two falcons gliding on high and no doubt describing sacred patterns together against the backdrop of clear blue. It was quite a magnificent sight and without taking my eyes off them, I took my camera out of the case always over my shoulder now, and took some photographs.

After taking a few shots, I put the camera away and started for home, glancing every now and then with binocular-hands to keep my eye on them as well as I could as they headed over towards the ravine. Stopping one more time to look up, I stopped dead in my tracks because the sky had changed... drastically.

It wasn't the sky anymore. Nothing had changed on the ground, the light was the same as it had been, but the sky was now a panoply of golden sparkles. They were everywhere! I stared for as long as I could, looking away only briefly and then back to see if anything had changed. They were still there and dancing across the sky until they eventually began to fade, and I watched as they slowly disappeared and the sky returned to normal. Time shuts off at moments like these, but I'd say it lasted one to two minutes.

I knew I was seeing something miraculous. I had a few experiences under my belt now to put it mildly, and I recognised the overall feeling of it as well as what my eyes were registering – it was soul stirring. The fact that I didn't even think of my camera during this, even though I'd just used it, is a testament to the level of astonishment. My mind had been blank with wonder.

I was reminded of gold dust from heaven that some people witness being manifested in churches by God or Angels and so on, but I thought I could look into that later if I wanted to, for now, I just wanted to slowly walk home and let it sink in.

This was a sign the size of the entire sky! And that it was a miracle from The Great Spirit, I had no doubt whatsoever. I tried to say thank you on a level that corresponded to the magnificence of this unforgettable vision.

༄ ༄ ༄ ༄ ༄ ༄

On Saturday it was the last day of this moon phase, and I realised this would be the last official day of the book if I stuck to the original plan. I'd completed some pages now and was happy with the result so far, and again it seemed weird to be leaving the range of the book in the physical world just as I'd started writing it.

I was just sitting there, mulling things over when Sri Bhundari did the same thing as before and very casually came up to me and placed the blue crystal inside my heart.

He'd spent almost the same length of time on this one as the green one, about three weeks, and once again I closed my eyes and let the "installation" take place in its own time until I knew it was completed.

I now had three, and this time I received a message regarding the use of this blue crystal energy to calm situations down if they seemed out of control or just jagged. He also sent me a vision of the crystal serpent from my old dream and let me know it was a turning point in my education all those years ago. I had a feeling he'd been there in that dream somewhere, possibly overseeing things.

I was fired-up! The last three hundred and twenty-three days were like something out of a book! I laughed at that and went outside saying hello to a couple of insect friends, and decided I really needed to go for a bike ride – that was definitely the thing to do!

Getting my bike, I felt a pressure change and a kind of whooshing sound in my right ear, and I remembered Seth mentioning this sensation as sometimes being an indicator of a probability shift. We were shifting from one time-line to another all the "time" anyway, but usually to another reality almost identical. Sometimes this sound/feeling meant a larger shift, and I shook my head at the mystery of it all as I closed the garage door and thought about the me who didn't go for a bike ride.

I flew around the neighbourhood with the chilly April wind in my hair, and I realised I was now fifty-four. I noticed I didn't really care what my earth-age was, and most of the time I had to stop and think about it for a minute to figure it out. For most of my forties, I'd thought I was in my fifties. We are timeless, limitless beings anyway – I thought, so I just let it all go and headed for the bridge and home.

Hi Mr. Groundhog! I haven't seen you much since I left my job but I hope you're okay – say hi to your family for me.

As I got to the bridge, I read the graffiti someone had managed to write hanging over the edge at the top by the train tracks. That must have been some trick, writing it upside down like that, and they'd done a great job, considering. It was written in green spray-paint and capital letters that must have been over a foot high, with it spanning more than half of the four-lane bridge.

Yes it is! – I shouted aloud in response to what was written there, and I thanked whoever had done this as I zoomed underneath and laughed into the wind.

You couldn't even call it real graffiti. It was a message, and it was a message for all of us as I ran it over and over again in my mind on the way home.

ANOTHER WORLD IS POSSIBLE

Epilogue
The Holding

I had an opportunity to use the blue crystal shortly thereafter and it really worked calming down the situation I found myself in at the time. My confidence in Sri Bhundari was unwavering and he followed the red, green and blue crystals with three more: yellow, black and then finally white. He set the white crystal in place on June 1, and so on the next day, my one year anniversary – I was complete. He wore a pristine red robe with a belt for this occasion, and had long dreadlock-style hair. I could see his face clearly all the time now – it looked like home and he was smiling.

In the alchemical tradition, red is the masculine polarity and the feminine is white, and regardless of the other adjustments and tunings, his underlying plan of action with the crystals had been to balance the two energies all along.

I still felt I crumpled a little too easily sometimes, but now I knew my overall functional emotional state was balanced, and I also knew all my strength resided there – with my feelings. We'd been taught that crying for instance was a weakness, when in essence it was as deep a strength as unbridled joy and bliss. Ecstasy was a fusion of all sensation somehow, and I had a "feeling" that we were highly regarded in the universe because of the depth of our emotions.

I found a Native North American medicine wheel and red represented spring with black signifying death. I was stunned by Master Sri Bhundari's ability to work on many levels at once, and I shook my head yet again at his skill and style of teaching. Not only had he flawlessly devised a way to balance the masculine and feminine to the best of his abilities, but he'd thrown-in a unity between life and death at the same time. Thank you.

Now if only he could help my physical balance – I joked. I still felt like I was onboard a ship a lot of the time and hadn't gotten my sea-legs yet. I felt tippy. It was okay... my life was the greatest show on earth and I could hardly wait to see what happened next. There was no complaining about anything once you'd assumed full responsibility for the creation of your own life and the events therein – it had to just drop away like the worry and the fear.

There was still a residue, concerns about this thing or the other, and a desire to make things better than they were – worry of a watered-down kind – but not this stomach-cramping dread and panic that was such a part of normal life previously... and for so many of us.

I figured maybe some of that just came with the territory as a being in a physical body that needed food and shelter and warmth... that needed to *survive*. Maybe worry was born right there.

Sri Bhundari then set himself to work on what looked like a huge opal egg – man size – containing a sword of light. This was how he wanted me to think of myself, as a colourful luminosity containing the power of light. I could slide the sword out like Arthur did with Excalibur if I needed to wield it, but most of the time it remained inside and the two worked together.

The egg represented the masculine: static existence or Shiva, the non-animated universe – sometimes referred to as a dead body. The sword of light was the feminine in this case: action, movement, Kundalini – Shakti. This is the creative evolutionary force that acts upon everything and denies stagnancy – the body alive.

I'd come a long way since the lightning and the water, and as it turned out, the feminine energy was the true assertive motivational energy all along, and was only gentle in the sense that all ramifications were taken into consideration. This power didn't blindly knock you over or push you, but tenderly encouraged learning and growth the way a mother does with her children. The spurious strength of competition and winning were nothing compared to the true power of cooperation and consideration for all.

So what was the lightning and what was the water? I saw that it really didn't matter as it took both for one to work with the other. Balance had always been the key no matter how you looked at it. One type of energy created the piano, and another type of energy played it.

There is no perfected ideal or final version of anything, the universe doesn't work that way and change is constant and everywhere. There is no final and perfect God either. We were made in the image of this creator, and while I think the human body is definitely some kind of supreme accomplishment as a form, I believe to be made in God's image means to have the same drive or propensity or disposition of spirit.

It's in our natures to create and discover and learn, to be always shifting and growing and trying new things. Soon we will understand the safety and security of change and the unknown, as opposed to believing that a rote routine will deliver comfort and contentment. We find a happy moment and we try to recreate it again and again, sometimes blocking new different happier moments – even while the routine itself has become stale but familiar.

Of course the fear of death is a major reason for not wanting anything to really change. As children we knew better and could hardly wait to get older. Soon we start to believe the time we wanted to advance as fast as possible is now betraying us, and we would prefer it to stop altogether – or at least seriously slow down.

We understood a lot of things as children, and then the struggles of the adult world begin and wonder turns to worry. Nature is the key for returning to that place of miracles and magic and awe. Just sit and be quiet.

Turn off the TV and take the dog to the park.

Sometimes life was still very difficult, as it is for all of us, and I prayed I hadn't lost sight of where I was going. Sri Bhundari had something to say about this:

you haven't lost sight – you've found vision

The foundation, the firming, the layering and the tuning – gave way to the settling and then the holding.

The advertisement just before the bridge "YOU HAVE THE POWER," deferred to a gasoline poster just across the street and under the bridge that stated – "YOU HOLD THE POWER."

Well that just fit right in didn't it? What else could you call all of this, except... magic.

My thoughts were different now, and I could feel around the edges of concepts somehow. Trying to remember something I'd forgotten now involved looking for the feeling or shape or the colour of the thought, and I knew there was thinking without words or images. I knew there was knowing without these thought patterns but it was still an alien concept, and would have to be experienced once words in linear form were discarded.

Then I remembered being a baby. It was so pertinent to remember this now. It was the earliest thought I ever had that I can remember, and I have to call it a thought.

I was in my pram and secured with a leather harness attached to the sides of the contraption and I couldn't move enough. I was unhappy and fidgety because of this, but I wasn't crying... yet. All I wanted to do was say to my mother – could you please loosen this thing, it's really getting on my nerves. And when I opened my mouth, all that came out was incomprehensible nonsense. Now I started to cry. Frustration has to be one of the overwhelming emotions as a spirit newly committed to the infant body, and reduced to this level of helplessness – this is what I was feeling.

The idea was so clear and concise in my mind with no words, and it's debatable whether I could have even formulated an image of how someone might undo the harness. It made me think of "pure thought" before language and any kind of rigid structure was adopted. I could think clearly in a way native to consciousness, and not yet moulded by three-dimensional images and sounds. Other ways of thinking depended on where you where and what kind of reality you had to deal with.

I was sure English would be with me for a while, and I knew symbols changed form pertaining to the reality, but I could feel combinations of mind processes from parts of me in other realms, and a multi-dimensional thinking in a way I simply couldn't comprehend. In the meantime – we start where we are and try to live with as much grace as possible, discovering the true joy that comes from helping others by giving of ourselves.

The crop circles did not let up and in the summer of 2008 we received pi to ten decimal places in a ratchet form, and a formation that showed the exact configuration of the planets as they would be on December 21, 2012. Other designs and geometries followed in 2009 and 2010 that are almost beyond description... you simply have to see them. We also received more formations that looked three-dimensional and were truly something to behold. I thought of how a three-dimensional object renders a two-dimensional shadow, and it made sense that what we were seeing were like "shadows" of higher-dimensional symbols and geometries. The circle makers were doing a truly extraordinary job, and the formations expanded your mind simply by looking at them.

I found a new Mr. Green in 2008 and 2009, and now it's August, 2010 and I've yet to see him this year but I know he's there.

Another tree face telescoped right up to my own from thirty feet away, and then drew my vision back to the trunk of the tree to reveal features that looked rather like a gnome. I found another tree face that looked like a man.

I felt access to the Akashic records, or they were becoming available, and I knew I had four hundred and seventeen lives on this earth. In visions, this information routinely appears as a book with your name on it in a magnificent library (I saw my name and the number 417), but there was a notion it was in the DNA.

DNA seemed to be the place where spirit connected to this physical form and the so-called "junk" was the dimensional spiritual aspect. No wonder there was so much more of it. There was so much more of "us" somewhere else. As usual, there were so many things to think about.

I saw a seagull and then merged with him to learn seagulls drink as they're flying through the rain.

On one particular rainy sunny day, I knew there was a rainbow somewhere because I heard a voice say – I'm here... look for me! And I knew it was the rainbow, who I found a minute later after going outside.

During the last week of writing this book the synchronicities were off the scale once again, and I would stare at a particular word giving me trouble and hear it on the radio (sung or spoken) at that second. This happened over and over again and I felt guided and reassured.

Right to the bitter end! – I thought, and could only laugh at how unrelenting these things were now.

I found an essay Officer Jane had sent me in late September 2006. I'd forgotten all about it and it was called "The Awakening." Oh my.

I saw another incarnation of mine, Giselle. She was outside a store putting on her knapsack and getting her bike, and our eyes fixed – same cropped hair and eyes I'd seen in my visions of her riding a bicycle in Paris – and then she was gone and a girl got on her bike and rode off.

Another incarnation – Isawa – a Native North American, began to visit me and not-so-gently encourage me to stick my head under the freezing cold water tap before I got out of the bath. This was really important to him and was the least I could do. I could see myself making sure my knife and bow were close at hand as I dunked my head in the river, and then threw my head back to get the hair out of my face so I could gaze at the Moon.

He died from an arrow in the neck after "accidentally" running into its path during a battle. It was from the bow of one of his own people. He learned about irony and humour at this moment and would have laughed – if he could have.

The last thing he saw as he was on the ground dying with his cheek on the earth – was a dog hiding. Their eyes found each other and locked... frightened eyes and dying eyes. The comfort and understanding he found gazing at this animal as he faded from the world, reverberated through all of our incarnations and explained much. He learned more in the last minute of his life than he ever had before... and one debt to the animal nation began there.

The photographs took another turn. Along with more Orbs and faeries I received a Dove of Light, spirit smoke in the form of a person (I called it a ghostie), and began to get a cylindrical prismatic "probe" or whatever you want to call it. I asked the Orbs to join me in a photograph, using the tripod and the timer, and they gathered around me.

A bus went by with "Keep Calm and Carry On" on the side, and Parvati had a word or two:

the year has wrapped around you – you are radiant

I heard the chorus:

let nothing stand in your way

I closed my eyes and smiled, seeing my grandma.

your face will stay that way!

I hope so Grandma.

I saw Edna.

"*I love you.*"

I love you too mum.

I bought the DVD of "An Affair to Remember" and my mother and I watched it together.

I wasn't sure what the last line of the book would be and I'd put quite a bit of thought into it. I was pondering this as "Into The Mystic" came on the radio and took me right back to the beginning and the very first thing I'd written inside the book. I could feel my hair standing up as the song took hold and it was so perfect.

>Smell the sea and feel the sky
>Let your soul and spirit fly
>Into the mystic

So many things had happened in those eleven moons and since then, and no matter what – we were all heading home one way or another. I was sure of that.

The arms of the universe, the arms of the Divine Mother, were reaching out for us to return... and then the song ended.

Had I ever noticed he'd tacked-on a line there... right at the end of that beautiful song? It wasn't even there most of the time if you looked-up the lyric, but there it was... and I had my last line.

>Too late to stop now

About the Author

Peter Nelson was born to a musical family in England and moved to Canada in 1964 at ten years old.

Discovering Jane Roberts and the Seth Material in the early 70s changed the direction of his life, leading to an ongoing journey of self-discovery and expansion of awareness through lucid dreaming and out-of-body states.

In 2007 a meeting with an old friend began a series of extraordinary events leading to a profound Kundalini Awakening and the dissolution of normal everyday reality. "Into the Arms of the Goddess" is the personal journal of someone learning to accept the greatest gift of all.

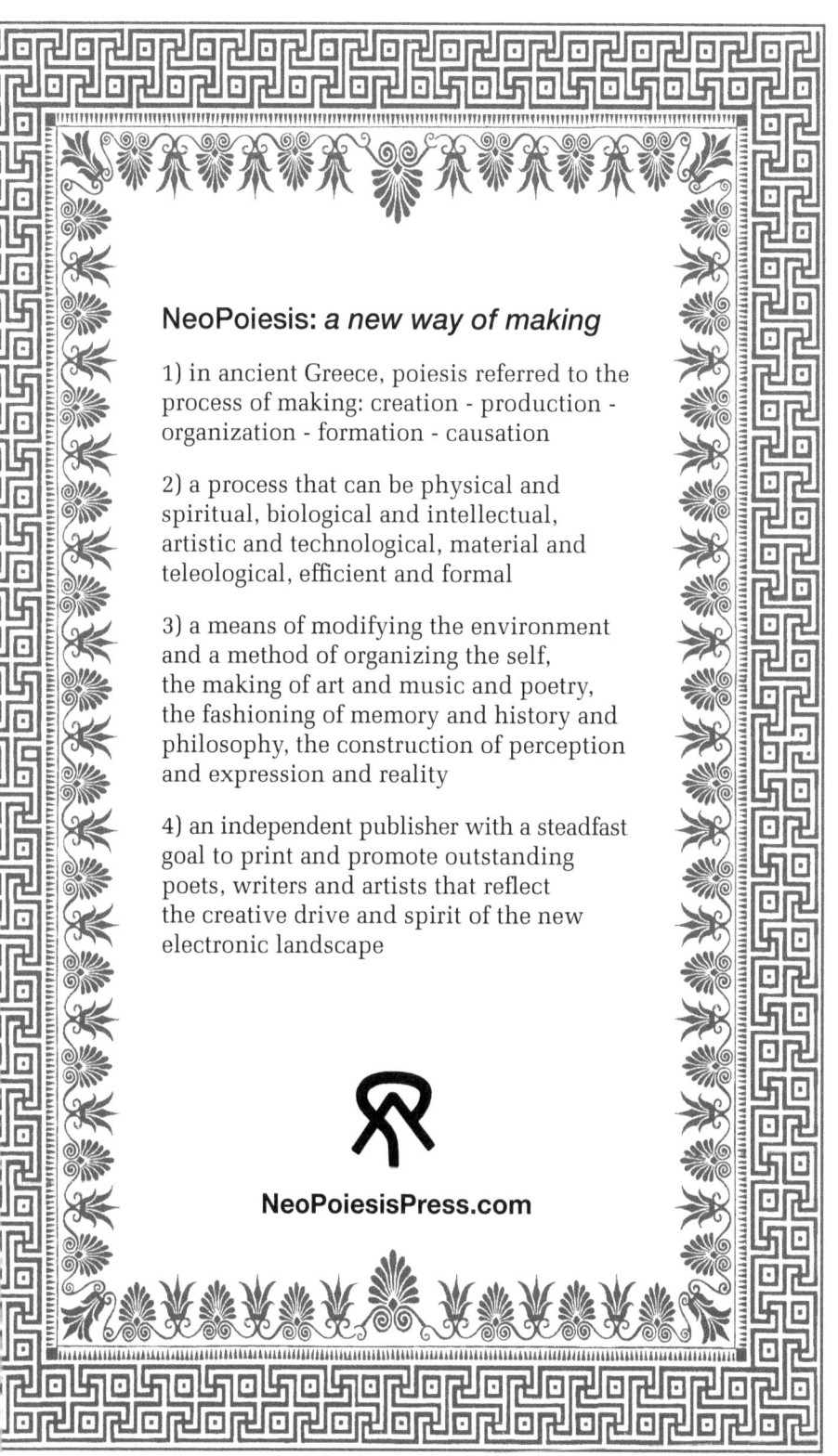

www.ingramcontent.com/pod-product-compliance
Lightning Source LLC
Chambersburg PA
CBHW071645160426
43195CB00012B/1367